ECONOMIC VALUATION
OF NATURAL RESOURCES

ABOUT THE SERIES

The *Social Behavior and Natural Resources Series* is about human adaptation to natural resources and the constraints these resources place upon institutions and work and play in everyday life. Natural resources, after all, are products of society. The very definition of natural resources arises from the interaction of population, culture, and the biophysical environment.

Biological and physical scientists are providing us with a clearer picture of the nature of species and habitats and the requirements of systems to function under varying management regimes dedicated to conservation and preservation. Social scientists are providing complementary information about the human species, our habitat, and how social systems respond to a wide range of resource management policies. The integration of social science with biological and physical science is the focus of this series.

Resource management issues are human problems that can only be solved with social science knowledge in combination with knowledge from the other sciences. The utilization of these different types of knowledge within the resource management arena depends upon the establishment of a partnership between scientists and managers. Sound management requires agreement on what information is pertinent, how information should be collected, and how information should be employed in decisionmaking.

Here the social sciences can help. Social scientists have a keen appreciation of the power, as well as the limitations, of science to resolve policy conflicts. This is important for understanding how managers filter the concerns of competing constituencies and their own professional cadre while managing the natural resources under their charge.

ECONOMIC VALUATION OF NATURAL RESOURCES

ISSUES, THEORY, AND APPLICATIONS

EDITED BY

Rebecca L. Johnson
and Gary V. Johnson

WESTVIEW PRESS
Boulder, San Francisco, & Oxford

Social Behavior and Natural Resources Series

This Westview softcover edition is printed on acid-free paper and bound in library-quality, coated covers that carry the highest rating of the National Association of State Textbook Administrators, in consultation with the Association of American Publishers and the Book Manufacturers' Institute.

Published in 1990 in the United States of America by Westview Press, Inc., 5500 Central Avenue, Boulder, Colorado 80301, and in the United Kingdom by Westview Press, Inc., 36 Lonsdale Road, Summertown, Oxford OX2 7EW

Library of Congress Cataloging-in-Publication Data
Economic valuation of natural resources: issues, theory, and
  applications/edited by Rebecca L. Johnson and Gary V. Johnson.
    p. cm.—(Social behavior and natural resources series)
  Includes bibliographical references.
  ISBN 0-8133-7838-9
  1. Natural resources—Valuation. 2. Natural resources—
Management. 3. Recreation—Valuation. 4. Recreation—Management.
I. Johnson, Rebecca L., 1955–   . II. Johnson, Gary V.
III. Series.
HC59.E375 1990
333.7—dc20   90-12114
                                                                        CIP

Printed and bound in the United States of America

The paper used in this publication meets the requirements
of the American National Standard for Permanence of Paper
for Printed Library Materials Z39.48-1984.

10   9   8   7   6   5   4   3   2

Contents

Tables

Figures

Acknowledgments

The editors would like to thank Jane M. Curran for her editorial assistance; Marilyn J. Adams, Eileen M. McCulley, and Dorine E. Nagy for their typing assistance; and the individual chapter authors for their patience.

Rebecca L. Johnson
Gary V. Johnson

Introduction

Rebecca L. Johnson

Gary V. Johnson

Allocation of natural resources has become a prominent concern at the local, state, and federal level. Competing uses for increasingly scarce resources are requiring that the relative values of those uses be investigated. Although many types of value are important in decision making, this book is concerned with the economic value of natural resources.

Economic values for certain natural resources are readily observable in markets. For others, however, market prices are not available, and estimates of value must be made through nonmarket valuation techniques. The progress that has been made in improving the theory, methods, and applications of these techniques has been remarkable. Along with the progress, however, come new problems that must be addressed. The chapters presented in this volume are a collection of examples of both progress and problems.

The first section of the book addresses issues and perspectives of resource valuation. Public agency decision makers, social psychologists, sociologists, and economists all have different perspectives on the valuation of natural resources. Even within the field of economics there are varying perspectives, such as the neoclassical approach versus the institutional approach. Part I includes chapters that discuss the different perspectives on resource valuation and their implications for resource allocation. They also raise many of the current issues in resource valuation, such as the comparison of nonmarket values to market values of resources.

Some of the chapters in Part I discuss whether economists are estimating demand and benefits in a vacuum, without regard to supply considerations or institutional constraints. Research that strives to make nonmarket values relevant for policy and management is thought by some of the authors to be lacking.

The chapters in Part I make it clear that the issues involved in resource valuation are challenging and dynamic. There are no easy answers to the questions that arise, and the possibilities for future research are abundant.

Part II presents examples of progress and problems in valuation theory and method development. Included are discussions of both the contingent valuation method (CVM) and the travel cost method (TCM) for estimating nonmarket values. Richard Bishop and Thomas Heberlein have an excellent overview chapter of the CVM at the beginning of this section. Many of the authors address problems with bias in the CVM from a number of different perspectives, and potential solutions to these problems are suggested.

The authors in Part II have done a particularly good job of showing the relevance of their studies to policy and management of natural resources. The implications of the theoretical properties of the models for use in policy analysis are made quite clear.

In the final section of the book, empirical applications of nonmarket valuation techniques are presented. The chapters include applications of the CVM and TCM to a number of different natural resource valuation problems. The applications include benefit estimates for air and water pollution control policy, whitewater recreation, recreational fishing, and marine mammals.

The chapters in Part III include good overviews of the valuation methods and their strengths and weaknesses. Two of the chapters are particularly concerned with the policy context in which the methods are applied. Alan Randall and Warren Kriesel introduce their "national policy evaluation referendum model," which they argue is most appropriate when the relevant policy to be evaluated is national in scope and usually decided upon through referendum. Karl Samples and James Hollyer study the application of the CVM in the presence of substitutes and complements. They explore, conceptually and empirically, the sensitivity of wildlife value estimates to partial equilibrium assumptions.

Given the need for natural resource value information in planning and policymaking, the number of empirical studies that are being completed is quite encouraging. However, as theories and methods are applied, new problems emerge, which provide the impetus for future research in this area. There is also the potential for empirical results to get misused, or applied to situations for which they are not suited. Current research is addressing this problem, and studies like those found in this book are making progress toward defining appropriate valuation methods for different types of policy situations. Progress is being made, and as natural resource allocation becomes even more of a policy issue, that progress should continue.

Part I Issues and Perspectives

1 The Benefits and Costs of Recreation: Dollars and Sense

George L. Peterson

Beverly L. Driver

Perry J. Brown

Introduction

The goal of this chapter is to reduce confusion about the benefits and costs of outdoor recreation. Because the words *benefit* and *cost* represent different ideas to different people, hidden premises often cause semantic disagreement. We have tried to clarify such premises by describing the richness of ideas involved. If we can agree on what we are talking about, we can define, measure, and produce the benefits of recreation more effectively.

The discussion is divided into four major parts. The first section describes the different information requirements of different kinds of recreation decisions. Agreement about what question is being asked will reduce disagreement about the answer. The second section organizes the analysis of recreation costs and benefits into qualitative analysis, quantitative analysis, and valuation. Failure to separate these different kinds of information often causes needless confusion. The third section examines several concepts of value that are sometimes mixed in valuation of recreation costs and benefits. Mixing different concepts of value interferes with effective communication. Section four organizes the content of the first three sections into a simple mathematical model. This model aids systematic thinking about a complex and often baffling subject, and it demonstrates the kinds of definitions and measurements needed for rigorous analysis.

Different Decisions Need Different Information

A decision is an act of making up one's mind about something—for example, deciding to do something now that causes desirable changes in the conditions of the future. Recreation decision makers need to know what their alternatives are. They also need to know the beneficial and detrimental consequences of each alternative. What information is needed depends on the context and objectives of the decision.

For example, each of the following may require different kinds of information about the consequences of participation in recreation activity: (1) ranking alternative recreation investments according to a specific criterion such as economic efficiency, (2) describing the distribution of benefits among different people, (3) informing and educating people so they can make choices that more effectively serve personal objectives, (4) designing improved recreation alternatives, (5) predicting what people will choose, (6) designing advertisements and incentives that influence what people choose, and (7) improving theoretical understanding of what recreation is and is not.

Economists concerned with ranking alternative public investments according to economic efficiency define *economic benefit* in terms of one kind of "assigned value" (Randall 1984a; Brown 1984). *Economic value* is defined as "willingness to pay" or "compensation demanded" for the changes in question. It is simply the sum of money one is willing to trade for changed conditions.

When asked to measure the "value" of a meal, an economist will simply state a sum of money, say $12.50. In answer to the same question, a nutritionist will describe the nutritional consequences of eating the meal. These answers demonstrate two different points of view. When the different purposes are made clear, it is obvious the two people are answering different questions. However, if either the economist or the nutritionist assumes the other is answering the same question, communication will break down.

Definition and Measurement of the Costs and Benefits of Recreation

The words *cost* and *benefit* imply preference relationships. Recreation is a means by which people achieve desired objectives (Driver and Tocher 1970; Brown, Dyer and Whaley 1973; Driver and Harris 1981), although for many people the objective may simply be to participate in recreation.

Following the most common dictionary definitions, a recreation *benefit* is "anything contributing to an improvement in condition" (World Publishing Company 1968) or "something that guards, aids, or promotes well-being" (G. & C. Merriam Company 1965). A *cost* is a "loss, sacrifice, or detriment." When recreation activity causes conditions to change in ways that promote or protect well-being, the activity is beneficial. To the extent that it imposes costs, it is detrimental.

For some decision purposes it is sufficient to know simply what forms of recreation are desired. For other decisions, however, it is necessary to describe and assign value to the beneficial and detrimental consequences of the activity. There are three ways to analyze such changes: qualitatively, quantitatively, and by valuation.

Qualitative analysis identifies the conditions changed by recreation. Recreation is instrumental in the achievement of human objectives, even if the objective is simply to escape the conscious pursuit of objectives. Where the recreation activity is an end in itself, the exercise of describing and valuing consequences may be degenerate. But even activity that is self-justified has consequences, and for some purposes it is useful to understand what they are.

Objectives can be defined in terms of specific variables or conditions that describe the state of being. For example, jogging causes beneficial and detrimental changes in the conditions of physical health. Qualitative analysis of the health benefits and costs of jogging identifies the kinds of changes that occur in the body.

The qualitative consequences of a particular recreation activity might include changes in physical conditions of the environment, changes in conditions of physical or mental health, changes in emotional and cognitive states, or changes in personal or governmental financial conditions. Complete qualitative analysis of recreation costs and benefits requires identification of all the variables on which human welfare depends, as defined by the philosophical point of view.

However, a given decision context may require only limited information about a specific subset of those variables. The relevant subset consists only of the conditions that differ significantly among the alternatives being considered. Because identification of the relevant set of variables requires identification of those variables that are of human concern and will change significantly, qualitative analysis, quantitative analysis and valuation are not fully separable.

Quantitative analysis measures the magnitude of change in each of the conditions of concern. While qualitative analysis of jogging identifies improved cardiovascular fitness as one of the changes, quantitative analysis uses the relational properties of numbers to describe the magnitude of a given change. Operational definition of the variables and measurement instrumentation are therefore necessary (Caws 1962; Stevens 1962). Quantitative analysis also requires ability to predict the magnitude of change in addition to simple observation.

Valuation measures the strength of the affective or preferential meaning of a change. According to Brown (1984), valuation measures the "assigned" values derived from an individual's "held" values and choice options. Assigned values describe the relative worth of objects or actions. They are measured by some quantitative unit of value and are generally demonstrated or observed in the choices people make. Held values are enduring beliefs about what is preferable and generally concern the sense of what is "virtuous, lovely, or of good report."

Valuation is thus assignment of value to recreation opportunities or to changes caused by participation in recreation activity. A positively valued change is a benefit. A negatively valued change is a cost. The type of change identifies the benefit or cost. Prediction and measurement of the magnitude of change quantify it. Valuation classifies the change or opportunity either as beneficial or detrimental and measures its relative importance to the decision objectives.

Valuation may be a technical exercise in which analysts measure the value responses of affected individuals or assign values by application of normative criteria. Valuation may also be the implicit by-product of behavior. Contingent valuation (Randall 1984b) or travel cost analysis (Rosenthal et al. 1984) of unpriced goods in benefit-cost analysis are examples of technical valuation. Another example is measurement of attitudes, preferences, and perceptions by psychologists in marketing studies. Assignment of prices by competitive market equilibrium, voting behavior in elections, and citizen participation in public hearings are examples of value assignment as the outcome of behavior. For some decisions technical value measurement is appropriate. As in the Resources Planning Act (RPA) of 1974 and amended by the National Forest Management Act (NFMA) of 1976, law may require benefit-cost analysis of public investment alternatives. However, in most cases, we the people reserve the right to make up our own minds about what we like and dislike about consumer goods or proposed government projects and programs. We express our values through market choices, voting behavior, and political activity.

Information about the kind and magnitude of change caused by recreation activity is important to people who want to make up their own minds about recreation alternatives, while reserving the right to express their value responses by actual choices. They want to know what the changes are; and they want to decide for themselves what those changes are worth. Environmental, economic, and social impact assessment are examples of processes intended to describe the consequences of proposed changes so that people can assign their own values through informed choices. Design of new recreation alternatives also requires criteria derived from valuation. To create desirable new options, designers need to know how design variables relate to achievement of human objectives. Description and valuation of the consequences of recreation activity are also needed for such administrative functions as prediction and management of behavior and design of effective public education services.

The Many Facets of Value

The meaning of the word *value* is central to valuation of recreation opportunities and their consequences. However, value has many different meanings and is often the cause of semantic confusion. Artists sometimes use the word to describe color intensity or darkness. In mathematics, value is often used to mean "magnitude," e.g., the value of pi is 3.1416. In ethical philosophy, value is tied to the concepts of right and wrong, good and bad, desirable and undesirable. Valuation as we use the word means measurement of the relative goodness or desirability of recreation opportunities and their consequences. However, valuation takes many forms, depending on the specific idea represented by the word value. In this section different ways of defining value are examined. Agreement on the definition of value is prerequisite to communication about costs and benefits.

In the domain of assigned value, Morris (1956) differentiates among *operative value, conceived value,* and *object value.* Operative value is the worth implied by the actual choices people make. Conceived value is the worth assigned by the choices people believe they ought to make. Object value is the worth implied by the choices of a perfectly informed decision maker whose choices and objectives are consistent.

Economic value is a special way to measure operative value in terms of monetary exchange, although not all operative decisions are necessarily made by economic methods or in monetary terms. Economic theory is not concerned with conceived or object value, but a theory of economics could be framed in these values as well. For people who are perfectly informed and whose choices are consistent with their objectives, there is no difference among the three definitions of economic value. In other words, for "economic man" there is no difference. In "actual man" the differences may be substantial (Simon 1985).

Santayana (1896) provides another philosophical perspective. He separates *aesthetic* and *moral* value. In his words, "morality has to do with the avoidance of evil and the pursuit of good; aesthetics only with enjoyment." A moral action is not desired for its own sake but only as an instrument to achievement of a higher good. For example, within the economic paradigm a hundred dollars worth of candy has the same "value" as a hundred dollars worth of education. Even though the candy can be sold for a hundred dollars and the money used to buy the education, some people might feel the education has greater "worth" than the candy.

Such a judgment suggests inconsistency between economic and moral valuation criteria. Education produces long-term enhancement of productivity and quality of life while candy gives short-term consumption of pleasure. Even though economic criteria clearly demonstrate the two have the same economic value and are exchangeable at parity, moral criteria suggest that long-term changes caused by education are of greater "worth" than the pleasure given by candy.

The Economic Definition of Value

The economic definition of value is one of the most commonly used bases for valuation. It is also the most rigorously defined concept and is derived from a well-developed framework of operational theory that not only interrelates concepts but also relates concepts to empirical phenomena. Yet, the economic definition of value may be the most misunderstood and abused concept of all. The theory is complex, and good understanding of it requires considerable specialized training. Economic value is also a familiar part of everyone's life, and confusion of familiarity with understanding is common.

Economic value is strictly and narrowly defined by economic behavior in a context of supply and demand (Randall 1984a; Just, Hueth, and Schmidtz 1982). It is simply the amount of money (or the other goods that could be purchased with the money) a person is willing to give up in order to get a thing, or the amount required in compensation for the loss of a thing. This sum of money is demonstrated or implied by the choices people make.

Market transactions measure economic value at the margin if the market is free of distortion, the goods in question are capable of market exchange, and the transactions do not cause prices to change (i.e., are marginal). Some goods and services, such as public education, national defense, flood control, and wilderness preservation, have the nature of "public goods," and real markets cannot assign prices to them effectively (Randall 1983; Samuelson 1954).

Some changes in the supply of recreation opportunity, especially those proposed by government, may cause prices to change significantly. Marginal prices are not adequate to measure the value of such changes. Because of market imperfection and nonmarginal change, it is thus often necessary to measure economic value by means other than market prices. Extra market methods for measuring economic value are simply attempts to predict economic choices among various conditions and various sums of money, thereby simulating how people would behave in a perfect market if one were available (Randall 1984b).

The economic value assigned to a good does not necessarily measure the value assigned to the objectives served by the good. Neither does it identify or measure the magnitude of the beneficial and detrimental consequences. It simply measures how much money one is willing to give up in order to get the good as an instrument for obtaining the objectives. As with air and water, the value assigned to the objectives may be great, while the economic value of a unit of the good is very low because of an abundance of low-priced substitutes.

The diamonds and water paradox illustrates the distinction between the price of a good and the value assigned to the objectives served by the good. The function performed by drinking water is of great value, but the price of water is zero when one is standing next to a free drinking fountain. Willingness to pay for a glass of water is also zero because of the free source nearby. Water is essential to life, but the specific glass of water in question will make no difference to life. The low price simply reflects the local context of supply and demand, not the importance of water in maintaining life.

People are not willing to pay more than the required amount to get what they want, no matter how important the function served. Compared with water, diamonds serve relatively trivial functions (as jewelry), but they are of great economic value because of short supply and high demand.

Given absolute exclusion from all goods that perform the desired function, price measures full willingness to pay for the functions served by the good, as constrained by ability to pay and other demands on the budget. But if substitute means are available, willingness to pay is no more than the price of a substitute. As soon as one asks more than that price, demand will transfer to the substitute. This discussion assumes, of course, that the market context is not one of outrageous extortion, i.e., that the transaction does not violate the limits of propriety. "Consumer sovereignty" justifies economic value. This is a fancy way of saying that economic value is implied by the choices people make. In Morris's (1956) terms, it is a form of operative value. Spinoza stated the idea behind consumer sovereignty when he wrote, "We desire nothing because it is good, but it is good only because we desire it" (Santayana 1896). While this is the idea behind consumer sovereignty, it is highly debated by philosophers of value theory. Whether one agrees or disagrees with the idea, it is the platform on which economic value stands. However, economic value is not independent of the objective characteristics of a good. As an instrument to the achievement of desired outcomes, the good must be capable of performing the needed function. Thus, economic value is a joint product of ability to pay, the value assigned to the desired end, the perceived efficacy of the good as an instrument to that end, and the availability, perceived efficacy, and price of alternative instruments. Nevertheless, from the anthropocentric and instrumental perspective of economics, there is no value without preference.

Welfare economics uses this definition of economic value to evaluate achievement of two objectives: efficiency and equity. Efficiency asks whether a proposed change produces more economic value than it consumes, and whether it produces more net economic gain than other changes with which it is compared. Equity questions the fairness of the distribution of gains and losses among people or regions. Two equally efficient actions may have different distributional consequences. They may also serve different ends for different people or for society as a whole, and may therefore have different values relative to objectives other than economic efficiency. Thus, efficiency information is important but not sufficient for public policy decisions (Randall 1984c). The definition of economic value assumes a behavioral model posited by neoclassical microeconomic consumer theory (Henderson and Quandt 1980). This behavioral model may not adequately describe human behavior. Simon (1985) contrasts the global rationality of "economic man" with the bounded rationality of cognitive psychology. Maslow (1968) and Tversky (1972) describe hierarchical or lexicographic choice processes. Slovic and Lichtenstein (1983) report risk-related decision behavior that is not consistent with economic theory. Tversky and Kahneman (1981) show that assigned values are dependent on how decisions are framed, as well as on the objects of choice. Knetsch and Sinden (1984) report more empirical disagreement between willingness to pay and compensation demanded than can be explained by income effects alone.

Basing policy decisions on economic value through benefit-cost analysis has political implications. (Mishan 1976; Randall 1984a; Sassone and Schaffer 1978; Randall and Peterson 1984; Randall 1984c; deNeufville and Stafford 1971). These political implications include "one dollar, one vote" and the assumption that the existing distribution of endowments is fair, with the possible consequence that the rich become richer while the poor become poorer. The same assumptions are implicit in actual market transactions, but overriding legislation based on political judgment often regulates real markets. Economic value depends not only on "short-run" personal preferences, but also on the long-run institutional context (Bromley 1982).

Because of the implied behavioral and political assumptions embedded in the theory, conclusions derived from economic value, especially in extra-market applications, tend to be normative rather than descriptive. Therefore, it is important to understand and evaluate the underlying assumptions and limitations.

Psychological Value

Valuation as we have defined it is a subjective human response to external stimuli. Psychologists of many persuasions have studied such value-related phenomena, including the description, explanation, and prediction of choices and preferences. In this sense, economics is a separate school of psychology, or perhaps those psychologists who study valuation behavior represent a separate school of economics. The approach of psychologists to valuation behavior is different from that of economists. Psychological theories and methods range from Freudian introspection to mathematical decision theory. Between these extremes are such topic areas as cognitive dissonance, attribution, social judgment, perception, motivation, and reasoned action. An overview of the theory of reasoned action (Ajzen and Fishbein 1980) illustrates one approach to psychological valuation.

The theory of reasoned action focuses on "attitudes," defined as favorable and unfavorable dispositions toward an object or behavior.

One way of classifying and explaining attitudes distinguishes three types of response: cognitive, affective, and conative. Cognitive responses manifest beliefs and perceptions about the characteristics and consequences of things. An affective response consists of positive or negative feelings toward the object in question. Conative responses are behavioral inclinations, intentions, commitments, and actions that involve the attitude object. Methodology is well developed for measuring these responses and inferring attitudes and values (Thurstone 1959; Thurstone and Chave 1929; Guilford 1954; Edwards 1957; Osgood, Suci, and Tannenbaum 1957; Torgerson 1958; Nunnally 1967; Fishbein and Ajzen 1975; Ajzen and Fishbein 1980).

According to the theory of reasoned action, the antecedent of behavior is behavioral intention. Strength of intention influences the likelihood that the behavior will occur and depends on attitude toward the behavior and on subjective norm. Attitude toward the behavior is a function of beliefs about the probability that specific consequences will occur, and of affective response toward those consequences. Subjective norm concerns the perceived expectations of others. These determinants of intention are sometimes called behavioral beliefs and normative beliefs. The relationship between intention and behavior is also a function of volitional control, the extent to which a person is free to make a decision.

What psychologists have learned about attitudes and behaviors can help improve the validity of economic valuation. For example, the theory of reasoned action demonstrates that measurement of economic value by hypothetical market methods (contingent valuation) requires correct identification of the valued object. When assigning economic value to a public good such as clean air, we must distinguish among (1) clean air, (2) policies that affect air quality, and (3) a behavior such as payment for a policy said to affect air quality. If a contingent valuation question is framed poorly, people may simply express attitudes rather than willingness to pay, and different people may express attitudes toward different components of the question (Ajzen and Peterson 1988).

The psychological approach to value helps explain economic value in relationship to other aspects of human behavior and affective response. Economic value has a very precise and rigorous definition, but it is often misunderstood, falsely accused, and incorrectly interpreted. Psychological examination of economic value as a special kind of behavioral response helps to clarify what it includes and excludes, thus leading to more enlightened application. The purposes for which information about economic value is useful become clearer, and the need for other kinds of information in certain situations is also shown. The model presented in the last part of this chapter illustrates these relationships.

Other Anthropocentric Definitions of Value

Economists and psychologists study valuation from the point of view of individual behavior, but anthropocentrically justified values are not limited to those assigned directly by individual preferences. Sociologists and anthropologists also study values, but from a social perspective (Kelly 1974, Cheek and Burch 1976). Other disciplines such as history, political science, art, music, and religion also study human values.

These social, ethical, and historical perspectives are important because they help assure comprehensive understanding of the costs and benefits of recreation. For example, many of the costs and benefits are not perceived at the level of individual behavior. In a complex society it is difficult for individuals to understand the social and long-term effects of their choices. Social science demonstrates the need for communal conscience, as with the "tragedy of the commons" (Hardin 1968), so that people can make more informed individual and institutional decisions.

Values Justified by Social Choice

Conflict between individual choices and social well-being is the basis for the "public interest" point of view often advocated by political ideologies, religious admonitions, economic theories, and philosophical maxims. The assigned and held values thus advocated may be different from those motivating individual behavior. Such values are often mixed unwittingly or by design in discussions of the costs and benefits of recreation.

These "public interest" values might be justified by right of might as in a dictatorial command economy or through due process and social contract in a democracy. If so, they are legitimate arguments. Public education, national defense, and preservation of wilderness areas are examples of products of social choice where "public interest" values are implied. In such cases, "social" values are products of individual decisions to apply long-run constraints on short-run behavior. However, where "social" values have no sovereignty other than logical arguments, their inclusion in technical evaluations is a political act.

Intrinsic Value

The definitions of value discussed thus far are based on human preferences. Philosophers of environmental ethics define another approach under the rubric *intrinsic value* (Callicott 1985, Rolston 1981, 1985). Unlike assignment of value by beliefs and preferences based on instrumental utility of an object in the satisfaction of human desires, intrinsic value is a product of belief that value is an intrinsic property of the object, independent of usefulness to humans. Valuations of actions and activities that affect environmental conditions sometimes mix anthropocentric justifications of value with intrinsic justifications, especially where unique and delicate ecosystems or endangered species are affected. Effective communication about costs and benefits requires clear separation of such arguments, and this, in turn, requires clarification of the intrinsic value argument. Definitions of intrinsic value vary in content, and stem from philosophical maxims, ethical beliefs, and held values. One proposition is that nonhuman entities have rights, that their preferences are therefore sovereign, and that values are assigned by those preferences. Another is that genetic information is intrinsically valuable ecological capital, because it is an improbable combination of the inherent and immutable properties of matter and energy, a product of eons of biological experimentation. Still another point of view is that humans, as moral agents with power to destroy or protect other species, have a duty to protect them (Stone 1974). Intrinsic value is often associated with reverence for life.

On philosophical and ethical grounds, these arguments are difficult to refute, but within the political framework, they are effective only as justified by due process. From the economic point of view, intrinsic value has meaning when human beliefs or preferences assign it to nonhuman things. For example, economists have defined *existence value* as value assigned by human preference to the existence of things, independent of their instrumental services.

Whether one agrees with these intrinsic value arguments, the task of measurement is formidable. Perhaps the best practical approach is for each person to express personal beliefs through the pluralistic processes of market and political equilibrium. People who believe in intrinsic value are thereby free to act as they choose. They are also free to advocate their beliefs and try to convince others.

A Model of Recreation Costs and Benefits

This section organizes analysis of recreation costs and benefits into a simple model. Figure 1.1 identifies five components: recreation opportunities, population, activity, other inputs, and consequences. It is also possible to specify the same model in terms of attributes of recreation opportunity, rather than the opportunities themselves.

People come to a recreation opportunity with the intention of participating in an activity to produce beneficial change, as judged by personal preferences. These people combine the recreation opportunity and other things (such as travel, equipment, and skill) in a recreation activity. Participation in the recreation activity is a production process that causes change in the person, environment, and society.

The choices people make express their operative preferences. A system of values may be assigned based on these observed choices. Such values are subjective and descriptive of behavior. However, the decision that creates the need for information about consequences might not aim at operative individual preference. The decision might require information about changes in variables identified by other objectives, perhaps at the level of societal welfare or relative to some normative point of view.

Assuming the purpose of the analysis is economic valuation, it is possible to assign economic value to opportunities, attributes of opportunities, input factors, activities, or objectives. For example, consider a Marshallian demand function specified for recreation opportunities. Finding that such a demand function can only predict the observed, Lancaster (1966) and Becker (1965) reformulated consumer demand theory in terms of characteristics of goods. Demand functions thus specified allow prediction of demand for new opportunities created by combining characteristics in innovative ways.

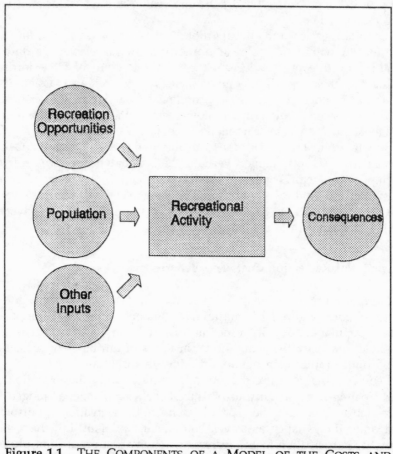

Figure 1.1 THE COMPONENTS OF A MODEL OF THE COSTS AND BENEFITS OF RECREATION.

Following a suggestion by Hicks (1956), Morishima (1959) described demand in terms of the objectives served by goods and their characteristics. Expression of demand functions in terms of the consequences of recreation activity allows economic valuation of those consequences. Economic value thus assigned is more useful than simple information about willingness to pay for recreation opportunities. It both measures economic value and also describes the reasons people prefer one opportunity over another. However, in the "normal" economic approach, economic value is assigned directly to the recreation opportunities. Assigning economic value to the consequences of participation in the opportunities is more complicated and does not necessarily lead to the same conclusion or serve the same purposes.

Information about economic efficiency does not satisfy the needs of all decisions. As with equity, some questions require exposure of specific changes. Different questions require different kinds of information. Thus, the "consequences" in Figure 1.1 represent many different things. They may be perceived or actual changes in physical or mental health, environmental or social conditions, distribution of income, or recreation experience. The question to be answered determines how to specify the outcomes and how to assign value. For some questions, the answer may stop short of valuation.

We are now able to state the model mathematically, although full theoretical development transcends the scope of this chapter. This simple mathematical statement is important because it identifies the operational definitions needed before the model can move from the domain of ideas to the domain of operations. Define the following vectors:

Q = the set of recreation opportunities
$$= (q_1, q_2, ..., q_j, ..., q_m), \tag{1}$$

A = the set of attributes of the opportunity
$$= (a_1, a_2, ..., a_k, ..., a_p), \tag{2}$$

S_π = a set of personal characteristics describing market segment π
$$= (s_{\pi 1}, s_{\pi 2}, ..., s_{\pi h}, ..., s_{\pi z}), \tag{3}$$

F_π = the set of recreation activities by which consumers produce desired outcomes
$$= (f_{\pi 1}, f_{\pi 2}, ..., f_{\pi g}, .., f_{\pi t}), \tag{4}$$

P = the set of other factor inputs that are combined with opportunities and attributes in activities
$$= (p_1, p_2, ..., p_r, ..., p_s), \tag{5}$$

O   =   the set of important (benefit-related) variables oj that change
        because of the recreation activity

    = $(o_1, o_2, ..., o_j, ..., o_n)$.   (6)

Identification of the elements of Q, A, S, P, and O is the qualitative
part of the analysis of benefits. Identification of the elements of O
specifies those benefit-related variables expected to change because of the
recreation activity. Definition of these variables in operational terms, so
that quantitative measurement is possible, is the first step in quantitative
analysis. It allows measurement of the magnitude of change. The symbol
$f_{\pi g}$ represents a process, not a magnitude. This process specifies the
functional relationship for market segment π and activity g by which
changes in Q, A, S, and P cause changes in O, the vector of benefit-
related variables. The model thus specified is

$$O = f_{\pi g}(Q, A, P, S_\pi).$$ (7)

Given a change in an input variable, say A + δ, the model predicts

$$O + \Phi = f_{\pi g}(Q, A + \delta, P, S_\pi),$$ (8)

and

$$\Phi = f_{\pi g}(Q, A + \delta, P, S_\pi) - f_{\pi g}(Q, A, P, S_\pi),$$ (9)

where

δ = a vector of changes in the elements of A, and

Φ = a vector of predicted changes in the benefit-related consequences.

Assume, for example, the recreation activity in question is river
floating. One of the important characteristics of a given opportunity is
the quantity of in-stream flow. Another important characteristic is water
quality. Let the initial magnitudes of these two characteristics be a_1 and
a_2, respectively. Assume a proposed change in water quality, from a_2 to
$(a_2 + \delta_2)$. What quantitative changes in the benefit-related elements of O
does the modification of water quality cause? At the initial condition of
water quality, a_2, a river trip causes the state or condition of the
participant to be the vector O. For the same river trip, a change in water
quality from a_2 to $(a_2 + \delta_2)$ causes the jth element of O to change from o_j
to $(o_j + \Phi_j)$. The benefits (or losses) through river floating caused by the
specified change in water quality is thus the vector Φ describing the
changes in each of the elements of O. Prediction of the magnitudes (Φ)
of change in the elements of O completes the quantitative analysis of

benefits (or losses). It does not, however, assign value to those changes. Quantitative analysis only states the magnitudes of change in those variables identified as important.

The above example describes the benefit-related consequences of a change in water quality. Another question is, what are the benefits of river floating. Here, the comparison of conditions is with versus without the float trip. To answer the question, first predict the vector O, assuming the trip does not occur. Then, predict O, given the trip does occur. The difference is the vector Φ describing the benefit-related changes caused by the river trip. In this example, the recreation activity (river floating) has the magnitude "zero" in the first case and "one" in the second case.

Because the elements of O are benefit-related conditions, the vector describes the beneficial and detrimental changes in state caused by the change δ. However, it is not a "valuation" model. It does not estimate the strength of preference for the change thus described. It simply states that the decision in question has caused a change of Φ_j in the benefit-related condition o_j. Thus, in answer to the question, "What are the important consequences of δ," we respond, "the important consequences of δ are Φ."

The next step is valuation, assignment of value (as opposed to magnitude) to the changes (Φ) identified qualitatively and predicted and measured quantitatively. There are several ways to accomplish valuation, depending on the purpose of the information. One way is to measure affective, cognitive, and conative responses and to infer attitudes and predict behavior, according to theories and methods of psychological value.

Another approach is to define some normative criterion of cost-effectiveness and rank alternative Φ vectors by that criterion (deNeufville and Stafford 1971). Still another approach is economic efficiency, with value defined by willingness to pay or compensation demanded for changes in Q, A, P, F, or O, depending on the purpose of the information and availability of data. The underlying relationship is the production process F by which demand for O causes derived demand for Q, A, and P.

Measuring the economic value of the elements of Q does not require description of Φ, the vector of changes in the benefit-related consequences. However, description of the vector Φ and measurement of the economic value of its elements assigns economic value to changes in Q, A, and P. Qualitative and quantitative description of Φ is also useful in many decisions where economic information is not sufficient.

Summary and Conclusion

Good decisions require knowledge of the alternative courses of action and their consequences. However, different decisions may have different objectives and different specific information requirements. Much disagreement and confusion about the benefits and costs of recreation occurs because different people are talking about different kinds of decisions.

Disagreement also arises from mixing different parts of the valuation problem. Decision makers are concerned about those variables that are important to the decision objectives and that differ in magnitude among the decision alternatives. Qualitative analysis identifies these variables. Quantitative analysis measures the magnitudes by which the decision alternatives change these salient variables. Valuation measures differences in the strength of preference among the decision alternatives, either by assigning value to the alternatives themselves or by assigning value to the variables that measure changes of state caused by the alternatives. Valuation requires criteria by which to judge strength of preference. Many different value theories and valuation processes are available. Different systems are appropriate for different purposes and situations. Hidden disagreement about decision purposes and situations or about the value system being used leads to fruitless controversy. Are values to be assigned by political equilibrium, market equilibrium, descriptive analysis, or normative analysis? Is value justified by operative preferences, normative beliefs, or authoritative directives? Is the definition of value economic, psychological, intrinsic, or something else? The objectives and context of the decision in question determine what is most appropriate.

The model presented at the end of the chapter embeds these questions in an organizing framework. Such a framework has two potential applications. It provides a paradigm by which to organize systematic thinking about complex and baffling topics, and it offers potential for operational application to those problems where the variables can be identified and defined, where the magnitudes of change can be predicted and measured quantitatively, and where numeric valuation is needed and feasible.

References

Ajzen, I., and M. Fishbein. 1980. *Understanding Attitudes and Predicting Social Behavior*. Englewood Cliffs, N.J.: Prentice Hall.

Ajzen, I., and G. L. Peterson. 1988. Contingent Value Measurement: The Price of Everything and the Value of Nothing. *In* Amenity Resource Valuation: Integrating Economics with Other Disciplines, edited by G. L. Peterson, B. L. Driver, and R. Gregory. State College, PA: Venture Publishing, Inc.

Becker, Gary S. 1965. A Theory of the Allocation of Time. *The Economic Journal.* (September):493-517.

Bromley, Daniel W. 1982. Land and Water Problems: An Institutional Perspective. *American Journal of Agricultural Economics.* 64:834-44.

Brown, Thomas C. 1984. The Concept of Value in Resource Allocation. *Land Economics.* 60(3):231-46.

Brown, Perry J., Allen Dyer, and Ross S. Whaley. 1973. Recreation ResearchSo What?" *Journal of Leisure Research.* 5(1):16-24.

Callicott, J. Baird. 1985. Intrinsic Value, Quantum Theory, and Environmental Ethics. *Environmental Ethics.* 7(Fall): 257-75.

Caws, Peter. 1962. Definition and Measurement in Physics. *In* Measurement: Definitions and Theories, edited by C. West Churchman and Philburn Ratoosh. New York: John Wiley and Sons.

Cheek, Neil H., and William R. Burch, Jr. 1976. *The Social Organization of Leisure in Human Society.* New York: Harper and Row.

deNeufville, R., and J. H. Stafford. 1971. *Systems Analysis for Engineers and Managers.* New York: McGraw-Hill.

Driver, B. L., and Charles C. Harris. 1981. Improving Measurement of the Benefits of Public Outdoor Recreation Programs. *In* Proceedings of the XVII Congress, International Union of Forestry Researchers. Kyoto, Japan.

Driver, B. L., and S. R. Tocher. 1970. Toward a Behavioral Interpretation of Recreation Engagements, with Implications for Planning. *In* Elements of Outdoor Recreation Planning, edited by B.L. Driver. Ann Arbor: University of Michigan Press.

Edwards, Allen L. 1957. *Techniques of Attitude Scale Construction.* New York: Appleton-Century-Crofts.

Fishbein, M., and I. Ajzen. 1975. *Belief, Attitude, Intention, and Behavior: An Introduction to Theory and Research.* Reading, Mass.: Addison-Wesley.

Forest and Rangeland Renewable Resources Planning Act of 1974. Pub. L. No. 93-378, 88 Stat. 476 (Codified at 16 U. S. C. 581h, 1601-1610(1976), as amended by 1976, Pub. L. No. 94-588, 90 Stat. 2949).

Guilford, J. P. 1954. *Psychometric Methods.* New York: McGraw-Hill.

Hardin, Garrett. 1968. The Tragedy of the Commons. *Science.* 162(December):1243-48.

Henderson, James E., and Richard E. Quandt. 1980. *Microeconomic Theory: A Mathematical Approach.* New York: McGraw-Hill.

Hicks, J. R. 1956. *A Revision of Demand Theory.* Oxford: Clarendon Press.

Just, Richard E., Darrell L. Hueth, and Andrew Schmidtz. 1982. *Applied Welfare Economics and Public Policy.* Englewood Cliffs, N.J.: Prentice Hall.

Kelly, J. R. 1974. Socialization toward Leisure: A Developmental Approach. *Journal of Leisure Research.* 6:181-93.

Knetsch, Jack L., and J. A. Sinden. 1984. Willingness to Pay and Compensation Demanded: Experimental Evidence of an Unexpected Disparity in Measures of Value. *Quarterly Journal of Economics.* 99(3):507-21.

Lancaster, Kelvin. 1966. A New Approach to Consumer Theory. *The Journal of Political Economy.* 74(2):132-57.

Maslow, Abraham H. 1968. *Toward a Psychology of Being.* New York: Van Nostrand Reinhold.

G. & C. Merriam Company. 1965. *Webster's Third New International Dictionary of the English Language Unabridged.* Springfield, Mass.

Mishan, E. J. 1976. *Cost-Benefit Analysis.* New York: Praeger.

Morishima, Michio. 1959. The Problem of Intrinsic Complementarity and Separability of Goods. *Metroeconomica.* 11(3):188-202.

Morris, Charles. 1956. *Varieties of Human Value*. Chicago: University of Chicago Press.

Nunnally, Jum C. 1967. *Psychometric Theory*. New York: McGraw-Hill.

Osgood, C. E., G. J. Suci, and P. H. Tannenbaum. 1957. *The Measurement of Meaning*. Urbana, Ill.: University of Illinois Press.

Randall, Alan. 1983. The Problem of Market Failure. *Natural Resources Journal*. 23:131-48.

Randall, Alan. 1984a. The Conceptual Basis of Benefit Cost Analysis. *In* Valuation of Wildland Resource Benefits, edited by George L. Peterson and Alan Randall. Boulder, Colo: Westview Press.

Randall, Alan. 1984b. Theoretical Bases for Non-market Benefit Estimation. *In* Valuation of Wildland Resource Benefits, edited by George L. Peterson and Alan Randall. Boulder, Colo.: Westview Press.

Randall, Alan. 1984c. Benefit Cost Analysis as an Information System. *In* Valuation of Wildland Resource Benefits, edited by George L. Peterson and Alan Randall. Boulder, Colo.: Westview Press.

Randall, Alan, and George L. Peterson. 1984. The Valuation of Wildland Benefits: An Overview. *In* Valuation of Wildland Resource Benefits, edited by George L. Peterson and Alan Randall. Boulder, Colo.: Westview Press.

Rolston, Holmes, III. 1981. Values in Nature. *Environmental Ethics*. 3(2):113-28.

Rolston, Holmes, III. 1985. Valuing Wildlands. *Environmental Ethics*. 7(Spring)-:23-42.

Rosenthal, Donald H., John B. Loomis, and George L. Peterson. 1984. The Travel Cost Model: Concepts and Applications. U.S. Department of Agriculture, Forest Service General Technical Report RM-109. Rocky Mountain Forest and Range Experiment Station, Fort Collins, Colo.

Samuelson, Paul A. 1954. The Pure Theory of Public Expenditure. *Review of Economics and Statistics*. 4:387-89.

Santayana, George. 1896. *The Sense of Beauty*. New York: Charles Scribner's Sons; reprinted by Dover, 1955.

Sassone, Peter G., and William A. Schaffer. 1978. *Cost-Benefit Analysis: A Handbook*. New York: Academic Press.

Simon, Herbert A. 1985. Human Nature in Politics: The Dialogue of Psychology with Political Science. *The American Political Science Review*. 79:293-304.

Slovic, Paul, and Sarah Lichtenstein. 1983. Preference Reversals: A Broader Perspective. *The American Economic Review*. 73(4):603-18.

Stevens, S. S. 1962. Measurement, Psychophysics, and Utility. *In* Measurement: Definitions and Theories, edited by C. West Churchman and Philburn Ratoosh. New York: John Wiley and Sons.

Stone, Christopher D. 1974. *Should Trees Have Standing: Toward Legal Rights for Natural Objects*. Los Altos, Calif.: William Kaufmann.

Thurstone, L. L. 1959. *The Measurement of Values*. Chicago: University of Chicago Press.

Thurstone, L. L., and E. J. Chave. 1929. *The Measurement of Attitude*. Chicago: University of Chicago Press.

Torgerson, Warren S. 1958. *Theory and Methods of Scaling*. New York: John Wiley and Sons.

Tversky, A. 1972. Elimination by Aspects: A Theory of Choice. *Psychology Review*. 79(4):281-99.

Tversky, Amos, and Daniel Kahneman. 1981. The Framing of Decisions and the Psychology of Choice. *Science*. 211(30):453-58.

World Publishing Company. 1968. *Webster's New World Dictionary of the American Language: College Edition*. New York: World Publishing Company.

2 Recreation Management Theory, Economics, and Resource Allocation: A Unifying Perspective

William G. Workman

Scott C. Matulich

Alan Jubenville

Introduction

Outdoor recreation research has failed to yield a cohesive decision tool that facilitates effective recreational resource planning. There has been no unifying effort to integrate the separate contributions of recreation management theory and economics. Further, much of the research by both recreation management theorists and economists has focused on demand issues without sufficient attention paid to resource characteristics and to the regulations and inputs over which managing agencies have control.

Recreation management theory has evolved as a social-psychological inquiry into user behavior and visitor motivations (Kaplan 1984). Typically, motivational studies have been funded by management agencies under the assumption that a better understanding of the user's motivations and behavior should help improve the quality of management programs. These investigations define output as the recreational experience of the individual, assuming that specific motivations lead to specific experiences and, ultimately, to benefits. A few researchers, such as Clark and Stankey (1979) and Driver and Brown (1978), have suggested that we also look at the supply, or management, side of the problem. Clark and Stankey focused on situational attributes that management could manipulate to produce various recreational opportuni-

This chapter was developed under the USDA Regional Hatch Project, W-133, Outdoor Recreation, Environmental Quality, and Public Interest: Benefits and Costs in Federal and State Resource Planning. Scientific Paper No. 7424, College of Agriculture and Home Economics Research Center, Washington State University.

ties. The concept of providing opportunities by mixing managerially controlled inputs was quickly adopted by federal agencies into a "cookbook" inventory process under the title Recreational Opportunity Spectrum, or ROS (USDA 1981).

Like the emphasis of recreation management theory, the focus of economic analysis of outdoor recreation has been on the user—on the value derived from recreation. Economists have made elegant theoretical advancements and have developed ingenious estimation procedures to measure nonmarket values of recreation opportunities, particularly as they apply to dichotomous, all-or-none decisions. Only recently has effort been made to isolate and value the marginal contribution of resource characteristics and management actions to visitors' welfare. Even more rare is any attempt to address cost or supply issues.

This chapter advances the managerial economics model as an appropriate analytical framework to discipline and unify the contributions of both professions. Elements of recreation management theory and economics are combined to illuminate the linkage between the recreation experience realized and the role of management in creating the quantity and quality of that experience. It is argued that the historically singular focus on valuation of user behavior will ensure continued failure to integrate managerial contributions with user choices, i.e., supply with demand. Thus, supply-oriented analysis is essential to realizing the potential of the managerial economics model.

Recreation Management Theory

The generic role of the recreation resource manager is to provide opportunities to potential users through the allocation of resources. Implicit in this view is the distinct role of the user in producing his or her own experience, given the opportunity presented. While this may seem to suggest that the user's choice of a site is exogenous to the manager, it is not. The resource manager has some control over biophysical and managerially determined attributes, such as improved access and facility development. These controllable inputs, taken together, presumably contribute to the value of the recreationist's experience on the land. The link between potential recreational value and a site's inherent and managerially determined characteristics must be known if management is to maximize a site's contribution to societal welfare. Armed with this knowledge, managers are in a position to dedicate for recreational or multiple use those sites which, due to their natural attractors, have a comparative advantage in producing desired recreational services. Societal well-being can be enhanced through the managerially determined attributes of the site.

Differentiating the Role of User and Manager

What seems to be needed is a conceptual framework that recognizes the recreational experience as a common interest of the user and manager yet differentiates their roles in the production of the experience. Figure 2.1 captures the ides of user/manager interaction through classification of inputs to the recreational experience. The first category Social Inputs, includes those inputs under control of the user/individual demanding a given experience. The Biophysical and Managerial Inputs reflect supply-related factors that are under control of the manager providing the recreational opportunity. Exogenous Inputs are uncontrollable or external factors that mitigate both the user-determined and managerially influenced recreational opportunities. The basic premise of this framework is that the user is in charge of his or her own experience, choosing a site and participating within whatever personal or nonsite constraints that are present to produce a satisfying outcome. Collectively these user inputs define demand. The manager, on the other hand, mixes the various Biophysical and Managerial Inputs to produce the opportunity or the generalized recreational experience obtainable at the site.

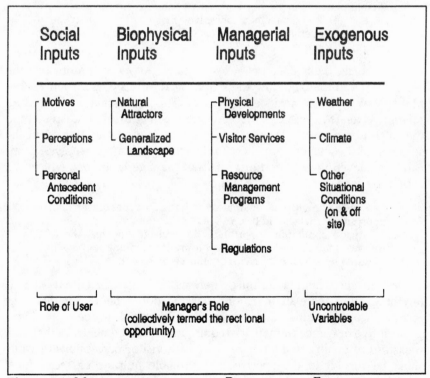

Figure 2.1 MODEL OF INPUTS TO THE RECREATIONAL EXPERIENCE.

ROS—An Attempt to Integrate the User and the Manager

Driver and Brown (1978), Brown, Driver, and McConnell (1978), and Clark and Stankey (1979) attempted to integrate the roles of the user and manager by developing a recreation resource inventory classification scheme known as the Recreation Opportunity System (ROS). The ROS framework recognizes the link between the environmental setting and the experiences or psychological outcome that users realize. It is based on the notion that recreationists choose to participate in those activities that are consistent with a particular environmental setting and that the setting may be managerially influenced to alter the recreation opportunities. Thus, ROS was intended as a "fundamental [aid] to multiple use natural resource planning and management decision" (Brown, Driver, and McConnell 1978).

Both the Driver and Brown (1978) and the Clark and Stankey (1979) conceptualizations of a resource-based opportunity spectrum advance the notion that the ROS planning and management process involves two steps:

> (1) inventory ORR's [outdoor recreation resources] in terms of their inherent potential to provide both activity and experience opportunities, and (2) set management objectives that specify what types of activity and experience opportunities will be provided at a particular location. (Driver and Brown 1978)

In other words, the manager chooses the target or anchor point along the continuum and then, holding the Biophysical Inputs constant, mixes the Managerial Inputs to achieve that point. This recommended procedure raises two related questions that have not been addressed adequately in the ROS literature: (1) What criterion is or should be employed in the selection of the anchor point? (2) To the extent that a given anchor point can be achieved through various mixes of Managerial Inputs, which mix should be chosen? Clark and Stankey (1979) go so far as to suggest that:

> The ROS is a helpful concept for determining the types of recreational opportunities that should be provided. And after a basic decision has been made about the opportunity desirable in an area, the ROS provides guidance about the appropriate planning approaches-standards by which each factor should be managed.

Despite such bold assertions, there is little evidence that ROS is anything more than an inventory classification scheme. It describes recreation opportunities that exist or are planned, but does not offer a prescriptive or choice framework required for management. To that end, measures of quality that are consistent with visitor perceptions of value must be related to the spectrum of possible outputs or recreational opportunities. These qualitative measures then must be related to a consistent, well-defined managerial objective that facilitates optimizing that objective, subject to biophysical, political, and economic constraints.

Clark and Stankey (1979) recognized that quality is a relevant notion across the entire spectrum, but argued, along with much of the profession, that having the objective of diversity assures quality. This ill-founded notion is rooted in the belief that recreational quality is so highly personal that management should not be dominated by mass or average tastes. As noted by Davis (1963), it is one of those "conceptual weeds that have grown up (and gone to seed) in the outdoor recreation movement." The fundamental problem with diversity is that it offers no criteria by which to judge management performance.

The use of diversity as a managerial criterion within ROS would be analogous to a farmer assessing land/soil quality, compiling a list of potential crops that could be produced, and then producing all of them to satisfy the diverse tastes and preferences of the market. While an inventory of output potentials is an important step in planning, it falls short of rational resource allocation. Farmers need to know how to produce and what to produce. That is, they need to know what combination and intensity of inputs promote optimal (profit-maximizing) quantities of each crop per unit of land, and what mix of crops will maximize profits for the entire farm. Such is the case with recreation managers as well.

One analytically tractable recreation management criterion is economic efficiency. A more or less traditional managerial economics approach to recreation resource planning and allocation would suggest that any given anchor point along the ROS continuum should be associated with a least-cost combination of Managerial Inputs. The efficient anchor point (or combination of anchor points) is that which maximizes net benefits to society. Viewed in this manner, the ROS framework has an element of consistency with the decision-making apparatus of managerial economics and involves integrating considerations of cost/supply and value/demand in establishing an objective choice criterion.[1]

Since the anchor point that the manager chooses represents the aggregate of the management objectives, one would assume that shifting that anchor point would represent a change in management objectives. The economic question to ask is "How does this management-induced change affect the aggregate net benefits to society or the aggregate value of the site?"

---

[1]We recognize that economic efficiency is not the sole criterion used in public sector resource allocation decisions. It may be, for example, that agencies willingly sacrifice some amount of net benefits (economic efficiency) in order to advance an equity goal or to offer a wider variety of recreational opportunities in a given location. Such a trade-off ought to be deliberate, though.

The Role of Economics

Economic research in outdoor recreation is synonymous with benefit estimation or nonmarket valuation. Accordingly, it shares a common orientation with recreation management theory—the user. There is, however, a fundamental difference between the contributions of these disciplines. The impetus for assessing the economic value of outdoor recreation was not to offer an economic perspective on user motivations, but was an attempt to improve benefit-cost ratios of multipurpose federal water projects. Initially, valuation involved assignment of some arbitrary unit/day value for each visit times the projected number of visits. Beginning with Hotelling, economists devoted substantial effort to develop nonmarket valuation methodologies that were more rigorously anchored in economic theory (Prewitt 1979). The travel cost method (TCM) (Clawson and Knetsch 1966) and survey or contingent valuation method (CVM) (Davis 1963) are products of these early efforts.

The early TCM and CVM techniques, and subsequent methodological refinements that continue today, have had profound impacts on two classes of public policy: ex ante project feasibility analysis intended to assist in design choice among alternative projects, and ex post construction audits designed to determine whether programmatic expenditures were warranted. These policy contributions are similar in that they center on discrete, often dichotomous, decisions—decisions markedly different from those most commonly addressed in the 1980s.

The watchword in state and federal resource agencies has shifted from project construction to multiple-use management. Thus, it is not surprising that policymakers confronted with multiple-use and even dedicated, single-use management decisions often fail to see the connection between nonmarket valuation and resource allocation. Even in the context of discrete project analysis, economists' measures of social welfare change have not been widely accepted. McConnell (1979) offered two explanations for this lack of acceptance. First, he suggested that the mercantilist attitudes of many public decisionmakers motivate them to choose projects on the basis of total expenditures rather than net benefits. Moreover, he argued that narrowly defining welfare changes in terms of pure Pareto efficiency ignores distributive impacts that also concern decisionmakers.

McConnell's comments beg the question "What function has economics served in its tradition of nonmarket valuation?" Apart from theoretical and methodological advancements, the answer appears to be that most economists have fallen into the mercantilist's trap by providing aggregate valuation or surplus measures that help to support (improve) feasibility studies or buttress agency budgetary requests concerning discrete, often mutually exclusive, alternatives. These nonmarket valuation studies assume as given some prior optimization that fixes project design(s). As such, aggregate measures of benefits are not well suited to address the broader social welfare questions involving optimum scale and mix of resource uses.

To some, this criticism may be an unfair indictment of nonmarket valuation research. Perhaps it is better to raise the question "When is the appropriate time to seek economic analysis?" Surely it is not after project designs are already decided. Maximizing social welfare from public investment and resource allocation decisions depends upon integrating nonmarket benefit measurements with scale and resource mix decisions. There are two types of recreational resource allocation decisions implied by recreation management theory and managerial economics: (1) allocation of resources under different management intensities and/or configurations for a single dedicated use, and (2) allocation of resource endowments among alternative multiple uses.

The failure of economists to develop methods and research results that fit into this decision-making framework is surprising. The efficiency-oriented neoclassical economics paradigm for market commodities is precisely the desired structure. It comes as a surprise to no one that the characteristics of a resource influence its productivity and capitalized value. This linkage is readily observable in markets for all classes of natural and capital resources from farmland and oil tracts to parking lots. Private entrepreneurs are aware of causal relationships between the conditions of resources, their productivity, and, ultimately, market values. Economists employ standard production economics techniques to analyze the implications of various private resource allocation options. Consider, for example, a rancher who contemplates spraying sagebrush on his pasture to increase the land's grazing potential. The traditional production economics treatment of this situation starts with the biological response function of forage to the spraying treatment and ends with an assessment of the change in net returns associated with the optimal level of treatment. The decision of whether or not and how much to spray hinges on (1) the biological response of forage to the introduced chemical; (2) the cost of various levels of treatment; (3) the value of the associated yields; (4) identification of the most advantageous level of treatment based on costs and returns; (5) computation of added annual net returns (rents) associated with this optimal treatment; and, possibly, (6) computation of the capitalized value of the investment.

If the rancher's range land has alternative uses (e.g., cattle grazing and elk habitat), and if these uses are competitive over some of the range, the resource allocation decision process is slightly more complicated. It involves maximization of net returns or rents from the combination of enterprises, assuming the rancher can capture the benefits from availability of increased elk numbers. The traditional production economics treatment begins with the physical trade-offs among enterprises as they compete for resources, and culminates in the identification of a solution to a net returns maximizing problem that yields the highest capitalized value of the land.[2]

The public sector recreation resource manager faces a decision-making situation very much like that which confronts the rancher; efficient resource allocation requires maximizing expected flows of economic surpluses (net benefits), only now the decision process is confronted by two special circumstances. First, while benefits of private sector allocations are captured by both private consumers and sellers, pricing policies for most publicly provided recreational opportunities allow the bulk of any economic surplus to accrue only to visitors. Nonmarket valuation techniques are essential to measure these consumer benefits. Second, measurement of biophysical responses to management is more difficult. Fundamental biological relationships such as mule deer population response to bitterbrush enhancement or salmon stock response to spawning gravel enhancement are not well developed. User response to altered biophysical conditions, access routes, or regulations also are not well understood.

Nonmarket Valuation

Explicit recognition of the role of resource characteristics and management actions in influencing recreation values is found as early as Clawson and Knetsch's (1966) seminal contribution. They observe, "The physical characteristics of these natural elements of the landscape affect their use for outdoor recreation, but they become resources for outdoor recreation only as they are useful for this purposes." Later they write, "The number of visits to a recreation area is generally influenced by the intensity of management. ..." And again, "A change in access or management creates a somewhat different recreation 'product'."

Despite the existence of this Lancaster-like (1966) perspective on recreation demand some twenty years ago, the economics profession has been slow in its adoption. However, there are a number of contributions to the literature that note the need to take stock of empirical methods used in recreation resource valuation and, in particular, to evaluate their utility to the resource manager. Gum and Martin (1975) recommended a de-emphasis of the development of improved methods of estimation and advocated that we instead concentrate on interpretation of benefit estimates in studies of resource allocation. This recommended pause to reflect upon whether techniques yield useful, as well as accurate, information, and the integrability of the economists' tool kit and resource management issues are also the theme of Batie and Shabman's (1979)

---

[2]Empirical measurement of physical trade-offs has proven elusive when one of the products is a nonmarket good. But as long as the benefits from elk usage can be internalized by the rancher, explicitly or implicitly trade-offs are considered.

review of recent methodological advances in nonmarket valuation. Specifically, they write, "economists have not established relative values for policies and inputs over which agencies have control (e.g., habitat management and fish stocking), and instead have focused research efforts on establishing values for recreational services." They add that "collectively economists have paid too little attention to the physical production and transformation linkages between public policies and recreation values."

Mendelsohn and Brown's (1983) assessment of revealed preference approaches to recreation valuation, however, seems more optimistic. They see such various techniques as simple travel cost, household production function, and advanced travel cost, e.g., demand system (Burt and Brewer 1971), own price/quality (Vaughn and Russell 1982; Freeman 1979), and hedonic travel cost (Brown and Mendelsohn 1980) yielding useful information to resource managers. They conclude that in the final analysis, "The principal factor in choosing among the approaches is the policy question to be answered." The perspective of the Mendelsohn and Brown evaluation is that the focus of valuation should be on the "quality and quantity of the public good, the recreation site." In this setting, they find the simple travel cost method well suited only for determining the all-or-none value of a single site in an unchanging environment. Quantitative and qualitative changes in site attributes, on the other hand, are best attacked with one of the advanced travel cost methods. The Mendelsohn and Brown view of the household production function approach is that it is "an unnecessarily cumbersome approach to measure the value of sites or their qualities" since its aim is to value such products as kill, catch, etc.[3]

The Mendelsohn and Brown emphasis on site valuation and the use of the advanced travel cost methods seems appropriate for a wide range of resource allocation issues. The efficient mix of livestock grazing, recreation pursuits, and timber-harvesting activities on a tract of Bureau of Land Measurement, Forest Service or other public lands is a case in point. Similarly, when conflicts exist between recreation and mining activities in and along a clear-water stream, the issue of which combination of uses maximizes the capitalized value of the resource site should be an important focal point for management agency discussion. The costs and benefits of variations in design and scale of public campground, and the regulations that govern its use, can also be summarized in the estimates of site value associated with the different configurations, and

[3]Mendelsohn and Brown (1983) also summarize some potentially serious econometric problems and stringent assumptions regarding production technologies that are associated with this framework.

as argued by Mendelsohn and Brown, techniques that yield estimated values of changing site characteristics show the greatest promise.

There are other instances, however, in which the attention to site value may be less compelling. For example, consider a salmon stock that may be harvested in various combinations by commercial fishermen in salt water or by sport fishermen in fresh water along the route to the spawning stream. It seems that the appropriate linkage to focus on in this case is that between the managerially determined allocation, the expected quality of fishing, and benefits of the fishing experience. Strong and Hueth (1983), for example, used the household production function framework to examine the effect of variation in catch on the value of steelhead recreational trips in Oregon.

The contingent valuation method (CVM) in principle offers considerable flexibility to evaluate a wide range of management actions and variations in resource characteristics. Questions may be written to yield data appropriate for conducting marginal analysis, or to address all-or-none issues concerning environmental quality (Brookshire, Ives, and Shulze 1976), site values (Hammack and Brown 1974), or the allocation of a flow resource such as water (Daubert and Young 1981). In the presence of the increased use of CVM in natural resource valuation, however, there remains a widespread skepticism concerning its validity due to the suspected presence of a number of biases associated with its use (Rowe and Chestnut 1983). For our purpose here, however, we note the potential for contingent valuation procedures to yield the kinds of information that are useful for managerial decisions.

The upshot of this brief review is that the most useful nonmarket valuation procedures for a recreation resource management perspective are those that will feed data to a traditional managerial economics framework. In evaluating the efficiency and distributional aspects of site selection and alteration, and of shifts in allocations of fish and wildlife stocks and other resource services among user groups, managers require estimates of the value of marginal productivities of the resource inputs and regulatory instruments at their disposal. Whether it is the intention to look for variations in net benefits as changes in capitalized site values or in the form of contributions to recreation experiences, the neoclassical model of the firm can appropriately discipline the structure of our analysis so that we are addressing the right questions in our valuation research.

Supply—The Missing Link

Nonmarket valuation never has realized its potential in allocation decisions because it has not been widely utilized in conjunction with supply-related analysis. Instead, most empirical studies have assumed implicitly that the recreational resource supply is perfectly inelastic or fixed. Those studies that do yield marginal values typically fail to develop or extend the scope of analysis to the fundamental allocation question confronting the manager: how to create different recreational opportunities of greater net social value by changing site attributes or altering management practices on a given site. Thus, the challenge for outdoor recreation research is to marry supply and demand concepts so as to clarify the relationships between the recreation experience and the management inputs that influence the quantity and quality of that experience.

Treating the quantity and quality of recreation opportunities as endogenous requires detailed knowledge of the underlying biological and physical responses to management, i.e., a production or supply response function. Agricultural economists have been conducting similar types of bioeconomic research for decades. Early examples include plant response to fertilization and animal feed response research. The response function is used to gain insight into the trade-offs inherent in the biological system, for purposes of controlling that system.

Most of the agricultural response research has centered on modeling the direct input/output characteristics of commercial agricultural production. In that context, response functions are properly specified as single output or separable joint products. The linkage between inputs that are applied through management and the output(s) extracted is direct; the biological/physical environment has no intrinsic value other than what it contributes to the final product. Unintentional by-products of the production process typically are assumed not to exist or are unimportant to the producer/consumer.

Outdoor recreation presents a very different scenario. Unlike production agriculture, the outdoor recreation product is, at least in part, the attractor(s) per se. The attractors are an integral part of the experience and, thus, have intrinsic value. Management actions are designed either to enhance one or more biophysical attractors directly or to augment indirectly the recreational opportunities one can derive from the attractor(s). However, the interdependence of biological systems is almost certain to result in both intended and unwanted environmental impacts from management. A detailed understanding of the direct effects and interdependencies is essential if short- and long-run biological consequences, including unwanted side effects of management, are to be avoided or mitigated. Attempts at modeling direct biological response to recreation management are few indeed, and almost no consideration has been given to indirect effects.[4]

---

[4]A relatively rich literature addresses at least the theoretical dimensions of unwanted side effects or externalities. One issue that would seem to be particularly onerous to the study of outdoor recreation is the problem of local optima and corner solutions. Baumol (1964), Baumol and Bradford (1972), and

How to measure empirically the highly interdependent production processes found in outdoor recreation is problematic. Lack of observational repeatability is a major operational problem that plagues bio-economic analyses of all kinds and is probably why economic analysis of outdoor recreation has addressed only the issue of nonmarket valuation. Measurement of biological responses to incremental changes in management is confounded in natural environments. Two principal culprits are the stochastic nature of population dynamics and, in the case of fish and wildlife, the fugitive nature of the resources. In contrast to production agriculture, experimentation is less controllable, and environmental responses to management are not always immediately observable. Sufficient data to formally estimate production functions that capture the complex interdependencies of biological systems are common.

In light of the data limitations, it is likely that statistical analyses of complex biological system will be limited to high levels of aggregation that grossly simplify the production process. Detailed (microlevel) production models of nonseparable, joint biological systems may be an ideal that will never be achieved. The extent to which such research may be successful surely will depend on the use of statistical tools that can extract the most from limited data as well as development of suitable data for analysis. For example, use of prior information may be essential to improve estimator efficiency. Since many aspects of biological systems are bound by know physical laws, logit or mixed estimation models that explicitly incorporate pertinent laws may prove invaluable.

Inability to measure statistically the interdependencies between environmental attractors and management does not deny their existence. It simply requires developing alternative frameworks to model the complex causal chains. Simulation offers a potential interim alternative. It circumvents the problem of sparse data and resultant statistical properties by avoiding that aspect of the problem altogether. However, any attempt to simulate the recreation environment must contend with the usual legitimate criticisms of documentation and transferability.

Simulation: An Alternative to Statistical Analysis

Several standardized biophysical simulators have been developed recently in response to legislative imperatives that government programs and projects be assessed for environmental impacts. For example, the Fish and Wildlife Service of the U. S. Department of Interior (1981) designed the Habitat Evaluation Procedures (HEP) as a systematic accounting tool to measure the quantity and quality of wildlife habitat displaced or altered by project construction. The Quantified Evaluation for Decisions

---

Starrett (1972) show that highly interdependent production processes can lead to either/or production choices that complicate public policy.

(QED) (Gum et al. 1982) was developed to measure the achievements of environmental quality objectives and to analyze the economic consequences of environmental improvement programs and/or actions.

Although specific procedures and methods differ among the various simulators, there is a common conceptual process to simulating complex causal chains that characterize biophysical environments and production processes. The environment is disaggregated into a hierarchy of component parts or attributes, where the most aggregated component is defined in terms of less aggregated components. Technical indicators quantify every component. Since direct physical measurement is possible for only the most elemental (least aggregated) components, these measurements are linked to standards of performance in terms of qualitative (0 to 1) indices that may be derived from published scientific data, expert opinion, and, in some cases, nonexpert opinion or perceptions of quality.

Any of the biophysical simulators that can be augmented with management practices may be expanded into a supply response model. It is through this linkage that the influence of management on biophysical productivity can be traced. That is, management practices alter the measurable environmental variables in predictable ways, which ultimately affect overall environmental quality or change the quantity of the available environmental resources or amenities.

Figure 2.2 stylizes this process in the context of a management-linked HEP model framework, as developed by Matulich et al. (1982) and Matulich, Hanson, and Buteau (1983). The production potential for a given wildlife habitat is quantified as Habitat Units (HU). An HU is comprised of both quality (suitability) and quantity (area) dimensions. Thus, total HU production can be altered in two ways. The total habitat area can be increased or decreased, or habitat quality per unit area (HSI) can be altered by employing management actions. In either case, it is HSI that embodies the complexity of biological production in the habitat being modeled.

Overall habitat suitability (HSI) depends on the suitability of life requisite needs. Each life requisite need may be supplied by several cover types. Since each cover type is different, a separate set of directly measurable environmental variables (habitat variables) is required to define the adequacy or suitability of each cover type. As with HSI, each of the intermediate suitability indexes are specified as dimensionless, 0 to 1 values.

Incorporating the influence of management on habitat suitability requires specification of actions that alter the overall habitat conditions in some observable way. There are two general categories of management activities: those actions that maintain or enhance existing habitat and those actions that convert habitat from one type to another. Maintenance actions may be construed as variable cost activities, whereas conversion of one cover type to another often (though not always) requires some form of capital cost or construction activity. Conversion may, in turn, require maintenance of the new condition. Associated management costs are a function of the intensity with which these practices must be applied to achieve a given biological outcome. Superimposing an optimization model on the simulated supply response framework and parametrically varying the biological output (HU) identifies that subset of least-cost management practices corresponding to given levels of output (Matulich, Hanson, and Bateau 1983; Matulich and Hanson 1986). Among that subset is the one that yields maximum net benefits.

A parallel HEP-like application may be conceived for a recreation site. The Recreation Opportunity Spectrum, discussed earlier, identifies somewhat different recreation products that could occur on a given site. For any given point or product along the spectrum, the potential suitability and overall quantity can be altered through management. An expanded HEP-like framework can be used to evaluate the mix and intensity of various management actions required to achieve a given recreation product of any technically feasible quality or suitability. Qualitatively different recreation opportunities will be reflected in both inherent value and use levels, i.e., demand. Thus, incremental valuation data from appropriate nonmarket valuation studies can be used in an optimization model to determine the welfare-maximizing resource allocation decision confronting the manager or agency.

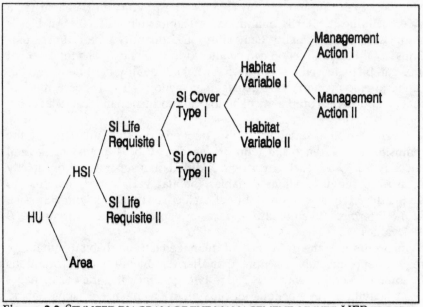

Figure 2.2 STYLIZED DIAGRAM OF THE MANAGEMENT-LINKED HEP PROCESS.

Summary and Conclusion

Improved management of public sector recreational resources is a multidisciplinary task. Much of the research by both recreation management theorists and economists has focused on demand issues without sufficient attention being paid to resource characteristics and to the regulations and inputs over which managing agencies have control. Recreation management theory, for example, has emphasized social-psychological underpinnings of visitor motivations and perceptions in attempting to explain recreation visitor behavior. Lacking has been any systematic attempt to understand the influence that management actions may have on user behavior.

Similarly, economists' contributions have focused on demand; nonmarket valuation procedures typically have yielded information useful only for all-or-none types of allocation decisions in benefit-cost analyses. Despite elegant theoretical advancements and ingenious estimation procedures, little effort has been made to isolate the effect of resource characteristics and management actions on either the benefits that visitors enjoy or the costs of associated management decisions. The traditional managerial economics framework of business firm decision making calls for due consideration of both demand (value) and supply (cost) in its prescriptions for efficient resource allocation. Adaptation of this framework to recreation resource management is consistent with contemporary problems calling for incremental choices.

The basic precept of recreation management is that the manager supplies the recreational opportunity from which the user produces and consumes the recreational experience. The optimal (efficient) point along the spectrum of recreational opportunities is that which generates the greatest net benefits to society. This depiction of the management system conceptually fits the managerial economics framework, and it is this framework that can discipline the structure of future research efforts. Emerging theoretical developments in nonmarket valuation procedures promise more useful demand—side valuation. However, even with marginal value estimates, decision makers will be deprived of adequate information to render efficient resource allocation decisions unless correlative supply response/cost functions are available. The usual assumption of perfectly inelastic supply is indeed a convenient artifice for most nonmarket valuation research but one that is untenable for public or private recreation policy analysis. Development of statistical supply response functions is certain to encounter serious obstacles. However, simulation seems to offer an interim framework capable of piecing together essential supply response relationships. Managers require estimates of both costs and values of marginal resource productivities and of regulatory instruments, if efficiency and distributional consequences of allocation decisions are to be evaluated.

References

Batie, S., and L. Shabman. 1979. Valuing Nonmarket Goods Conceptual and Empirical Issues: Discussion. *American Journal of Agricultural Economics*. 61(5).

Baumol, W. 1964. External Economies and Second-Order Optimality Conditions. *American Economic Review*. 54(3).

Baumol, W., and D. Bradford. 1972. Detrimental Externalities and Non-Convexity of the Production Set. *Economica*. 34(5):160-76.

Brookshire, D., B. Ives, and W. Shulze. 1976. The Valuation of Aesthetic Preferences. *Journal of Environmental Economics and Management*. 3(4).

Brown, P., B. L. Driver, and C. McConnell. 1978. The Opportunity Spectrum Concept and Behavioral Information in Outdoor Recreation Resource Supply Inventories: Background and Application. *In* Integrated Inventories of Renewable Resources: Proceedings of the Workshop, 73-84. U.S. Department of Agriculture, Forest Service General Technical Report RM-55.

Brown, G., an d R. Mendelsohn. 1980. The Hedonic Travel Cost Approach. University of Washington, Seattle. Unpublished paper.

Burt, O., and Brewer. 1971. Estimation of the Net Social Benefits from Outdoor Recreation. *Econometrica*. 39(5):5.

Clark, R. N., and G. H. Stankey. 1979. The Recreation Opportunity Spectrum: A Framework for Planning, Management, and Research. U.S. Department of Agriculture, Forest Service, General Technical Report. PNW-98.

Clawson, M., and J. L. Knetsch. 1966. *Economics of Outdoor Recreation*. Baltimore: Johns Hopkins University Press.

Daubert, J., and R. Young. 1981. Recreational Demands for Maintaining Instream Flows: A Contingent Valuation Approach. *American Journal of Agricultural Economics*. 63(4).

Davis, R. K. 1963. Recreation Planning as an Economic Problem. *Natural Resources Journal*. 3 (October):239-49.

Driver, B. L., and P. J. Brown. 1978. The Opportunity Spectrum Concept in Outdoor Recreation Supply Inventories: An Overview. *In* Integrated Inventories of Renewable Natural Resources: Proceedings of the Workshop. U.S. Department of Agriculture, Forest Service General Technical Report RM-55.

Freeman, A. M. 1979. *The Benefits of Environmental Improvement*. Baltimore: Johns Hopkins University Press.

Gum, R., and W. Martin. 1975. Problems and Solutions in Estimating the Demand for the Value of Rural Outdoor Recreation. *American Journal of Agricultural Economics*. 57(4).

Gum, R., L. Arthur, S. Oswald, and W. Martin. 1982. Quantified Evaluation for Decisions: Measuring Achievement Goals and Analyzing Trade-Offs. Technical Bulletin 145. Corvallis: Agricultural Experiment Station, Oregon State University.

Hammack, J., and G. Brown. 1974. *Waterfowl and Wetlands: Toward Bioeconomic Analysis*. Baltimore: Johns Hopkins University Press.

Kaplan, R. 1984. Wilderness Perception and Psychological Benefits: An Analysis of Continuing Programs. *Leisure Sciences*. 6(3):271-90.

Lancaster, K. 1966. A New Approach to Consumer Theory. *Journal of Political Economy*. 74(2).

Matulich, S., and J. Hanson. 1986. Modeling Supply Response in Bioeconomic Research. *Land Economics*. 62(3).

Matulich, S., J. Hanson and J. Buteau. 1983. Design and Management of Irrigation Projects for the Sustained Benefit of Wildlife. Report No. 53. Pullman: Water Resource Center, Washington State University.

Matulich, S., J. Hanson, A. Farmer, and I. Lines. 1982. HEP as a Planning Tool: An Application to Waterfowl Enhancement. Transactions of the North American Wildlife and Natural Resource Conference.

McConnell, K. E. 1979. Values of Marine Recreational Fishing: Measurement and Impact of Measurement. *American Journal of Agricultural Economics*. 61:921-25.

Mendelsohn, R., and G. M. Brown, Jr. 1983. Revealed Preference Approaches to Valuing Outdoor Recreation. *Natural Resources Journal*. 23:607-18.

Prewitt, R. A. 1979. The Economic of Public Recreation—An Economic Survey of the Monetary Valuation in National Parks. Washington, D.C.: National Park Service.

Rowe, R., and L. Chestnut. 1983. Valuing Environmental Commodities: Revisited. *Land Economics*. 59(4).

Starrett, D. 1972. Fundamental Nonconvexities in the Theory of Externalities. *Journal of Economic Theory*. 4(4):180--99.

Strong, E., and D. Hueth. 1983. An Application of the Household Production Function Approach to the Oregon Steelhead Sport Fishery. Paper presented at the Western Agricultural Economics Association Conference, July, Laramie, Wyoming.

U.S. Department of Agriculture. 1981. ROS Guide. Washington, D. C.: USDA, Forest Service.

U.S. Department of Interior. 1981. Standards for the Development of Habitat Suitability Index Models. 103 ESM. Washington, D. C.: USDI, Fish and Wildlife Service.

Vaughn, W., and C. Russell. 1982. *Freshwater Recreational Fishing: The National Benefits of Water Pollution Control*. Washington, D.C.: Resources for the Future.

3 Economic Efficiency and National Forest Planning

Dennis Schweitzer

Frederick Norbury

Gregory Alward

Introduction

Difficulties in estimating future economic costs and values, particularly for nontraditional management activities, result in unknown errors in estimates of economic characteristics of national forest plan alternatives. However, it is unlikely that such errors distort decisions on forest plans significantly. This is primarily because there are strong forces that heavily influence new plans of management to be quite "similar" to traditional plans of management.

In 1976, the National Forest Management Act (NFMA) directed the Forest Service to develop plans for each of the national forests. Subsequently, regulations that provided more specific direction were put into place by the U.S. Department of Agriculture. In combination with other applicable laws, such as the National Environmental Policy Act (NEPA), these legal rules gave the most detailed direction in history for analysis, planning, and management of the national forests (Wilkinson and Anderson 1985).

Forest plans are legal documents that define the schedule and combination of multiple-use activities to be applied during the next decade to forests that, on average, are larger than the state of Delaware. Programs to monitor the consequences of management are included so the plans can be modified if necessary. In any event, each plan will be completely redone within 15 years.

A lengthy and exhaustive process of planning with public participation is used to develop each plan. Indeed, in attempting to meet all legal requirements, a demanding rational-comprehensive model of planning is followed (Iverson and Alston 1986). This means alternative goals are explicitly defined, the widest possible ranges of management options and

43

plan alternatives are explored, and the consequences of each plan alternative are defined in detail. All of this information is made available for public review and comment and, perhaps, for challenge.

By regulation, a significant feature of the analytical process supporting forest planning is the use of economic analysis. In this chapter, we discuss some of the difficulties encountered in developing estimates of economic costs and of economic values, the fundamentals of economic analysis. We then discuss the general implications of those difficulties.

Requirement for Economic Efficiency

One requirement of the regulations guiding forest planning is that the most economically efficient set of management activities be selected to achieve the goals of each forest plan. From the perspective of the economist, this is a problem in achieving a constrained or local optimum, rather than a global optimum, for two reasons. First, potential efficiency is reduced because all plans must meet non-economic, legal standards of environmental protection, vegetative conditions, and (usually) nondeclining, forestwide timber harvest flow patterns. Second, procedures for defining the multiple-use goals to be achieved within the remaining decision space are specified by regulation, and a major portion of those goals always are non-economic.

Within these constraints or, more properly, while achieving these nationally and socially significant non-economic goals, the task is to satisfy the subordinate requirement for economic efficiency. More specifically, the surplus of economic values over the costs of production, when discounted for time, must be maximized. The Forest Service calls this surplus "present net value."

There are numerous difficulties in estimating both the economic costs and the economic values that are fundamental to calculating present net value.

Estimating Economic Costs

Our ability to estimate the economic costs of forest management tends to be taken for granted. After all, in the aggregate we do know how much it costs to carry out management on the ground; we know what we spent last year. And as long as we continue to do what we did last year, we can estimate with reasonable confidence how much things will cost, at least in the near future. However, in conducting the analysis necessary to support forest planning, we have to look at other possibilities as well.

The quest for reduced federal budgets and for economic efficiency in management requires that we explore a wide range of management options. NEPA requires that we define and analyze the widest possible range of plan alternatives, that is, of combinations of kinds and intensities of management practices. But as we consider departing from the ways we managed the forest last year, we also depart from our experience and bookkeeping records. Cost estimates become more speculative.

Research and experimental results provide only clues to the actual costs of applying nontraditional practices on a wide scale. Consider the case of helicopter applications of nitrogen fertilizers to forest stands to increase growth rates. Early operational applications led to growth responses that averaged about 85 percent of those promised by a considerable body of careful research. The major sources of this discrepancy were eventually traced to differences between the techniques of application of fertilizer used for research purposes and those used for operational purposes (Schweitzer 1972). The consequences of differences in techniques could not be quantified until operational applications were attempted, and the development of satisfactory rule-of-thumb corrections to cost (and benefit) estimates required several years of trial and error.

In current forest planning, there is a much less satisfactory research base supporting many practices we must explore for possible use in management. For example, the research or empirical knowledge base ranges from nonexistent to highly speculative when we consider the yield functions and operational costs of timber management without herbicides or under uneven-aged harvest systems on the West Coast. As a consequence, economic analyses of forest plan alternatives that contain such practices undoubtedly are in error.

Economists are fundamentally concerned with yield or production functions. If we do thus-and-so at a given cost, what quantity of economically valuable outputs will be produced? Unfortunately, we often do not know enough about the way complex ecosystems respond to management to answer this question with much confidence. For example, wildlife biologists know a great deal about how to create forest conditions that will benefit animals. However, their ability to define the increase in the number of animals that will result from XX acres of habitat improvement type YY is less certain. And even this estimate is not sufficient for an economic analysis. We also must know how the presence of more animals will affect the behavior of people (whose actions are the focus of economic analysis). This means we must estimate the change in the number of hunters or other users of animals that would occur. Quantifying the linkages between changes in habitat conditions and changes in the numbers of wildlife users is often an artistic, rather than scientific, endeavor.

We can confidently define correlations among existing habitat conditions and wildlife-user populations; this tells us a good deal about average relationships. But we are not at all confident in defining causal relationships or how users would change in response to habitat changes; we know little about marginal relationships. Because planning deals with changes from present conditions, our ignorance of causal relationships introduces considerable uncertainty into estimates of both physical and economic changes.

In combination, our imperfect understanding of existing production functions and our need to explore nontraditional management activities imply that planning estimates and projections of costs contain unknown, but possibly significant, errors.

Estimating Economic Values

To calculate measures of economic efficiency, economic values or the economic benefits of forest management must also be estimated. Our practice is to attribute economic values to all forest goods and services that are sold for cash or that could be sold for cash if national laws or policies permitted their sale. If we imagine a fence built around a national forest, our definition of economic value (used in efficiency analysis) is the fee that could be collected from forest users who want to go through a gate in the fence. (The analogy is not perfect, for it excludes off-site users of mobile forest resources such as fish and water.)

Under current policies, full fees generally are collected only for timber and minerals. The law limits the fees that can be charged to those who graze livestock and to recreationists. And there is no mechanism to charge distant users for water flowing from the forest. To measure the economic value of not-sold outputs requires estimating the fees that users would be willing to pay rather than to give up using them.

One approach is to assume these hypothetical fees are the same as fees actually collected elsewhere for similar uses, perhaps after making adjustments for minor differences. This is how we estimate fees for grazing livestock. A second approach is to base estimates on the "value added" to industrial products that are sold by a forest user after processing and transportation to a market. This approach is used to estimate values for commercial fish and for water used in hydropower generation and agriculture and is the basis for the "residual value" system of timber appraisal. A third approach includes a variety of techniques to estimate the fees recreationists would be willing to pay, such as the travel cost method and hedonic pricing.

Our confidence in estimates decreases as we move farther away from actual market transactions. We know for certain what is paid for national forest timber. We progressively lose confidence as we move from extrapolating from "similar" markets to calculating economic values added to marketed products to hypothesizing nonexistent markets for many kinds of recreation.

A few years ago, the Forest Service conducted an exhaustive survey of all published and known studies of recreation values across the country (Sorg and Loomis 1984). It turned up fifteen reasonably competent estimates of the economic value of big-game hunting; a single study yielded the only estimate for the northeastern quarter of the United States. Similarly, there were only five existing studies of the economic value of nonmotorized boating, all conducted west of the Continental Divide.

Relatively few studies comprised the major data base for our current forest planning. After they were collapsed into representative values for rather diverse kinds of recreation and sorted out for large regions of the country, they were used in developing most of the plans for national forests. Sufficient expertise and funding were available for a relatively few forests to conduct studies that yielded estimates of economic values specific to those forests.

Unfortunately, even these custom-fit economic values are really not very appropriate, for they are based on some existing or past set of forest conditions. In planning for the future, the problem is to predict what would happen under a wide range of alternative forest conditions. Again, existing correlations are important to know, but the real need is to understand causal relationships so we can predict what would happen if conditions changed.

The most promising approach seems to be basing estimates of value on hedonic pricing techniques. A forest output—recreation opportunity—is viewed as a bundle of attributes rather than as a single entity, and econometric techniques are used to define a value for each attribute. If some attributes or conditions of the recreation opportunity can be equated to physical conditions that can be varied across planning alternatives, unique economic values specific to each plan alternative can be defined.

A study on the Black Hills National Forest found that variables representing vegetative conditions could be related to the economically important behavior, or to the willingness to pay, of deer hunters (Wilman 1984). They were willing to pay more as the number of new forest openings with particular characteristics increased and as the prospects for successful hunting improved. The study identified vegetative conditions as independent variables in a way that could be related to forest planning alternatives.

While the study showed what could be done, the methodology is probably too expensive for widespread application. Simply to deal with deer hunting required the periodic services of a first-rate econometrician over several years and the cooperation of numerous employees of federal and state agencies to compile nonstandard data. Nevertheless, the hedonic pricing approach is worth further exploration.

We are more confident of our estimates of the economic value of timber than of any other resource, but even these estimates are debatable. They must be based on some historic starting point and then projected into the future. But the starting point is uncertain because of recent extraordinarily low prices, and projections are speculative because demands and prices for timber are the result of interest rates and other fundamentals of our entire economic system that have been, and probably will continue to be, extremely volatile.

The analytically most critical characteristic of valuation applied to national forest planning is that all resources be treated equally so that analysis does not significantly distort actual relationships. Solutions to the forest planning problem must define the relative portions of each national forest's resources to be spent on producing a long list of outputs. Particularly when the production of valued outputs is physically competitive, we should be confident of their relative values. Unfortunately, our estimates must be regarded as suspect.

Implications of Imperfect Estimates

Given the problems outlined above, it is clear that we cannot claim success in ensuring that forest plans are economically efficient in meeting their goals. However, the important question is not the purity of analysis. It is whether economic estimates and their imbedded errors lead to distorted decisions or provide useful clues to the best courses of action.

It is our belief that economic analysis is unlikely to distort the analytical basis for decisions to the extent that major errors in decisions will be made. One reason is that decisions are based on comparisons of the planning alternatives. Many errors in estimates of input-output relationships are likely to be constant in all alternatives and to disappear or be minimized when attention is focused on the differences among alternatives. A second reason why economic analysis is unlikely to distort decisions is that economic information is but one of many bases for judgment; social, environmental, and other consequences of the alternatives must also be examined. But the most important reason for our belief is that there are powerful forces in the forest planning process that influence most forest plan decisions to be similar to traditional types of forest management.

Earlier we pointed out that procedures to be followed in defining the goals of forest plans are specified in regulation. These procedures require that each forest respond (in different ways in different alternatives) to "issues" raised by the public and to "management concerns" defined by the professional managers of the agency. Nearly all of the issues and concerns that are guiding current planning reflect the same debates that have surrounded the management of national forests for at least the last twenty years. It is unlikely that forest-planning decisions will come up with answers that are much different from the traditional or current answers to these debates.

Current schemes of forest management represent some sort of "balance" among the competing claims on each forest that has been accepted well enough—with some specific exceptions—to work. And new forest plans must also find solutions that are publicly and politically acceptable. Radical change, as a result of forest planning, is extremely unlikely. In those instances where ecological slack has been used up or other conditions have changed so that all competing interests cannot be as satisfied as they have been in the past, there will be marginal changes. But we believe that changes will be evolutionary rather than revolutionary.

To the extent that selected forest plans are similar to current management, economic analysis will be most useful because the most important questions are focused on small changes from our most recent experiences. It is here that our estimates of costs and economic values, primarily based on current forest conditions and practices, are least likely to err. And if errors in estimate still distort analytical results, it is here that forest analysts and managers can rely most confidently on their professional judgment to recognize they are being led astray.

Documented evidence that economic information is influencing planning results is scanty. Economic information clearly has led to significant changes in the national forests in the lake states. It has resulted in planning decisions to replace a traditional and costly emphasis on the production of red pine timber with a much less expensive emphasis on aspen production. There are also signs that economic analysis, given recent prominence by public concerns about "below-cost timber sales," is influencing proposed levels and techniques of timber production. Finally, anecdotal evidence suggests that many forest managers are being influenced by combinations of economic and other analytical information.

On the other hand, few forest managers have selected the planning alternative with the highest present net value, where the surplus of economic values over costs is greatest. Indeed, chosen alternatives occasionally promise present net values lower than what could be obtained by simply continuing current management. In addition, comparisons of expected near-term cash receipts to expected costs show that many forests will continue to be managed at a sometimes substantial cost to taxpayers. This implies considerable weight is being given to non-economic issues and concerns in an attempt to maintain the balance necessary for forest management to be acceptable to the public. It also suggests that the influence of economic information on planning decisions is not dominant.

Summary

It is necessary that plans for the national forests be economically efficient in achieving the established goals. But difficulties in estimating and projecting both costs of management and economic values of outputs that could be produced suggest that the degree to which the requirement has been met is problematic.

When the first regulations to implement NFMA were published in the *Federal Register* in 1979, it was noted that many requirements were goals for the Forest Service to try to attain in the future. It was explicitly recognized that existing data and analytical techniques were not then up to the task. We believe that the difficulties are so fundamental that fully satisfactory efficiency analyses probably never will be achieved.

Nevertheless, this does not mean efficiency analysis is not useful. To the extent that forest plans lead to marginal, rather than radical, changes from current conditions, available economic information probably is most useful because we can be most confident about estimates that are "close to" recent experience. And it is in considering relatively small changes that professional judgment is most useful in detecting analytical errors.

References

Iverson, D.C., and R.M. Alston. 1986. *The Genesis of FORPLAN: A Historical and Analytical Review of Forest Service Planning Models.* U.S. Department of Agriculture, Forest Service General Technical Report INT-214. Ogden, Utah: Intermountain Forest and Range Experimental Station.

Schweitzer, D.L. 1972. Forest Fertilization in the Pacific Northwest: A Case Study in Timber Production Under Uncertainty. *In* Uncertainty in Forestry Investment Decisions Regarding Timber Growing, edited by A.L. Lundgren and E.F. Thompson. Publication FWS-1-72. Blacksburg: Virginia Polytechnic Institute and State University, Division of Forestry and Wildlife Management.

Sorg, C.F., and J.B. Loomis. 1984. *Empirical Estimates of Amenity Forest Values: A Comparative Review.* U.S. Department of Agriculture, Forest Service General Technical Report RM-107. Fort Collins, Colorado: Rocky Mountain Forest and Range Experimental Station.

Wilkinson, C.F., and A.M. Anderson. 1985. Land and Resource Planning in the National Forests. *Oregon Law Review.* 64:1-373.

Wilman, E.A. 1984. Recreation Benefits from Public Lands. *In* Valuation of Wildland Resource Benefits, edited by G.L. Peterson and A. Randall. Boulder, Colorado: Westview Press.

4 The Propriety of Applying Economic Methods to the Allocation of Public Amenity Resources: Paradigms, Property Rights, and Progress

Charles C. Harris

Mary McGown

Introduction

Resource economics has invested the last several decades in the development of methods for valuing and allocating public amenity resources, such as clean air and water, wildlife, recreation attractions, and other public goods. These methods for valuing environmental goods include the contingent valuation method (CVM), in which survey instruments directly elicit from people the monetary values they place on nonmarket goods, and two other indirect approaches, the travel cost method (TCM) and the hedonic price method (HPM), which estimate people's monetary values on the basis of their behaviors.

Despite the considerable effort that has been made over the years to improve these approaches to economic valuation of nonmarket goods, a variety of concerns have been raised about their efficacy and applicability for valuing public amenity resources. The intent of this chapter is to expand upon the issues that actual policymaking, as well as evolving theory and methods in economics and other social sciences, suggests should be addressed if those concerns are to be resolved.

We focus our discussion on the CVM, for three reasons. First, all of the monetary valuation approaches developed to date have a common theoretical basis in the neoclassical school of economic thought. While our discussion of alternative paradigms will focus on the CVM, the basic points we make at this broad conceptual level are also applicable to other valuation methods. Second, methodological, conceptual, and statistical concerns have been raised about whether the TCM and HPM, which attempt to develop empirically based models for measuring values, adequately do so; questions about the assumptions underlying these models, problems of proper model specification, the data collection requirements of these methods, and the complexity of their implementation have yet to be resolved after two decades of research. Third, these two empirically based modeling approaches are limited in their applicability, given their dependence on private consumption bundles having market prices; the potentially wide applicability of the CVM suggests that of all the economic valuation methods being developed, this approach could be the most useful.

The theme of this chapter is that the field of resource economics is evolving in a period of intellectual ferment that we hope will promote improvement of traditional approaches to analysis of resource amenity values and allocation, and perhaps the development of new approaches. Our purpose here is to foster that ferment and spur on development of valid, acceptable techniques for policy analysis and decision making.

Adopting a multidisciplinary perspective, we organize our discussion on the basis of three levels of analysis. One concerns the broad philosophical issues raised for the CVM by its underlying paradigm and assumptions, particularly when they are contrasted with the paradigms of other schools that might be considered. At a second, more specific level, we consider the methods of these schools, the CVM in particular, and the concerns raised about the validity and efficacy of this particular approach in light of alternative approaches and the theory and findings of psychologists, sociologists, and political scientists studying human information processing and decision making. At the third and most pragmatic level, we briefly consider issues surrounding the application of these methods for agency policymaking in terms of their actual use and that of the values they provide. The chapter concludes with a summary of major issues that need to be addressed and some tentative suggestions about future directions that thought and investigation might take toward resolving those issues.

The Neoclassical Model and Alternative Schools of Thought: Paradigms, Methods, and Applications

At the broadest, most basic level of analysis, questions are increasingly being raised about the neoclassical paradigm underlying the CVM. The last decade has seen increasing discussion of alternatives to this dominant school of economic thought. The growing prominence of these alternative schools of economic thought, whose differences from the neoclassical mainstream are philosophically rooted in the questions they ask about man and society and the means they deem appropriate for answering those questions, underscores the subjective and normative basis of the paradigms that shape economics as a social science.

Ironically, although the neoclassical school was founded with the spirit of nineteenth-century optimism about the usefulness of the scientific method for achieving social progress, two other schools of economic thought are now gaining influence in America because of concerns that the neoclassical mainstream has been unsuccessful in achieving that progress. These schools are the individualist school of public choice and the institutionalist school. Significantly, while both of these schools are viewed as being outside the positivist philosophical mainstream characterizing the neoclassical school, both are built upon a neoclassical core. Nonetheless, we would contend that the differences in these three schools are truly paradigmatic, in that they represent different concepts of human progress and how to achieve it, and thus differing ideologies.

These paradigmatic differences have important implications for evaluating the propriety of applying economic valuation methods to the problem of allocating public amenity goods. Traditionally, environmental goods and amenity resources have been allocated as public goods with nonmarket mechanisms. All of the outputs of the national forests (e.g., timber, forage, recreation, etc.) are public goods that are subsidized by government and thus allocated in ways that differ from market-based processes—despite the perception that some (e.g., timber) are market commodities requiring monetary measurement of output (McLaughlin and Saunders 1987). Implicitly, government has chosen to base its management and production decisions about all forest resources (not just amenity ones) on criteria other than efficiency, thereby asserting their position as social, merit goods.

Yet, because economic valuation methods are based on the neoclassical model, they tend to cast these goods in the neoclassical mold of "commodities" that can be allocated through quantitative analysis per the private market mode. Despite claims that other "values" (e.g., environmental, social, etc.) or accounts are considered, our perception is that the market-based paradigm gives great weight to certain normative judgments underlying it that counter those values. Implicit in the private market, as opposed to public allocation mechanisms, is the emphasis (and thus valuing) of the individual over the group, self-interest over altruism and commitment (Sen 1977), competition over cooperation, efficiency over equity, the status quo over progressive change, the short term over the long term, and laissez faire over social control.

Given these distinctions, we question whether the capitalist paradigm (developed vis-à-vis the exchange of private goods) is an appropriate foundation on which to base processes for valuing public amenity resources. The long-standing tradition of government intervention through its dominant role in resource management is evidence that this question is a significant one. A look at other schools of economic thought provides a broader perspective for considering this question; Table 4.1 summarizes the differences in the three schools in terms of their paradigms, methods, and applications.

Basic Philosophy

We begin our comparison of the paradigms of these schools with their basic philosophies. The neoclassical, rational planning school of economic thought has been described as "unabashedly reductionist" and thus located "firmly in the mainstream of post-enlightenment western thought" (Randall 1985, 1023). Neoclassical economics presupposes that the universal truth of theoretical propositions is a valid question; accordingly, it follows the positivist lead set by the physical sciences, where the separation of theory and methodology from ideology is not an issue. Reductionism encompasses elementalism (wholes are sets of individuals, atomistic units), universalism (establishment of universal and constant relationships, or laws), deductivism, and empiricism, and it is manifested in the social sciences in the adoption of the hypothetico-deductive model.

This reductionist perspective disregards the possibility that economic phenomena are neither as predictable nor as universal as those in the physical world. Married to the development of a capitalist system, it has evolved a scientism of economic behavior manifested in the growing reliance of agency policymakers on analytical methods (particularly benefit-cost analysis and the monetary evaluation methods it requires). Currently, the American economic system is best depicted as a mixed capitalist one. It attempts to join the microeconomic principles of a capitalist, self-regulating, and thus free market system to the Keynesian principle that government intervention is needed to correct failures of that system and ensure its smooth operation. All neoclassical methods of taking monetary measurements of the value of nonmarket goods reflect the principles of the pure capitalist system, wherein a private market structure is a useful and appropriate vehicle for analyzing changes in welfare and measuring people's values for any good with a common, comparable metric (e.g., dollars).

Unlike the neoclassical mainstream, with its reductionist basis that accommodates conservative and liberal thought alike, the fringe schools of individualism and institutionalism reflect a clear difference in basic philosophy. The individualist school combines some elements of reductionism (e.g., the atomistic, elemental, and individualistic) with a natural rights ideology that espouses individualism and faith in market and private property institutions. In reflecting Austrian economics' combining of positive economics with libertarian policy positions, it clearly represents a position to the right of the American political center.

Table 4.1 A COMPARISON OF MAJOR SCHOOLS OF ECONOMIC THOUGHT

Points of Comparison	Schools of Economic Thought		
	Institutionalist	*Neoclassical*	*Individualist*
I. *The Paradigm*			
A. Basic Philosophy:	Romantic/Anti-Positivist Ideology	Reductionist/Positivist Ideology	Reductionist/Natural Rights Ideology
B. View of Man:	Culturally Bound Man	Rational Economic (and Political) Man	Atomistic Man in Context
C. Mechanism for Social Progress:	Institutional Failure/Fix Government Fix	Market Failure/	Market Fix/ Government Failure
II. *Methods*			
A. Unit of Analysis:	Collectivities	Individual/Household	Individual
B. Measurement & Analysis:	Holistic/Pattern Modeling	Axiomatic, Deductive, Mathematical	Subjective
C. Aggregation:	Not an Issue (Synergism)	An Issue (Problimatic)	Not an Issue (Individualism)
III. *Application of Methods*			
A. Benefit-Cost Analysis:	Nondominant: Efficiency as Dubious Social Goal	Dominant: Efficiency as Social Goal	Rejected: Efficiency Irrelevant
B. Property Rights:	Property Claims (Inalienable Human Rights)	Property Rights	Natural Rights (Privatization)

In contrast, the institutionalist school, which is the focus of social reformers, can be located at the left end of the American political spectrum. Given its roots in the romanticism of the German Historical School, it totally rejects reductionism, instead asserting the philosophy that organic realities cannot be comprehended by analysis of relationships among their components. The founders of institutionalism in this country, John Commons and Thorstein Veblen, disagreed with the Cartesian view that the real world is characterized by order and rationality and thus is best apprehended through an appeal to human reason alone. Implicit in the mainstream, neoclassical theory that evolved from this Cartesian view is the position that truth about reality lies in the logic of the theory. Institutionalists reject this paradigm because it focuses on the logic of a formal model, emphasizing rational behavior and competition while ignoring custom and habit and the evolving nature of technology, business organization, and the role of the state (Wilber 1978).

Within the classifications of philosophy of science, most standard economics, including logical positivism and a priori rationalization, falls into the category of formalism. In contrast, institutional economics, at the most general level, can be categorized as holistic, systematic, and evolutionary (Wilber 1978): It is holistic because it focuses on the pattern of relations among parts and the whole; it is systemic because it believes that those parts make up a coherent whole and can be understood only in terms of the whole; and it is evolutionary because changes in the pattern of relations are seen as the very essence of social reality.

Mechanisms for Progress

The neoclassical, individualist, and institutionalist paradigms also differ in their perspectives on mechanisms for achieving social progress through economic analysis. The "market failure/government fix" approach of the neoclassical mainstream reflects a commitment to the rational, scientific process of policy formulation and implementation, whereby progress can be promoted by maximizing efficiency via the objective collection and analysis of factual information for optimum decision outcomes. Although this view, as held by rational planners and neoclassicists, is now depicted by some as "naivete . . . now clearly in eclipse" (Randall 1985, 1022), recent discussions by land-management agency analysts and planners (e.g., Haught 1984, Schweitzer and Cortner 1984) would suggest otherwise.

In contrast to this mainstream conceptualization, the individualists espouse what might be termed "market fix/government failure." True to their laissez-faire, libertarian ideal, the individualists believe that social progress can best be achieved by maximizing individual choice and responsibility; for this school, the role of economic system should be that of maximizing individual freedom and minimizing waste through privatization.

Institutional economics, unlike the other schools, takes a broader view of societal mechanisms for promoting progress. This third school expands its focus beyond the role of markets and government as major actors in the economic system and views the economic system as a subset of human relations and institutions.

Placed in this societal context, economic exchange is seen as a minor (but important) form of human interaction. Exchange is a valid form of social interaction, but it is not conceived as an adequate model for all human interaction. The constellation of interactions involved in political activities must also be considered. For institutionalists, political activities are valid ways of expressing one's values, and political outcomes are valid sources of information about what people value. In contrast, the other paradigms discount the role of political and legal processes in their focus on market and regulatory mechanisms.

The CVM, as one product of neoclassically based economic valuation methodology, reflects the paradigm underlying the mainstream rational planning approach to public amenity resource allocation. It thus requires the assumptions about the nature of man of the neoclassical school of economic thought as well as its presumptions about societal progress and key mechanisms for achieving it. Our contention is that attending to other schools of thought and understanding their implications could help in improving the CVM and resolving problems it currently poses.

Methods

The methods of any disciplinary approach are grounded in the paradigm upon which the approach is based; the paradigm necessarily shapes the methods used to operationalize and apply the approach. The neoclassical mainstream, because it is founded on reductionism, is guided in its measurement and analysis by the deductive process of the scientific method and an emphasis on mathematics and quantification that reflects its emulation of the physical sciences.

Neoclassical methodology builds upon a hierarchical model of theory construction, which is predictive in intent. The components of a hierarchical theory are arranged in a pyramid, with basic principles or postulates (e.g., assumptions of utility and profit maximization) at the top and deductions drawn from them at lower levels in the theory. Individual behavior is explained when it is deduced from basic postulates (e.g., utility functions) and initial conditions (e.g., income distribution and prices of goods). The predictive model is then tested empirically by comparing deductions (quantitative predictions) with observations.

Given this focus on developing predictive models, neoclassical economists de-emphasize structural realism.

Accordingly, neoclassical units of analysis tend to be individual ones, whether persons or households. The treatment of groups, as in the case of households, as simple aggregations of individuals is a critical feature of the mainstream; it is this conception of the social unit (i.e., the group can be represented as the sum of its individual members) that informs its attempts to derive a social welfare function by aggregating across individuals. Unfortunately, Arrow (1949) debunked the possibility of deriving such a function in this manner with his Impossibility Theorem.

The individualist school of economic thought, whose paradigm places the atomistic individual at the center of its theory and analysis, extends the individualism of the neoclassical's self-interested capitalist to its furthest limits. Its individualism is methodological as well as ideological, with subjectivism the hallmark of this school:

> The subjectivism of the Austrians (individualists) leads them to reject, for a variety of reasons, the various reductionist-positivist doctrines on the testing and validation of theories... Mises pronounced the basic axioms of economics to be self-evident facts of subjective experience and therefore true a priori. Empirical testing of the premises of theory is absurd, if one takes the a priorist position.
>
> While the modern hypothetico-deductive/falsificationist methodology seeks to test theories by denying their predicted consequences, modern Austrians view the predictions of their theories as admittedly unfalsifiable. Since there are no constants in the social "real world," empirical studies serve only to determine if a particular theory is applicable in a given situation. Falsification of universal theories about society is far too much to ask. (Randall 1985, 1024).

Given its subjectivist, methodological individualism, the question of aggregation to provide a quantitative indicator of social welfare is not a reasonable one for the individualist school; as Randall notes, "it [the aggregation question] presupposes the unthinkable: that it is ethically acceptable for a collectivist decision rule to be logically derived from diverse individual preferences and then imposed, coercively, on each of these same individuals" (Randall 1985, 1025).

The romantic holism of the institutionalist school shares the anti-reductionism, anti-scientism perspective of the individualist school, but institutionalists are at the other end of the methodological as well as ideological spectrum from the individualists.

In direct opposition to public choice individualists, institutional-ists do not see the individual as the appropriate unit of analysis. Rather, individuals are seen as a part and a product of the culture and institutions to which they belong. Individuals realize their potential through collective action, which provides an environment for individual actions.

Institutions are seen as a stimulus and a guide to individual behavior. Further, because individual preferences are not original or fundamental causal factors, they are not the place to initiate theory (Dugger 1979). "A thirst for power and adventure, a sense of independence, altruism, idle curiosity, custom and habit may all be powerful motivations of economic behavior. Thus, the institutionalists have been particularly critical of the economic man assumption of neoclassical economics" (Wilber 1978).

The methods of measurement and analysis of the institutionalist school reflect this perspective. They are based upon the development of concatenated models, which describe patterns and thus are the basis of the pattern modeling and holistic characteristic of institutionalism. The components of a concatenated theory form an identifiable pattern (a culture), which generally converges to some central point (an institution). Individual behavior is explained when it is shown to fit into an institutional structure of behavioral norms, and institutional structure is explained when it is shown to fit into a cultural context. The pattern model is tested empirically by comparing hypothesized institutional structures (qualitative patterns) with observations. In building pattern models, institutionalists spend a great deal of effort in making the pattern or theoretical structure realistic.

Because of their perception of culture as a manifestation of social synergism, the institutionalists do not regard the aggregation question as even being an issue. The question reflects a reductionist perspective; consequently, the institutionalist school views it as absurd and thus irrelevant.

Based on their methodological differences from the neoclassical mainstream, the other schools of economic thought would view economic valuation methods like the CVM as problematic, if not irrelevant. For both the individualists and the institutionalists, valuing public amenity resources is ultimately a reductionist exercise. The results of an effort grounded in scientism are of little value—especially so because their aggregation (whether through averaging, as most research results are reported, or adding, as welfare and public choice theory discuss) is of little meaning.

Additional issues concerning the viability of the CVM reflect an institutionalist perspective, in that institutionalism focuses on the application of broader, sociopsychological theory to questions of resource valuation. The extent to which people have the ability to process value-elicitation information correctly, the degree to which respondents' valuation responses are influenced in unknown or undesirable ways by value-elicitation methods when those people may lack well-formulated values, and the role of stress on the quality of people's evaluative judgments are all questions that psychological research raises for the adequacy of current forms of the CVM (Harris, Driver, and McLaughlin 1987; Harris, Tinsley, and Donnelly, in process).

Applications of the Methods

The explicit purpose of economic valuation methods is to provide value measurements that agencies managing and regulating amenity resources can use in their policy and decision analyses. For the neoclassical school, benefit-cost analysis is the dominant tool for ensuring efficiency in resource management, and efficiency is viewed by the mainstream as the primary social goal.

This current emphasis on neoclassical economics by land management agencies is part of a larger tradition of rational planning based on the possibility of an objective, scientific approach to policy formulation and implementation (Randall 1985). Throughout the evolution of the U.S. Forest Service's integrated, comprehensive approach to strategic planning for the national forest system, for example, the role of economic analysis in that agency's decision making has been lauded as growing in importance (Johnson 1985).

At the level of nationwide forest planning, in particular, that role has been depicted as central to the development and selection of a national management program (Haught 1984). Yet, at the forest level, a study of forest plans (at least those produced in the state of Idaho) suggests the difficulty of tracking the criteria and logic actually used to select the final planning alternative—much less the role of economic analysis—despite the considerable amounts of dollars and time that are devoted to generating economic data based on the value of various forest outputs. One must question the propriety of neoclassical methods whose ends are pursued but never fully realized, due to the difficulties for agency analysts in applying the technical and data-hungry procedures of these methods and to the skepticism of agency decision makers about the value estimates obtained with them.

The viability of analytical and decision-making processes of other federal agencies, such as the Army Corps of Engineers and the Environmental Protection Agency, can be similarly questioned. They also claim the pursuit of a means-ends approach to decision making based on disinterested benefit-cost analysis, but their pursuit is hardly as simple and straightforward as theory would suggest. (Witness the reactions of some lawmakers, for example, to the implicit values subsumed within these methods, as when Rep. James J. Florio, D-N.J., recently judged the EPA's attempt to place a dollar value on the life of a child to be "barbaric.")

In contrast to the neoclassical position, the individualists pronounce that—given the irrelevance of efficiency, the unacceptability of utilitarian decision rules, and the view that benefits and costs are totally subjective—benefit-cost analysis lacks any usefulness. The institutionalist school takes a more extreme position on efficiency than the individualists but a less extreme one on the utility of benefit-cost analysis. Institutional economists emphasize the normative implications of the efficiency criterion: even though any particular efficiency solution represents one of many configurations of allocation, distribution, and pricing, efficiency analysis promotes the status quo and is thus a questionable social goal. Nonetheless, institutionalists regard benefit-cost analysis as a useful tool, although they caution that it should not be regarded as dominant, thereby bestowing improper influence of current prices and income distribution on policy formulation.

Perhaps the most fundamental issue for applications of the methods of the three schools to land management problem analysis is raised by the differences in their positions on the nature of property rights. Definition of property rights determines the extent to which private market mechanisms are applicable to the allocation and valuation of public amenity goods. Neoclassical thinkers presume that principles of private property rights can be extended to common property rights like those characterizing public resources. It is then admissible to apply the CVM and ask people their willingness to be compensated for the loss of their "rights" to endowments or entitlements like clean air or water.

The individualists take an even more extreme position than mainstream thinkers and assert a concept of "natural rights," which in effect are the rights of man, including property rights. Because this school holds that the right of property is an expression of a fundamental right of man, it opposes any scheme that would limit the freedom of individuals. The belief follows logically that all institutions, including public resources, should be privatized.

The institutionalists differ sharply with the other paradigms over the role of property rights in economics and society. Institutionalists, preferring the less emotional term *property claims*, have long considered this concept to be an important one, but in a broader sense than the other paradigms. Property is an idea, rather than an object; it refers to all of the rights that extend over an object. These rights have important meanings and identify important relationships between and among individuals and the society. The institutionalists see the role of society as essential in the idea of property: "While there are variations in how property claims are viewed, the common element is that each society must specify property claims, and the structure of those claims influences the behavioral relations. Further, the property claims are evolutionary and must be sanctioned by society" (Reynolds 1985, 945). Problem solving has often required changes in property claims.

The variations in perspectives among the three schools of economic thought on the application of the efficiency criterion and benefit-cost analysis suggest, even among economists, that the basic tenets underlying an economic valuation method like the CVM are in question. An analysis of the three schools suggest that the propriety of pursuing particular social goals and means for achieving those goals is questionable, given the different normative stances of the schools. Understanding of the normative issues raised by a particular approach like the CVM through an understanding of the neoclassical, individualist, and institutionalist positions can help to clarify the problems and questions that must be resolved before it will be a widely accepted and applied method.

Needed Research

Future research should promote the cross-disciplinary fertilization from which can spring new ideas and improvements in the conceptual and methodological development of resource valuation methods. If the neoclassical paradigm's dominance is to be fully credible, current price theory must be expanded to resolve normative issues raised by other schools like the institutionalists (Boudling 1977).

In addition, the issues raised for resource valuation and allocation need to be clarified and addressed. The applicability of private property structures to common property rights and to larger issues of universal, inalienable human rights (i.e., health, happiness, etc.) associated with public resources like clear air and water have only begun to be addressed and their implication for resource valuation explored. A basic conception of assessing trade-offs among resource use may be a more tenable theoretical foundation for nonmarket valuation than that of estimating the outcomes of property exchanges implicit in the CVM. In a similar vein, measures of willingness to accept compensation for losses of nonmarket goods are likely to be a more conceptually sound measure than willingness-to-pay measures predominantly used in CVM applications; however, even applying these kinds of measures to questions involving the surrender of inalienable rights may be viewed by some as unreasonable and improper.

If progress is to be made in the area of resource valuation, the implications of other economic schools for neoclassical approaches like the CVM need to be examined further. Transactive approaches (whereby legislators, agency analysts, and resource economists work together as partners in a decision making process that is as subjective, interactive, and political as it is objective, rational, and quantifiable) reflect institutionalist concerns and could be implemented to achieve a consensus about acceptable methods. Quasi-privatization of public resources, whereby the individualists' faith in the market could be tested by private leasing of public resources under well-defined contractual agreement, could be considered; this approach would render the CVM unnecessary, but its problems as well as potentialities need to be clearly identified. Finally, progress in resource valuation and allocation could be advanced by more in-depth analyses of the economic analysts' current and potential role in policy and decision making, an approach that Shabman (1985) has initiated but that others could expand upon in the context of economic valuation methods.

Conclusions

Our contention is that the nonreductionist paradigms represented by individualism and institutionalism and their implications for the relationship between market and government solutions need to be addressed in the context of amenity resource valuation and allocation. The single-minded embracing of the neoclassical paradigm by land managers, resource policymakers, and the researchers studying refinements of economic valuation methods is curious in light of Randall's assertion that the "market failure/government fix" naïveté of the neoclassical/rational planning paradigm is now in decline. We would propose that the ideological and methodological pluralism that is emerging as an increasingly vital force in economics holds the seeds for further multidisciplinary efforts of the kind needed to promote progress in the area of resource valuation. Thus, we fully concur with Randall's conclusion that while "the persistence of rivalry among noncomparable research programs is the reality to which we need become accustomed," "cross-program disagreements are powerful stimuli for within-program progress" (Randall 1985, 1028). We would even assert that attention to nonreductionist programs may provide the wedge for attending to theories and findings of other social sciences and their implications for resource economics programs.

We perceive resource economics to be particularly open to expanding its perspectives. Indeed, much to its credit, it is already doing so in its development of economic methods for valuing nonmarket goods, where researchers are working to improve the CVM and increasingly heeding and even enlisting the ideas and methods of non-economic behavioral sciences. The ongoing research on nonmarket valuation approaches can be defended—to some extent—from Kuttner's (1985) charge that economics fears dissension. The flowering of new experimental approaches and integration of sociopsychological theories in current valuation research (see, for example, Peterson, Driver, and Gregory, in process) is significant: it is indicative of the willingness of resource economists developing the CVM—perhaps because of their self-imposed contact with applied, real-world problems that are subject to observation and disputation—to bear the risks and also the fruits of dissension.

Given that all three schools of economic thought, as previously noted, have a common theoretical core in neoclassical theory, this commonality could provide a basis for clarifying, addressing, and perhaps resolving fundamental issues that exist for the estimation and use of nonmarket values derived with methods like the CVM. We would assert, however, that economists researching methods for resource valuation must crack their investigative window a bit wider and begin to address the implications of these larger issues if the efficacy of these valuation methods is to be established.

References

Arrow, K.J. 1949. *Social Choice and Individual Values.* 2nd ed. New York: John Wiley New York.

Boulding, K.E. 1977. Prices and Other Institutions. *Journal of Economic Issues* 11(4):809-21.

Dugger, W.M. 1979. Methodological Differences Between Institutional and Neoclassical Economics. *Journal of Economic Issues.* 13(4):899-09.

Harris, C.C., B.L. Driver, and W.J. McLaughlin. 1987. *Assessing Contingent Valuation Methods from a Psychological Perspective.* Department of Wildland Recreation Management, University of Idaho, Moscow. Draft manuscript.

Harris, C.C., H.E.A. Tinsley, and D.M. Donnelly. In process. Research Methods for Public Amenity Resource Valuation: Issues and Recommendations. Draft manuscript of a chapter in a book tentatively titled *Integrating Psychology and Economics in Valuing Public Amenity Resources,* edited by G. Peterson, B.L. Driver, and R. Gregory. U.S. Department of Agriculture, Forest Service, Rocky Mountain Forest and Range Experiment Station, Ft. Collins, Colo.

Haught, A. 1984. Economic Analysis for National Land Planning in the United States. *Proceedings for Economic Value Analysis of Multiple Use Forestry, International Union of Forestry Research Organizations,* edited by F. Kaiser, D. Schweitzer, and P. Brown, 132-45. Corvallis: Department of Resource Recreation Management, Oregon State University.

Johnson, K.N. 1985. Integrating Economic Analysis into Strategic Planning on the National Forests. *In* Foresters' Future: Leaders or Followers? Proceedings of the 1985 Society of American Foresters National Convention, 276-79. Bethesda, Maryland: Society of American Foresters.

Kuttner, R. 1985. The Poverty of Economics. *The Atlantic Monthly.* 255(2):74-80, 82-84.

McLaughlin, W.J., and P.R. Saunders. 1987. Effects of Below-Cost Timber Sales on Outdoor Recreation and Related Tourism. *In* Below-Cost Timber Sales. Conference Proceedings, edited by D.C. LeMaster, B.R. Flamm, and J.C. Hendee, 179-94. Washington, D.C.: The Wilderness Society.

Peterson, G., B.L. Driver, and R. Gregory, eds. In process. *Integrating*

Psychology and Economics in Valuing Public Amenity Resources. U.S. Department of Agriculture Forest Service, Rocky Mountain Forest and Range Experiment Station, Ft. Collins, Colorado. Draft of book manuscript(s).

Randall, A. 1985. Methodology, Ideology and the Economics of Policy: Why Resource Economists Disagree. *American Journal of Agricultural Economics.* 67:1022-29.

Reynolds, R.L. 1985. Institutionally Determined Property Claims. *Journal of Economic Issues.* 19(4):941-49.

Schweitzer, D.L., and H.J. Cortner. 1984. Evolution of Planning Requirement for National Public Forestry in the United States. *In* Proceedings for Economic Value Analysis of Multiple Use Forestry, International Union of Forestry Research Organizations, edited by F. Kaiser, D. Schneitzer, and P. Brown, 112-22. Corvallis: Department of Resource Recreation Management, Oregon State University.

Sen, A.K. 1977. Rational Fools: A Critique of the Behavioral Foundations of Economic Theory. *Philosophy and Public Affairs.* 614:317-44.

Shabman, L. 1985. Natural Resource Economics: Methodological Orientations and Policy Effectiveness. *American Journal of Agricultural Economics.* 67:1030-034.

Wilber, C.K. 1978. The Methodological Basis of Institutional Economics: Pattern Model, Storytelling, and Holism. *Journal of Economic Issues.* 12(1):61-89.

5 Valuing Changes in Environmental Assets

Robin Gregory

Donald MacGregor

Introduction

It now has become commonplace for measures of the value of an environmental asset to be included as part of the benefit-cost analysis of natural resource investment options. For example, recent studies investigate the value of changes in hazardous waste risks (Smith, Desvousges, and Freeman 1985), water quality (Mitchell and Carson 1981), and visibility (Rowe, d'Arge, and Brookshire 1980) that could result from alternative public decisions. Tests for the validity of these procedures have emphasized comparisons with methods more akin to conventional market-based analyses, and in general these tests have confirmed the results obtained using survey measures of value (Cummings, Brookshire, and Schulze 1986). As a result, information derived from surveys increasingly is used to assist decision makers in allocating public funds and in selecting the socially preferred choice from among competing project alternatives.

We worry that these tests may ignore important issues of measurement validity and reliability, and therefore we are less confident that the value measures they provide accurately estimate the worth of environmental assets. One set of reasons for this concern has to do with how expressions of value are interpreted; in fact, it is not clear to us that meaningful economic values, at least as normally defined, actually exist for many of

Funding for this project was provided in part by a grant from the Sloan Foundation. Any opinions and recommendations expressed in this paper are those of the authors and do not necessarily reflect the views of the Sloan Foundation.

the goods in question. This concern has been noted elsewhere (Brown 1984; Gregory 1986) and will be discussed further only in the final section of this chapter. A second set of reasons for our unfashionable skepticism stems from several sources of difficulty that we believe have not been addressed sufficiently as part of the design and analysis of amenity environmental surveys. These concerns have to do with (a) how the assets in question are perceived, (b) how they are conceptualized, and (c) how change itself is understood by survey participants. These issues will be explored, in turn, in the following sections.

Issues of Perception

Consider a survey in which people are asked to state the value of a proposed change in visibility, perhaps due to a change in the operating regime of a nearby coal-fired power plant. Typically, individuals will be asked either their willingness to pay to obtain an improvement in visibility or their willingness to pay to avoid a decline in visibility conditions (e.g., Brookshire, Ives, and Schulze 1976; Rowe, d'Arge, and Brookshire 1980). Photographs depicting different states of the environment (e.g., different visual ranges) will be shown, possibly for each of several vistas or for different times of the day or year. In this case both the asset in question (visibility) and the selected stimuli (photographs) are certainly familiar to most people, and the notion that visibility change and money payments are linked (e.g., through utility bills) also is likely to make sense.

Yet even in this relatively straightforward elicitation environment, a number of perceptual issues may complicate the estimation of values for a proposed visibility change. A first problem relates to the size of the change under consideration, because in most cases the expected annual change in visibility is fairly small and the impact on environmental conditions is anticipated to occur only gradually. For example, an existing plant may plan to double emissions (due to a corresponding increase in production) over an eight-year period, or a new facility that is proposed for construction may not attain full output capacity until the sixth year of operation. Photographs comparing before and after visibility conditions may show quite a dramatic change (e.g., decreases in visual range from 90 to 45 km.). For individuals living in the area, however, the annual change in conditions will be experienced as a more gradual process (e.g., an annual change of 6 or 7 percent). Unless a convenient touchstone is and remains accessible, the results of psychophysical studies that investigate the smallest increment (or Just Noticeable Difference) in a stimulus producing a noticeable psychological response (Stevens 1971) suggest that a change of this magnitude may not be perceptible. For return visitors to an area, the time between visits may be sufficiently long that the memory of prior conditions is not sharp and the change therefore will not be noticed; first-time visitors, not knowing what to expect, are unlikely to miss what they don't know is there. It therefore appears possible, and perhaps even likely, that results obtained from surveys that depict the visibility change as occurring instantaneously may not be consistent with individuals' experienced change in welfare.

A corollary issue raised here has to do with adaptation levels, and the conditions (including stimuli, timeframe and incentives) under which individuals are motivated to adapt to a particular reference level (from which positive or negative changes in visibility are valued). Kahneman and Tversky emphasize this aspect of the valuation process in the descriptive model of choice they term "Prospect Theory" (Kahneman and Tversky 1979; 1984), which provides a framework for analyzing preferences that emphasizes a person's subjective evaluation of alternative states. Two features are especially important in the context of assigning values to nonmarket environmental goods. First, outcomes are expressed not in terms of final asset positions (as in utility theory) but in terms of the positive or negative deviations (i.e., gains or losses) that they represent from a neutral reference level. This construct emphasizes the importance of a person's perceived change in status, rather than the absolute level of a good or activity. Second, the value function is steeper for losses than for gains, so that an unpleasant change in status will elicit a more extreme response than will an "objectively" equivalent desirable change.

Exactly how a valuation problem is encoded or "framed" relative to a subjectively determined reference point therefore is posited as a critical concern. However, very little is known about how environmental decisions are framed or how reference points are established in the context of choices between alternative options. Furthermore, prospect theory provides no specific guidance as to why a particular reference point might be chosen or the mechanism by which adaptation could occur to a new reference level. As a result, it is usually not possible to predict with any accuracy how individuals are likely to perceive a proposed change in the status of an environmental good.

The issue also relates to how a selected change in an environmental asset is operationalized—i.e., to the choice of an independent variable by which the change is expressed. In the case of visibility, the most frequently selected independent variable used by economists is visual range (measured in miles, or kilometers), followed by measures of particulate emissions or the intensity of haze. Most laypersons, and probably many experts as well, are not sensitive to relatively small changes in these measures: we probably can tell the difference between a visual range of 50 miles and a range of 10 miles, but unless a notable landmark is obscured, it is unlikely that we will distinquish between a range of 44 miles and a range of 37 miles (a decrease of about 15 percent). Indeed, general statements of air quality, such as "visibility of five miles," are probably meaningless to all but a few highly trained individuals, such as weather observers and airline pilots. When the selected measure is less familiar or less easily observed (e.g., airborne SO_2 concentrations), a given change is likely to be even more difficult to perceive.

These questions raise some tough problems for survey designers who seek to elicit meaningful measures of how people value a small change in an environmental asset. If the change is depicted on an annual basis, it might be sufficiently small that it will not be perceived and, therefore, not valued. If changes are aggregated over a period of years so as to increase their salience, people may both notice and value the difference but lose the link to their real-world experience. Results obtained by researchers in closely related fields suggest that an intermediate option, in which participants are shown the smaller (annual) changes but told something more about possible cumulative effects, is unlikely to yield more satisfactory data. Morgan et al. (1985), for example, in a survey of risk perceptions, found that it was impossible to give participants neutral information about the possible health effects of exposure to electromagnetic radiation from high-voltage transmission lines. It appears that individuals' expressed values for unpriced goods may be easily swayed by informational cues, such as changes in question context or format (Brown and Slovic 1986): just knowing that they are rating different levels of visibility, for example, may artificially increase individuals' valuation of a proposed air quality change.

Issues of Conception

We are naturally compelled to attribute meaning to the perceptual events in our lives. Indeed, one can characterize the history of psychological inquiry in terms of theories that propose to account for the organizational structure people give to perceptual stimuli in their environment. According to many such theories, experience over time is aggregated into a psychologically coherent and highly linked framework that is used as a basis for organizing our memories and giving meaning to our perceptions (e.g., Rosch 1973, 1975; Collins and Quillian 1972; Tulving 1972). What we come to develop in the way of a world view about something as complex as the natural environment, therefore, is represented psychologically in terms of a relatively stable conceptual organization that forms a perspective by which we interpret new events. Although current theories in cognitive psychology differ on many details of how that organization takes place (e.g., Chang 1986), they tend to agree (by and large) that organizational properties are strong and play a central role in facilitating important mental activities such as memory, recognition, interpretation, and reasoning.

Conceptual problems typically arise in the context of large changes. One feature of large changes that makes them difficult to comprehend psychologically is that they may require a high degree of mental reorganization to be understood. Recent research in the cognitive sciences suggests that single events activate multiple pathways in our mental organizational structure and that the extent of that activation is in part a function of both the strength of those events and the strength of pathways linking associated concepts (e.g., Collins and Loftus 1975). Thus, large changes tend to require major shifts in one's conceptual organization if they are to be integrated and understood. When the changes are both large and involve concepts that are unfamiliar or that are difficult to grasp conveniently, chances increase that they will be either misunderstood or ignored entirely.

Consider, for example, the problem of communicating information about the risks of radon and eliciting judgments of people's willingness to pay for proposed reductions in the associated radiation hazard. Radon is a colorless, odorless, naturally occurring gas that until recently has been largely unknown to most of the public. Quite suddenly, it has emerged as a major health risk for many thousands of people living in the eastern United States. Yet much of the available empirical evidence on public views of the radon problem suggest that there may be a pervasive tendency for people to seriously understate the actual risks that they face. Preliminary evidence also suggests that this undervaluation of risks may be quite persistent, even in the face of information specifically designed to encourage a more appropriate level of investment in protective measures (University of Maine 1983).

One reason for this may be the difficulty that people have in conceiving of the costs of radon exposure. A major impediment to conception has to do with the fact that radon risks, along with many other health risks, are probabilistic. There is extensive literature in the field of risk perception and analysis which emphasizes the problems people have in understanding low probability events, even if the associated consequences are high or, in the extreme, catastrophic (e.g., Slovic, Fischhoff, and Lichtenstein 1981). The problem, demonstrated in study after study, is not that people are stupid or cannot count the number of zeroes after a decimal point, but that information comparing low probabilities simply is not meaningful to them. Attempts to present aggregate estimates of probabilities, such as informing people of the risks associated with not wearing a seatbelt over a lifetime of driving, rather than on the basis of a single trip (Slovic 1985), make sense from an analytical standpoint but apparently still are not meaningful from the standpoint of the individual.

This problem is amplified in the context of radon risks by the fact that radon enters buildings invisibly (through infiltration of the water and soil), and by the technical difficulties and uncertainties faced by the homeowner who wants to make his or her house measurably safer. Not only is the prescription uncertain (in one widely publicized case, for example, more than a million dollars has been spent on a single house with little effect), but so are the alternatives: the owners of a house exhibiting high radon levels cannot automatically be reimbursed by the government for protective expenditures, nor can they simply put a "for sale" sign on the front lawn and expect an immediate sale. Furthermore, there is no one to blame for the surprise, no obvious poor decision on the part of industry or an error of government that has led to the problem.

As a result, to conceive of the radon risk and to value reductions in that risk in an appropriate manner are not easy tasks. They require an individual to recognize that his or her house—a most important possession, both emotionally and financially—and perhaps his or her entire community may be unsafe places to live because of an invisible danger that is represented only in probabilistic terms. This "truth" is difficult to translate into something that actually is experienced: it is hard to conceive of in terms of more common day-to-day cause and effect relationships, and it is difficult to conceive of because it is sufficiently unpleasant that there are strong reasons to deny its existence and thereby maintain an existing view of the world.

In many ways, economics is ill-prepared to address this type of valuation decision because economic models of choice are based on the study of routine behavior. Actions taken by people in the marketplace tend to be repetitive and deal with known commodities; furthermore, purchase or sale decisions tend to be both incremental (involving a little more or less of discrete units of a good) and reversible. When the participants in a survey are asked to value a proposed change in radon risks, they are dealing in a new universe of exchange: the good is unfamiliar and absolutely intangible, the valuation exercise itself typically occurs only once, the impacts of incremental changes (in exposure levels, or in protective expenditures) are not known, and the effects (in terms of mortality) are irreversible. It may well be that very few of us are well prepared to evaluate any such proposed exchange.

In a fundamental sense, economic measures of value are based on exchange. There are other ways to think about the worth of something, such as the withdrawal and replacement studies conducted by psychologists interested in valuing gambles, but in general all methods that share both economic and psychological meaning involve some form of give-and-take, some sampling from a distribution followed by a testing of the good and its physical or mental comparison to other goods in the set. When valuing changes in visibility or in radon risks, individuals have very little opportunity to do comparison shopping: survey participants are assigned one task and are asked to respond, as if they either had or quickly could develop a value in the given context, and they are given a stimulus that is itself either changing, probabilistic in nature, or both.

Economic exchanges typically occur in an essentially static world, with one factor (the price or quantity of a specified good) changing while everything else stays much the same. Larger changes, or changes to one part of a closely linked system, imply more far-reaching alterations in the status quo. Our general hypothesis in this regard is simply that environmental changes will be more difficult to conceptualize whenever their comprehension requires a major revision in the experienced world. As a common example, consider the situation faced by the residents of a town who are asked to value a change in recreational opportunities associated with the construction of a major hydroelectric dam. The problem here is that the proposed changes will occur on more than a single dimension, so that in many important ways life before construction of the facility will not be like life after its construction. For example, construction of the dam will bring new people into the area and new social and economic opportunities; these in turn could affect such wide-ranging considerations as residents' occupations, the stability of their families, or the general pace of life in the town.

As a result, people are not being asked to conceive just a change in recreational opportunities, any more than they are asked in the radon case just to conceive a change in fractional mortality, or in the visibility case just to conceive a change in visual range. Instead, people are asked to compare a familiar and individually coherent version of what life is like to a quite different version of what life could become: a change in visual range may directly affect haze intensity or the color of the air but indirectly affect employment opportunities or the agricultural crop mix in an area; a change in radon mortality probabilities may affect how long people live but also the sense of dread they feel or, less directly, the degree to which they perceive their life and its risks to be under their control. A proper valuation of the proposed change therefore requires imagining alterations to a multidimensional and interrelated world, rather than to a unidimensional one.

To return to the discussion at the start of this section, a central difficulty with cognitively constructing such a scenario is the high degree of linkage between the basic concepts that form our existing ideas of what life is like. As a result, people's imaginations may be much more limited than we assume when asking how they would feel about a world that looks somewhat different than the one with which they are familiar. Indeed, empirical studies of decision making indicate that even experts in a subject matter often have difficulty stretching their thinking to create "what if" scenarios: one result is that solutions to problems often are overlooked because they lie outside of the experts' imaginative capabilities (e.g., Fischhoff, Slovic, and Lichtenstein 1978).

In short, asking people to compare a version of life to which they have become accustomed with one that contains novel or unfamiliar elements requires a conceptual leap that involves much more than a change in one of the elements of a static picture. Clearly, the changes most important for society to understand are those that are most meaningful to people. However, it also may be that meaningful changes are those most difficult for people to value because they are the most difficult to conceptualize fully.

Issues of Change

In each of the valuation situations discussed above, participants in a survey typically would be asked to compare alternative states of the world. A pre-payment state would show low levels of visibility, for example, or high radon exposure levels; a post-payment state would show higher visibility levels, or lower radon exposures. In determining their valuation, participants would try to trade off the perceived benefits of the post-payment state against the monetary costs associated with its provision.

This is essentially a static deliberation, asking survey participants to choose between alternative bundles that each consist of two goods, an environmental amenity and a sum of money. However, the implicit policy question is dynamic rather than static: it asks people to value a proposed change in environmental conditions (e.g., a 50 percent increase in visual range, or a decreased probability of mortality due to lung cancer) rather than to choose between final asset states. This means that people must first think about what a future environmental state will be like (and also what their life in it will be like) and then decide on the value they wish to assign to it (so that the benefits they derive just match the stated monetary cost). Tools such as photographs or risk diagrams can compare some aspects of different environments, but outside of very limiting laboratory situations, one cannot simultaneously experience two different environmental states: the ease with which the change to a second state can be imagined therefore may be very important.

This static/dynamic distinction is relevant to valuation for other reasons as well. For the most part, people interact in and experience an environment that is ever-changing. Some aspects of that environment are experienced in the concrete, but many others are only known in the abstract: for example, people experience weather but not climate; they experience individuals but not society. The relevance of a proposed change to some element (large or small) of the environment can be understood only in terms of its impact on people's actual experience of that environment. Thus, changes in visibility due to air quality alterations are really most properly expressed against a dynamic, fluid background comprised of, for example, day-to-day changes in weather, seasonal changes in climate, daily variation in attention given to air cleanliness, changes in personal perspectives and mood, and the like. The myriad of changing elements in one's perceptual environment make it difficult to adequately evaluate a statically expressed change to a single element without seeing that element actually change in concert with the entire environment. Indeed, it may be that the proper expression of environmental change for the sake of valuation can only occur in the context of a simulation-like presentation, in which key macro-elements of the environment are modeled for the individual both with and without alterations of essential amenities.

In much the same way, people's preferences for different goods and their budgets for discretionary expenditures also are subject to change. Stated expenditures for improved visibility or reduced health risks therefore are likely to be affected by a number of considerations in addition to the typically introduced criteria, such as expenditures for other public goods. For example, everything from the recent occurrence of salient events (such as the Chernobyl melt-down) to the time when a paycheck was last received could affect how much an individual was willing to pay for improved visibility or reduced health risks. Moreover, alterations in key variables will not stop while the supposed change takes place, so that the value assigned to it will remain relative rather than absolute. One implication may be that expressed values are more valid to the extent they can be tied to less variable indicators; income-based estimates therefore may provide less reliable expressions of value, for example, than would rank-orders of preference or importance ratings among different goods.

Conclusion

Change in the natural environment may place an unusual demand on those individuals asked to value it to the extent they are asked either (a) to value something small, big, or new, or (b) to value something in a novel manner. In the case of nonmarket environmental goods, people often will be asked to do both these things: not only is the good itself new because it is evolving rather than static, but also the valuation approach is new because it requires a different way to think about value. Most often, we are simply told by others how to look at and think about changes in the natural world: improvements in visibility, we are informed, can be measured by changes in visual range; the risk of radon is that the probability of dying from lung cancer may increase.

The unasked question is how does all this relate to the way that people naturally perceive and think about and value environmental assets? After all, this would seem to be the true test for the validity of any measurement approach—how well it fits with the way that people customarily code a change. Such "psychonatural" valuation procedures, for want of a better term, might ·turn out to be considerably more expensive, and to yield considerably less tidy or more idiosyncratic output, than those currently employed. In some cases, a single value may not even exist: if changes in the natural environment are sufficiently small or large that substantial problems of perception or conception exist, or if the asset itself is changing over time, then the best that might be done is to report a range of different parts of an individual's value puzzle. Policy analysts then could select the value that corresponds most closely to the conditions.

The important recommendation, it seems, is that those involved in developing these more psychonatural measures look at people for what they are, and with the basic perceptual/cognitive apparatus that they have. It is not that our ability to perceive or to conceive change limits who we are, but rather that these abilities define who we are and, in a real sense, are who we are. Economic measures of environmental value need to reconcile themselves to this fact.

References

Brookshire, D., B. Ives, and W. Schulze. 1976. The Valuation of Aesthetic Preferences. *Journal of Environmental Economics and Management*. 3:325-46.

Brown, T. 1984. The Concept of Value in Resource Allocation. *Land Economics*.
60:231-46.

Brown, T., and P. Slovic. 1986. Effects of Context on Economic Measures of
Value. *In* Amenity Resource Valuation: Integrating Economics with Other
Disciplines, edited by G. L. Peterson, B. L. Driver, and R. Gregory. State
College, PA: Venture Press, Inc.

Chang, T. M. 1986. Semantic Memory: Facts and Models. *Psychological Bulletin*.
99:199-200.

Collins, A. M., and E. F. Loftus. 1975. A Spreading-Activation Theory of
Semantic Processing. *Psychological Review*. 82:407-28.

Collins, A. M. and M. R. Quilian. 1972. Experiments on Semantic Memory and
Language Comprehension. *In* Cognition in Learning and Memory, edited by
L.W. Gregg. New York: Wiley.

Cummings, R., D. Brookshire, and W. Schulze. 1986. *Valuing Environmental
Goods: An Assessment of the Contingent Valuation Method*. Totawa, NJ: Rowman
and Allanheld.

Fischhoff, B., P. Slovic, and S. Lichtenstein. 1978. Fault Trees: Sensitivity of
Estimated Failure Probabilities to Problem Representation. *Journal of
Experimental Psychology: Human Perception and Performance*. 4:330-44.

Gregory, R. 1986. Interpreting Measures of Economic Loss: Evidence from
Contingent Valuation and Experimental Studies. *Journal of Environmental
Economics and Management*.

Kahneman, D., and A. Tversky. 1979. Prospect Theory: An Analysis   of
Decision Under Risk. *Econometrica*. 47:263-91.

Kahneman, D., and A. Tversky. 1984. Choices, Values and Frames. *American
Psychology*. 39:341-50.

Mitchell, R. and R. Carson. 1981. An Experiment in Determining Willingness to
Pay for National Water Quality Improvements. Draft report to the U.S.
Environmental Protection Agency.

Morgan, G., P. Slovic, I. Nair, D. Geisler, D. MacGregor, B. Fischhoff, D. Lincoln, and K. Florig. 1985. Powerline Frequency Electric and Magnetic Fields: A Pilot Study of Risk Perception. *Risk Analysis*. 5:139-50.

Rosch, E. 1973. "On the Internal Structure of Perceptual and Semantic Categories. *In* Cognitive Development and the Acquisition of Language, edited by T.E. Moore. New York: Academic Press.

Rosch, E. 1975. Cognitive Representations of Semantic Categories. *Journal of Experimental Psychology: General*. 104:192-233.

Rowe, R., R. d'Arge, and D. Brookshire. 1981. An Experiment on the Economic Value of Visibility. *Journal of Environmental Economic Management*. 7:1-19.

Slovic, P. 1985. Only New Laws Will Spur Seat-Belt Use [Editorial]. *Wall Street Journal*. 30 January.

Slovic, P., B. Fischhoff, and S. Lichtenstein. 1981. Perceived Risk: Psychological Factors and Social Implications. *In* The Assessment and Perception of Risk, edited by F. Warner and D. H. Slater. London: The Royal Society.

Slovic, P., B. Fischhoff, and S. Lichtenstein. 1985. Charaterizing Perceived Risk. *In* Perilous progress: Technology as hazard, edited by R. W. Kates, C. Hohenemser, and J. Kasperson. Boulder, Colorado: Westview Press.

Smith, V. K., W. Desvousges, and M. R. Freeman, III. 1985. Valuing Changes in Hazardous Waste Risks: A Contingent Valuation Analysis. Draft Interim Report to the Environmental Protection Agency.

Stevens, S. S. 1971. Issues in Psychophysical Measurement. *Psychological Bulletin*. 78:426-50

Tulving, E. 1972. Episodic and Semantic Memory. *In* Organization of Memory, edited by E. Tulving and W. Donaldson. New York: Academic Press.

University of Maine. 1983. Radon, Water and Air Pollution: Risks and Control. Orono: University of Maine, Land and Water Resources Center. Unpublished report.

Part II Valuation Theory and Method Development: Progress and Problems

6 The Contingent Valuation Method

Richard C. Bishop

Thomas A. Heberlein

Introduction

The contingent valuation method employs survey techniques to ask people about the values they would place on nonmarket commodities if markets did exist or if other means of payment such as taxes were in effect. All other methods of valuing publicly provided goods and services require linkages to actual market transactions. For example, the travel-cost method uses market expenditures for transportation and other trip-related items to infer a demand function for recreation. No such connection to market transactions is required for contingent valuation. This makes contingent valuation the most flexible of the valuation techniques. However, this flexibility is gained at a cost. Once the link to actual payments is lost, questions arise about the validity of the values estimated. Doubts have focused on both the willingness and ability of people to state accurate dollar values for environmental assets and other nonmarket commodities.

Questions of validity arise at two levels. First, even if the technique itself is sound, it will not provide accurate values if the data gathering

The research for this chapter was supported by the College of Agricultural and Life Sciences, University of Wisconsin—Madison, Resources for the Future, Inc., the Graduate School of the University of Wisconsin—Madison, the Electric Power Research Institute, and the Wildlife Management Institute. An earlier version of this paper was presented at the National Workshop on Non-Market Valuation Methods and Their Use in Environmental Planning, University of Canterbury, Christchurch, New Zealand, December 2-5, 1985. Larry Murdock and Gary Johnson made many helpful comments on earlier drafts.

and subsequent analysis are not adequately designed and executed. In the first part of this chapter, we address the basic issues that must be resolved in any successful application of the contingent valuation method. Second, if the method itself has inherent flaws, even the most carefully done studies will not produce accurate values. This will lead to a discussion of recent experimental evidence on the validity of contingent valuation.

The Mechanics of Contingent Valuation

Any good contingent valuation study must successfully deal with six issues: (1) What will be the population of people whose values will be estimated? (2) How will the item to be valued be defined? (3) What payment vehicle will be appropriate? (4) How will the contingent valuation question be posed? (5) What supplemental data will be gathered? (6) How will the data be analyzed? These issues will be addressed here in terms of willingness-to-pay measures of value. This is partly a matter of convenience, but also reflects the fact that most—though by no means all—contingent valuation studies have measured only willingness to pay. Nevertheless, it should be recalled that in welfare theory minimum compensation demanded has equal status as a value measure. Everything that is said here can easily be translated to apply to compensation demanded, and the valuation experiments reviewed later on provide evidence regarding the validity of both contingent willingness to pay and contingent compensation demanded. The discussion follows Anderson and Bishop (1986) closely.

Population Definition

Assuming that a specific policy issue requiring resource values has been clearly delineated, the first step in contingent valuation research is to define whose values are to be counted. Most past studies have dealt with obvious user groups, such as hunters, anglers, people living in areas affected by air pollution, and park visitors. More recently, there has been growing interest in the "nonuser" or "intrinsic" values (Fisher and Raucher 1984). This is explicit recognition that those who are not current users of the resource in question may still place some value on the option to use the resource in the future or on the knowledge that the resource will continue to exist. Option and existence values are discussed in chapter 4 of Fisher and Raucher and in many recent publications including Bishop (1982, 1986), Randall and Stoll (1983), and Boyle and Bishop (1987). Of course, once the population for the study has been defined, satisfactory sampling strategies must be designed and implemented.

Product Definition

If contingent values are to be valid and useful, the object being valued must be appropriately defined to reflect the policy issue being addressed. Thus, good studies involve carefully presented descriptions of the resources or changes in environmental quality that are to be valued. Verbal descriptions are standard, and visual aids such as photographs, charts, and maps are often used.

Product definition often involves compromises between detailed presentation of technical information, on the one hand, and the need to convey information in a form that is understandable to respondents, on the other. An interesting example is presented in Figure 6.1. The water quality ladder has been used in actual studies by Mitchell and Carson (1981) and Desvousges, Smith, and McGivney (1983) during personal interviews to describe various levels of water quality. This visual aid attempts to convey, in simple terms, complex technical information regarding such parameters as dissolved solids, toxic levels, coliform counts, water clarity, and fishing success rates. People need as complete a concept of what they are valuing as possible in order to come up with realistic values, but there is also a need to present information in simple, understandable terms.

Payment Vehicle Definition

It is generally agreed that in order for respondents to express valid values, some specific mechanism for payment, called the "payment vehicle," must be specified as part of contingent valuation questions. For example, if hunting opportunities are being valued, the payment vehicle could be increased hunting license fees or increases in hunting trip expenses. In air and water quality studies, an often-used vehicle is the increased prices and taxes that might be necessary to pay for pollution control. In dealing with the environmental effects of electric power generation, one possible payment vehicle would be electricity rates paid by respondents.

Mitchell and Carson (1987) have suggested two criteria for choice of a payment vehicle: realism and neutrality. Contingent valuation researchers have reasoned that the more realistic the situation, including the mechanism for payment, the easier it will be for people to respond accurately. Thus, the actual means of payment should be used where it is possible to do so. Higher taxes and prices in air and water pollution studies reflect this rationale. At the same time, however, it is important that payment vehicles be neutral. Use of taxes as the payment vehicle may be inappropriate in this regard if people use the contingent valuation question to express general dissatisfaction with tax rates rather than to express a value for the resource. It is hoped that people will respond to contingent valuation questions in ways that reflect the values that they place on the resource and not some emotional or other reaction to the payment vehicle itself. As the tax example illustrates, the twin criteria of realism and neutrality may conflict. If so, compromises are inevitable, but leave the researcher uncomfortable about how to interpret the results.

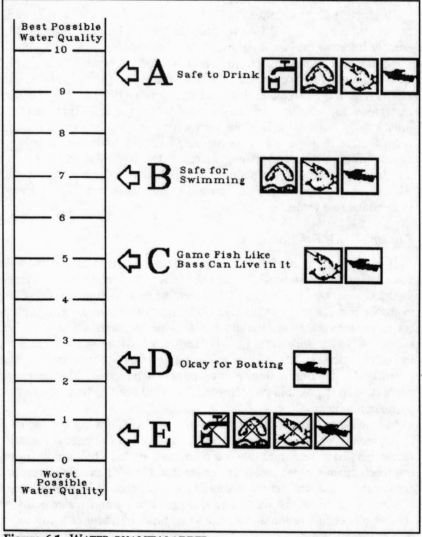

Figure 6.1 WATER QUALITY LADDER

Alternative Ways to Ask Valuation Questions

While there are numerous variations, five different approaches to asking contingent valuation questions can be distinguished: bidding games, open-ended questions, payment-card formats, dichotomous-choice questions, and contingent-ranking techniques. Each of these techniques requires a brief explanation.

A *bidding game* was used in the first contingent valuation study, that conducted by Davis (1963, 1964). Until recently, bidding games have been the most widely applied contingent valuation technique. In a standard bidding game, the first step is to ask a respondent whether she or he would be willing to pay a specified amount, known as the "starting point." If the response is affirmative, the amount is increased to successively higher levels until a maximum willingness to pay is reached. Likewise, if the starting point elicits a negative response, the amount is lowered in predetermined increments until the respondent indicates an acceptable amount.

Despite its wide application, there has been considerable dissatisfaction with the bidding game technique. For one thing, personal or telephone interviews are required in order to conduct the bidding process. This has led to research on techniques that can be applied in less-expensive mail questionnaires. Also, concerns have been voiced about possible "starting-point bias." The purpose of the starting point is to initiate the bidding process, and a bias exists when the initial bid, as stated by the interviewer, affects the final bid stated by the respondent. Mitchell and Carson (1981) and Boyle, Bishop, and Welsh (1985), among others, have presented empirical evidence of starting-point bias.

One alternative is the *open-ended question*. After the product has been defined and the vehicle described, respondents are left to devise their maximum values without the aid of additional information, bidding, or other processes. This technique is amenable to mail surveys and avoids influencing respondents by stating a starting bid. Perhaps the earliest study involving open-ended questions was that by Horvath (1974), dealing with fish and wildlife in the southeastern United States.

Most contingent valuation researchers have been reluctant to use open-ended questions because they fear that such questions do not provide sufficient stimuli and information to help people thoroughly consider the values they would place on environmental resources if a market were created. Study participants have rarely if ever valued such resources before and may never have considered what their economic worth might be. Expecting respondents to come up with accurate values "out of the blue" may be expecting too much. A number of contingent valuation studies that used both bidding games and open-ended questions found that open-ended questions consistently produced lower values (Cummings, Brookshire, and Schulze, 1986).

To avoid starting-point bias, yet to provide information and stimuli to help respondents think more clearly about their values, Mitchell and Carson (1981) proposed the *payment card*. After defining the product (in their case, nationwide improvements in water quality), the interviewers handed study subjects a card similar to that shown in Figure 6.2. This is an "anchored payment card," in that it shows amounts spent by people in the respondent's tax bracket for some publicly provided goods and services like highways and education. After considering the card, each study subject was asked the maximum she or he would be willing to pay each year for various changes in water quality. Whether or not there is an "anchor-point bias" in payment-card results analogous to starting-point bias in bidding games is a question deserving more research. Mitchell and Carson (1981, 1987) have concluded from their research that no evidence of bias exists. Boyle and Bishop (forthcoming) found that bidding-game and payment-card questions used to value the same environmental asset yielded statistically indistinguishable results. One plausible explanation was that both values were biased upward due to starting-point bias and anchor-point bias, respectively.

$ 20,000 - $ 29,000		
	Average Annual Taxpayer Expenditures for Selected Public Services	
$ 0	$ 300	$ 870
-National Parks		
30	360	960
-Space Program		
60	420	1,050
90 -Highways	480	1,140
-Public Ed.		
120	540	1,230
150	600 -Health Care	1,320
180	660	1,410
210	720	1,500
		-Defense
240	780	1,590

Figure 6.2 SAMPLE PAYMENT CARD.

A fourth alternative is to use a *dichotomous-choice format*. Bidding games, open-ended questions, and payment-card questions all require study subjects to express exact maximum dollar amounts. Respondents may find it difficult to come up with precise amounts and are likely to find it easier to respond to questions that ask them whether or not they would be willing to pay a specific amount. The dichotomous-choice technique, which was originally suggested by Bishop and Heberlein (1979), gives respondents specific dollar amounts, termed the "offer amount," and asks them to say whether they would be willing to pay that amount or not. Subjects are assigned different offer amounts at random, and the offer amounts are designed in advance to span a large part of the range of possible values for maximum willingness to pay. This question format is easily incorporated into mail surveys and can be used in interviews as well. However, analysis of the data to estimate maximum willingness to pay is more difficult than for previously mentioned techniques, as we shall see in a moment.

Contingent ranking is a relatively new technique. Here, respondents are not asked to value environmental assets directly, but rather to rank various combinations of environmental quality and monetary outlays. Examples include Rae (1981a, 1981b) and Desvousges, Smith, and McGivney (1983). Respondents are asked to rank the alternatives from most preferred to least preferred, and values are inferred through statistical analysis of the rankings.

Researchers continue to disagree about which of these techniques is best. Each researcher has his or her favorite, and variations on the five basic techniques discussed here are constantly being developed. Bishop et al. (1984) compared open-ended questions and bidding games and found no significant difference. Boyle and Bishop (forthcoming) compared bidding-game, payment card, and dichotomous-choice results. The bidding-game and payment-card means were not significantly different. Dichotomous choice values were significantly lower, but the difference may be due to an interview bias problem and starting-point bias in the bidding game. As noted previously, Cummings, Brookshire, and Schulze (1986) cited results that seem to indicate that open-ended questions produce relatively low values. They also claimed that bidding games tend to yield higher values regardless of whether a starting point is specified or subjects set their own starting bids. They argued that a bidding process is necessary in order for respondents to carefully consider their preferences. Boyle, Bishop, and Welsh (1985) would question such a conclusion given their evidence of starting-point bias. More will be said about this in the section on validity. Desvousges, Smith, and McGivney (1983) compared contingent ranking results with results from bidding games and open-ended questions and found that the three techniques yielded roughly comparable mean values. At this stage, choice of questioning technique is still largely a matter of individual judgment.

Supplementary Data Needs

Most contingent valuation studies go beyond simply asking valuation questions. Several objectives may be satisfied by expanding the questionnaire or interview form. Researchers often estimate "bid equations" to investigate the validity of their results. Such equations typically have willingness to pay as the dependent variable and socioeconomic variables like income, age, level of interest in the resource in question, recreational participation, and location of residence as explanatory variables. Data to use in estimating bid equations most often come from the questionnaire, and needs for such data should be considered carefully during survey design. In addition, resource managers may have information needs beyond those related to estimation of dollar values.

Analysis

Analysis of data from bidding games, open-ended questions, and payment-card questions is normally straightforward. The most difficult issue is what to do about extreme values including both zeros and expressions of willingness to pay that seem unusually high. Current practice calls for presenting zero bidders with follow-up questions to ascertain whether they really place no value on the resource, are expressing a protest bid against valuation, found it too difficult to arrive at a value, or had other difficulties. Zeros that are judged to be legitimate expressions of value are included in the analysis, while other zeros are excluded. Traditionally, expressed values that are judged to be excessive have been excluded from the data set as protest bids, but standards of excessiveness have been rather arbitrary. More systematic approaches to identifying outlier have been suggested by Desvousges, Smith, and McGivney (1983) and Edwards and Anderson (1984). Once protest bids and other outlier have been eliminated, sample means and variances are generally adequate to estimate values for the population. As noted above, bid equations are often estimated as well.

Analysis is rather more difficult for responses to dichotomous-choice questions. Data on values are in the form of "yes" or "no" responses to specific, randomly assigned offer amounts. How are such responses to be used to infer *maximum* willingness to pay? Logit or probit regression models are normally estimated. These models predict the probability of rejecting the offer as a function of the offer amount and other explanatory variables. The probabilities are then used to calculate the mathematical expectation of willingness to pay or the median offer amount (at the median the probability of rejection equals 0.5).

The calculation of values from dichotomous-choice responses is illustrated in Figure 6.3. The vertical axis measures the probability that a randomly selected respondent will answer "no" when asked whether she or he would be willing to pay a given offer amount (x), measured on the horizontal axis. Rejecting an offer means that the respondent's maximum willingness to pay is less than x. Thus, F(x), which is the function estimated using logit or probit, is upward sloping to reflect the increasing probability that a randomly selected study participant will reject the offer as the offer amount (x) increases. Since a refusal to pay x implies a refusal to pay all amounts greater than x, F(x) can be interpreted as a cumulative density function on the probability of rejecting x. As Hanemann (1984) has pointed out, one property of cumulative density functions is that the expected value of the random variable equals the area above the cumulative density function and below the line for F(x)=1. Thus, the estimated expected value of willingness to pay per individual in the subject population equals the shaded area in Figure 6.3. However, two methodological issues immediately arise with respect to this calculation.

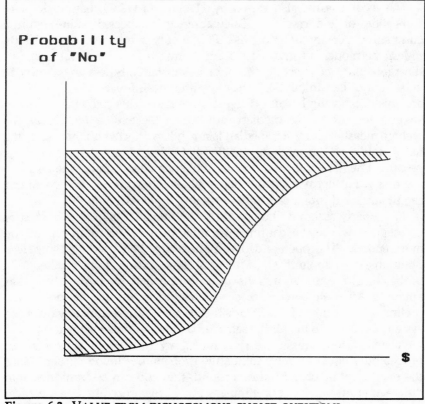

Figure 6.3 VALUE FROM DICHOTOMOUS-CHOICE QUESTIONS.

First, it is possible to link the specification of F(x) rather closely to economic theory. Hanemann (1984) developed a "random utility model" and discussed functional forms that would be fully consistent with known possible specifications of the utility function. He also showed that the specific form of the logit function used by Bishop and Heberlein (1979) is not consistent with any known function that would meet the full requirements of utility theory. There is room for disagreement about how serious this shortcoming is. Some might go so far as to say that welfare measures are meaningless if based on specifications of F(x) that cannot be shown to be consistent with utility theory. We would argue that as long as F(x) slopes upward and has statistically significant coefficients, the minimal requirements of theory are met. To accept a much poorer fit to be sure that the axioms of utility theory are met would not be advisable. However, to the extent that an acceptable fit can be obtained using a functional form that is consistent with utility theory, no one would quarrel with the conclusion that the results are stronger. Thus, the researcher who uses the dichotomous-choice technique should strive to find a functional form that is consistent with utility maximization and fits the data.

The second issue, also raised by Hanemann (1984), has to do with truncation of the model. Calculating the expected value from a cumulative density function like F(x) involves integration to infinity unless the model is truncated. If the estimated F(x) has a "fat tail" (i.e., the probability of rejecting the offer is substantially less than unity at very high dollar amounts), then integration to infinity is likely to yield an unjustifiably high value for the resource. This led Hanemann to suggest the use of the median rather than the expected value as the welfare measure, since the median is much less affected by the size of the tail. However, the median is difficult to defend on welfare grounds because it neglects the dollar values of the people who value the resource the most. Furthermore, truncation problems have been avoided in our recent studies through carefully designing the offer amounts.

To properly assign dollar amounts, the first step is to do a pretest of the survey, where the contingent valuation question or questions are open ended. The open-ended responses are then used to estimate a preliminary version of F(x). If the final sample size is to be N, then N/2 probabilities are drawn at random from the unit interval. The dollar amounts associated with these probabilities are found using the preliminary version of F(x) from the pretest. These dollar values are assigned at random to half the sample. Dollar amounts for the remaining members of the sample are determined by calculating a new set of probabilities equal to unity minus the probabilities found earlier. Once the second set of probabilities is found, they too can be translated into dollar amounts using the preliminary F(x). This procedure has the effect of giving a balanced set of observations across the relevant range of dollar amounts for arriving at the final estimate of F(x). It has now been applied in four studies including work described in Boyle (1985), Boyle and Bishop (1987), and Bishop et al. (1987), as well as work in progress. The resulting estimates of F(x) have then consistently produced expected values of willingness to pay that have not been affected by "fat tails" when the models were truncated at a probability of 0.99.

Validity

The Issues of Bias

Concerns about the accuracy of contingent valuation have focused on potential "biases." If contingent valuation could produce values comparable to those that would be obtained from a well-functioning market for the environmental asset in question, most economists would be satisfied. To the extent that contingent values diverge from this standard, they are considered biased.

There are a great number of potential sources of bias. Many of these are endemic to survey research in general (Dillman 1978). Examples would be interviewer bias and nonresponse bias. These need not concern us here beyond a very explicit warning that good survey research is not as easily achieved as one might conclude at first glance. The neophyte would do well to obtain the aid of trained professionals in designing and executing a contingent valuation survey. The researchers who pioneered the contingent valuation method would have avoided many pitfalls had they done so more often. Let us assume that these general pitfalls are avoided through the application of sound survey methodology, and focus on the potential biases that are peculiar to contingent valuation. The terminology is still developing in this area. For alternative taxonomies of the potential biases, see Schulze, d'Arge, and Brookshire (1981) and Mitchell and Carson (1987). We will proceed using the general terms "strategic bias" and "hypothetical bias" to categorize the major potential sources of inaccuracy.

Strategic bias is present if survey respondents *intentionally* mislead the researcher. Fears relating to strategic behavior can be traced back to Samuelson's (1954) classic article, which argued that rational economic agents have strong incentives not to reveal their true demands for public goods. Extending the argument to the current context, if a respondent rightly or wrongly believes that actual fees which he or she will be assessed are dependent upon contingent valuation responses, an incentive exists to state a value much lower than the true value. On the other hand, if a respondent recognizes that all payments expressed in a contingent valuation exercise are purely hypothetical and that stating a very high value will promote supplying of a desired public good, a value much higher than his or her true value may be stated. In either case, contingent values will diverge from values that would be expressed in an actual market.

Hypothetical bias, on the other hand, stems from the inability of respondents to accurately predict how they would behave if a market were created. In most situations where contingent valuation is employed, respondents may have never attempted to express their preferences in monetary terms before. Even if they are quite willing to reveal their true values, they may not be able to assess what those values are without having experience in an actual market. Starting-point bias is a possible example of hypothetical bias. One explanation for starting-point bias is that respondents do not know their true values and use the bidding game's starting point as information about what their values ought to be. In actual markets, participants have the opportunity to engage in repeated transactions over time, gain experience in consuming the good or service at various levels, have opportunities to explore in some detail the markets for substitutes and complements, have the opportunity to acquire substantial information, and may consult repeatedly with other household members, friends, and even experts. Obviously, all this experience and information is impossible to duplicate in a brief question-naire. To the extent that values expressed in contingent valuation surveys diverge from true values because of the lack of this information and experience, hypothetical bias is present.

It is to be emphasized, however, that so far all we have done is speculate about potential biases. Whether such biases actually exist and whether they are large or small are empirical questions. Thus, the discussion now turns to empirical evidence on the validity of contingent valuation. Making actual market behavior our standard for accurate contingent valuation, however, creates an immediate difficulty. If it were easy to establish markets for environmental assets, contingent valuation would not be needed. Researchers have nevertheless been able to go part way toward actual market behavior by creating "simulated markets." In simulated markets, actual commodities are exchanged for actual money, so that resulting values can be used to evaluate the performance of contingent valuation. Simulated markets are not real markets. The richness of experience and information associated with fully functioning markets is not present. For example, it is most often feasible to engage in only one transaction per participant. Also, experiments involving simulated markets are often conducted in the laboratory and may involve commodities and procedures that seem highly artificial to participants. However, the use of real money should reduce both strategic and hypothetical biases to the extent that they exist. Real money makes potential strategic behavior expensive in terms of both money and actual, foregone recreational opportunities. Hypothetical bias should be reduced since participants in simulated markets have much stronger incentives to search and assess their preferences. For these reasons, simulated market results constitute the most potent body of available evidence on the validity of contingent valuation. A lion's share of our discussion of validity will focus on simulated market results, and especially the results of our own work in Wisconsin. Before turning to those studies, however, it is worthwhile to mention some other research that has relevance to the issue of validity.

First, notice should be taken of a large number of laboratory experiments involving public goods and the possibility of strategic behavior. See, for example, Bohm (1972), Scherr and Babb (1975), Smith (1977), Schneider and Pommerehne (1981), Marwell and Ames (1979, 1980, 1981), Alfano and Marwell (1981), Brubaker (1982), Tideman (1983), Isaac, Walker, and Thomas (1984), and Kim and Walker (1984). It is difficult to do justice to all this literature in a short discussion (see Welsh 1986 for a more detailed summary). In general, strategic behavior was difficult to document and appeared to be much less influential than economic theory would lead one to expect. Taken together, these studies suggest that under most circumstances, strategic bias is not a major threat to contingent valuation.

Second, many contingent valuation studies have themselves endeavored to test the validity of the method. As noted previously, many studies, including several cited in this chapter, have estimated bid equations. The primary reason for doing so is to see whether willingness-to-pay values as expressed by study participants are related to socioeconomic variables in ways that theory would lead one to expect. As previously mentioned, an obvious example would be income, a variable which could normally be expected to have a positive effect on willingness to pay. Proxies for tastes and preferences such as place of residence (urban, small town, or rural), education, age, and number of visits to a recreation site being valued are also sometimes used. In general, hypothesized relationships are often found not to be significant, but beyond that, analysis of bid equations has not uncovered evidence that would lead one to doubt the validity of contingent values. More powerful tests have compared contingent values with values determined by using other valuation techniques. In general, the results of such comparisons have been positive. For instance, contingent values have been shown to be roughly comparable to values derived from travel-cost models (Knetsch and Davis 1966; Desvousges, Smith, and McGivney 1983; Sellar, Stoll, and Chavas 1985), hedonic price models (Brookshire et al. 1982), and costs and prices of substitutes (Thayer 1981). Such comparisons are always worthwhile, but they leave doubts. Everyone knows, for example, that results from travel-cost and hedonic-price models can vary widely depending on the assumptions made in specifying and estimating the models. To the extent that two valuation techniques yield roughly similar values, there is always the chance that both techniques are biased. Given that values from actual market transactions are the criterion of validity here and given that such values are not available, the next best alternative is to do simulated market experiments.

Three Simulated Market Experiments

In our simulated markets, actual hunting permits and actual money were exchanged. Experiment I involved hunting permits which authorized the bearer to take at most one Canada goose between October 1 and October 15, 1978, in the Horicon Zone, an area surrounding the Horicon Marsh in central Wisconsin. A hunter could legally receive only one such permit, and a total of 13,974 permits were issued by lottery by the Wisconsin Department of Natural Resources. The permits were free, and over 50,000 hunters applied to hunt geese in the Horicon Zone in 1978, so permits were allocated by lottery.

A random sample was drawn of 237 hunters who had been issued a permit in the state lottery. Each received an actual cash offer to give up the permit. Cash offers were randomly determined ranging in roughly log-linear intervals from $1 to $200. The letter of offer explained that the hunter should return by mail either the enclosed check or his permit, postmarked no later than September 29, when the offer would expire. Note the dichotomous-choice format used in this question. A total of 221 people (94 percent) returned either their check or their permit.

A second sample of 353 hunters with permits was mailed a contingent valuation survey employing a similar, dichotomous-choice question. The question was worded to sound as much like the actual cash offers as possible, except that the hypothetical nature of the proposed transaction was emphasized. The amount offered again varied randomly from $1 to $200. Each respondent was asked to state whether he or she would surrender the Horicon permit for the amount specified. Later in the survey, each respondent was also asked a dichotomous-choice willing-ness-to-pay question with the offers again ranging from $1 to $200. With an incentive of $5 per questionnaire, 94 percent of this group responded prior to the opening of the hunting season on October 1. (See Bishop and Heberlein 1979 and Bishop, Heberlein, and Kealy 1983 for a more complete description of this experiment and subsequent analysis.)

The Sandhill Wildlife Demonstration Area, again located in Wisconsin, served as the site for Experiment II. Sandhill, which is set aside for wildlife research, contains twelve square miles of land surrounded by a deer-proof fence. For several years, special one-day hunts for deer of either sex were held there on the Saturday preceding the opening of the regular deer season. In order to hunt deer at Sandhill, regularly licensed hunters also needed a special permit. These permits were issued free to winners of a lottery.

The 1983 Sandhill hunt for deer of either sex was held on November 12. A total of 5,349 applications was received. Prior to the hunt, the staff of the Wisconsin Department of Natural Resources held a random drawing to determine the 150 applicants who would be allowed to hunt. State regulations relating to the 1983 hunt not only authorized the issuance of these 150 either-sex permits but also the issuance of four permits to us at the University of Wisconsin for research purposes. Because only four permits were available to us, it was necessary to use an auction process in both the simulated and contingent markets.

The 150 applicants randomly selected by the state to receive permits were divided into two groups of equal size. The first group participated in a sealed-bid auction, and the four lowest bidders were paid their bids in return for giving up their permits. The second group participated in a hypothetical sealed-bid auction. Such a sealed-bid format is very similar to open-ended contingent valuation questions. A total of 73 respondents in the real auction and 73 respondents in the hypothetical auction submitted bids. To determine willingness to pay, a random sample of 150 applicants who were *un*successful in the state lottery participated in a sealed-bid auction. Half were informed that they were part of an actual auction for a total of four Sandhill hunting permits and that their sealed bids would be entered into the auction at the amounts they stated. Bid contracts for this group expressed a commitment to pay the University of Wisconsin the amount of the bid if it was one of the four highest. The other half of this group submitted hypothetical sealed bids on contract-like forms. Responses from a total of 68 participants in the actual auction and 71 participants in the hypothetical auction were received.

Bidding-game formats were also tested. In one of our bidding games, a random sample of 150 additional unsuccessful applicants (i.e., applicants not drawn in the state lottery) were assigned to either a real or a hypothetical auction. The first step of this bidding game was to solicit sealed bids in exactly the fashion just described except that the contract specified that it would be possible to change the bid later. This made it possible to avoid stating a specific starting bid. Respondents were not informed that telephone bidding or any other mechanism for reconsidering their offer would be instituted. A total of 66 individuals in the actual auction and 70 individuals in the hypothetical auction returned the contract. Telephone interviews were then conducted. The telephone interviewers were provided with scripts to follow when conducting the interviews and attempted to ascertain the subjects' maximum willingness to pay using an iterative bidding process. A total of 65 individuals in the real auction and 62 individuals in the hypothetical auction were contacted in this manner. Their final bids were entered into the willingness-to-pay auction. For further details about this experiment, including results from a standard bidding game, see Bishop et al. (1984) and Welsh (1986).

Experiment III was conducted at Sandhill a year later. As in 1983, 150 permits were issued by lottery for the 1984 one-day hunt for deer of either sex. However, in 1984, the University of Wisconsin was issued up to 75 permits to be used in the research. This allowed the use of dichotomous-choice procedures similar to those used in Experiment I rather than auctions.

Half of the 150 hunters who received free 1984 Sandhill permits in the state lottery also received a letter explaining the study and a valid check made out in the subject's name. The members of this group were told they had the choice of cashing the check and returning their permit or returning the check. The amounts of the checks were selected at random and ranged from $16 to $539. The other half received similar dichotomous choice offers except that all offers were hypothetical. They were asked *if* a check for $___ had been included, would they give up the permit? The blank was filled with a randomly assigned value drawn from the same interval as the cash offers. This provided dichotomous-choice contingent value data.

To test willingness-to-pay measures, 150 hunters were selected at random from the population of applicants who did not receive a Sandhill permit in the state lottery. Half received a contract and explanatory material. If they executed the contract, it would allow them to buy one 1984 Sandhill permit for the amount stated in the contract. The offer amounts ranged from $18 to $512. The other half received the same offers except that all offers to this group were purely hypothetical. Over 95 percent of the willingness-to-sell group and 93 percent of the willingness-to-pay group responded.

Values were generated with logit models in the dichotomous choice situations (see Bishop, Heberlein, and Kealy 1983 and Welsh 1986 for statistical details) and by computation of the arithmetic means in the auctions (Bishop et al. 1984). The comparisons between contingent values for selling permits and actual values for permits sold (or offered for sale) are displayed in Table 6.1. Using dichotomous choice, goose hunters' contingent values were $101, or 60 percent higher than the actual cash value of $63. This difference was statistically significant. When an auction was used for deer permits, the situation was reversed. The contingent values were lower ($833 compared to $1,184), although both values seemed very high for a one-day hunt. The difference was not statistically significant, however, since the variances were quite large. On the other hand, when dichotomous choice was used to sell permits, both values came down substantially and the mean contingent value was much higher (almost 175 percent) than the actual cash value. This is a statistically significant difference.

For willingness to pay, contingent values were much closer to the simulated market values (Table 6.2). In the sealed-bid auction and the dichotomous-choice experiment, contingent values and simulated market values were not statistically different, although the contingent value estimates were 33 percent higher in the former case and 13 percent higher in the latter case. Perhaps a larger sample size would have permitted us to establish statistically significant differences, at least in the open-ended case. The introduction of bidding further expanded the difference to the point where the contingent values were 126 percent higher than the actual cash measure, and this difference is statistically significant.

Table 6.1 CONTINGENT VALUES AND SIMULATED MARKET VALUES FOR COMPENSATION DEMANDED

Experiment	Commodity	Method	Dollar Values	
			Contingent	Simulated Market
I	Goose Permits	Dichotomous Choice	$101	$ 63
II	Deer Permits	Sealed-Bid Auction	$833	$1,184
III	Deer Permits	Dichotomous Choice	$420	$ 153

Table 6.2 CONTINGENT VALUES AND SIMULATED MARKET VALUES FOR WILLINGNESS TO PAY

Experiment	Commodity	Method	Dollar Values	
			Contingent	Simulated Market
I	Goose Permits	Dichotomous Choice	$21	—ᵃ
II	Deer Permits	Sealed-Bid Auction	$32	$24
		Sealed-Bid Auction and Bidding	$43	$19
III	Deer Permits	Dichotomous Choice	$35	$31

a. No Permits were available for us to sell so this value cannot be estimated.

In summary, these experiments indicate that contingent values for willingness to pay may be somewhat high, but for open-ended and dichotomous-choice questions the difference was not large enough to be statistically significant, given our sample sizes. Bidding seemed to introduce a substantial upward bias. On the compensation-demanded side, the results were quite discouraging. Contingent compensation demanded tended to produce excessive values when an open-ended question was asked and values that were biased substantially upward compared to values obtained from actual cash transactions when dichotomous choice questions were used.

Other Experimental Results

Four other studies deserve special mention here because they compared contingent values to values from simulated markets. The first is a laboratory experiment conducted at the University of Wyoming using undergraduates as subjects (Coursey, Hovis, and Schulze 1987). The goal was to simulate in the laboratory an unpleasant environmental stimulus. The commodity used to accomplish this was a bitter, unpleasant, but harmless, substance called sucrose octa acetate (SOA). This substance has been used previously in psychological experiments where the experiencing of an unpleasant flavor was desired. Part I of the experiment consisted of verbally describing SOA to respondents and asking them how much they would have to be paid hypothetically to taste SOA (i.e., their compensation demanded) or how much they would pay hypothetically to avoid tasting the substance. Compensation- demanded and willingness-to-pay groups were kept entirely separate throughout the experiment. Part II required three steps. In the first step, each subject tasted a few drops of the solution. In the second step, each was asked for her or his revised compensation demanded to taste a full, one-ounce cup of SOA or revised willingness to pay not to taste a full ounce. In the third step of Part II, monitors attempted to bid down subjects in the compensation-demanded group and bid up subjects in the willingness-to-pay group in $0.25 increments. In Part III, groups of eight individuals participated in an auction designed to elicit actual individual cash bids to either taste or not taste. At the end of the bidding, those in compensation-demanded groups that won the auction with minimal bids were actually paid and drank the one ounce cups of SOA. Those in willingness-to-pay groups who were the high bidders paid and those who were on the low end of the willingness-to-pay side had to drink the SOA.

On the willingness-to-pay side, contingent valuation performed quite well. Bids in Parts I, II, and III were quite close. On the compensation-demanded side, initial bids were, on average, quite high relative to willingness-to-pay, but through the bidding process in Part III mean compensation demanded collapsed and became statistically indistinguishable from willingness to pay.

The second simulated market study (Dickie, Fisher, and Gerking 1987) involved the sale of fresh strawberries.   One sample of Laramie, Wyoming, households was contacted at home and given an opportunity to purchase strawberries.   A second sample was contacted in the same fashion, except that hypothetical bids for strawberries were elicited. Each household, regardless of the sample, was given a set price for the strawberries and asked how many pints would be purchased. By varying the price across households, data for estimating demand functions were gathered.   The demand function based on actual cash transactions was not statistically different from the demand function estimated on the basis of hypothetical transactions. No data on compensation demanded were gathered during this experiment.

The remaining two experiments to be discussed here are reported in papers by Kealy, Dovidio, and Rockel (1987 and forthcoming).   These studies involved separate groups of undergraduate students and were conducted in a laboratory. Only willingness to pay was estimated. One of their studies involved a well-known brand of candy bar; the other dealt with donations to reduce damage to aquatic ecosystems in the Adirondack Mountains from acid rain. Both studies involved the same basic steps. In the first step, subjects were randomly assigned to two groups, a group to engage in actual transactions and a group to engage in hypothetical transactions. The "actual-transaction groups" were told from the beginning that their members would have an opportunity in the future to actually engage in the behavior being described, either buying the candy bar or making a donation to reduce acid-rain damage. The "hypothetical-transactions groups" were asked to imagine that the respective opportunities existed. The proposed actual and hypothetical transactions were stated in the dichotomous-choice format and data were analyzed using probit regression models. In addition, all four groups were asked open-ended contingent-valuation questions, and the candy-bar experiment included a bidding game as well.

The second step in both studies involved inviting the subjects back two weeks after the first step was completed. All groups were asked an open-ended contingent valuation question focusing again on either the candy bar or the donation. In addition, each member of the actual-transaction groups had the opportunity to complete an actual deal at the dichotomous-choice offer amount that had originally been specified in step 1, two weeks before. Again, a probit model was used to analyze the dichotomous-choice responses.

The contingent values of the candy bars were very close across dichotomous-choice and open-ended questions, across the actual-transaction and hypothetical-transaction groups, and across time. The expected value of a candy bar was between $0.76 and $0.85, and the various contingent estimates were not statistically different. However, when it came time to actually pay for and receive a candy bar, there was a tendency on the part of members of the actual-transactions group to back out. As a result, the value based on actual exchanges was only $0.57, which is significantly less than the contingent values. The bidding games in step 2 were conducted after the actual or hypothetical dichotomous-choice transactions. The bidding-game expected value for the actual-transaction group was somewhat lower than for the hypothetical-transaction group ($0.64 and $0.79, respectively), but the difference was not statistically significant.

Results for the acid-rain donation were surprisingly different. In step 1, the actual-transaction group had an expected value of $6.83, while at step 2, it was $5.37. This is not a statistically significant difference. On the other hand, the hypothetical group's expected value dropped from $15.51 at step 1 to $10.11 at step 2. The difference here is significant (t=2.76). The values of the two groups are statistically different at both steps (t=2.61 at step 1 and t=1.72 at step 2). Thus, in dealing with the acid-rain donation, contingent valuation overestimated the value compared to actual cash donated, but the tendency became less severe on the second iteration. Kealy and her colleagues attributed this result to a combination of hypothetical and strategic biases. They suspect that their contingent values in the acid rain case were biased upward because respondents lacked the time and/or adequate incentives to fully consider their preferences. On the other hand, they suspect that their simulated market results were biased downward because of free riding (Kealy, Dovidio, and Rockel, forthcoming).

Conclusions

Twenty years of research on contingent valuation have borne considerable fruit. First of all, though major issues—such as whether one question format works better than others—remain unresolved, great progress has been made in standardizing the mechanics. So long as proper attention is given to the well-understood, general principles of survey design and execution and to population definition, product definition, determination of the payment vehicle, and the other issues covered earlier in this chapter, odds are good that contingent valuation studies can be completed without major methodological problems. Nevertheless, it is worth stressing once more that survey research is never simple or easy. This field is at least as capable as others of attracting incompetents as well as outright charlatans. Careful examination of the methods underlying value estimates is always desirable. The other side of this coin is that researchers should always carefully explain all their procedures as well as report final results.

Furthermore, validity research, though it is still in its infancy, is already providing rich insights. When used to estimate willingness to pay for well-defined products with private goods characteristics—hunting permits, SOA, strawberries, and candy bars—contingent valuation appears promising. It does sometimes show a tendency toward overvaluation. This tendency showed up strongly in the candy-bar study and may have been present at times in the hunting-permit experiments as well, although the evidence there was less clear-cut. More research is needed to document this tendency, if it exists, and to better understand where and why it occurs and how large the bias is likely to be under specific conditions. In the meantime, except for questions raised by the candy-bar experiment, the overwhelming weight of the evidence from simulated-market experiments favors the use of contingent valuation for estimating willingness to pay for well-defined commodities with private-good characteristics.

Unfortunately, these rather encouraging results do not extend to contingent measures of compensation demanded. Such measures seem to be unstable and heavily dependent on question format. Dichotomous-choice questions appear to work best for estimating compensation demanded, but even using this format, contingent measures of compensation demanded have a strong upward bias when applied to well-defined, private goods. However, even this largely negative result has a positive side. All the evidence to date would strongly support using contingent compensation demanded as an upper bound on true compensation demanded. This result could be very useful in policy analyses.

Regarding willingness to pay for less welldefined products and products with public-good characteristics, an optimistic attitude tempered with a healthy skepticism is warranted. That contingent valuation has performed as well as it has for private goods is encouraging. However, the acid-rain donation study cautions against uncritical generalization to public goods of results from simulated-market experiments for private goods. More research would be highly desirable in this important area.

All in all, the prognosis is favorable. Most environmental assets lie outside the market system. Things without market value tend to be valued at near zero or near infinity, depending on which side of the policy debate one hears. Contingent valuation deserves acceptance into the set of tools that can be used to narrow this range and, as a result, facilitate sound public decisions. When environmental values must be weighed against more traditional economic values, contingent valuation can help assure that environmental values are adequately represented.

References

Alfano, G., and G. Marwell. 1981. Experiments on the Provision of Public Goods III: Non-divisibility and Free Riding in 'Real' Groups. *Social Psychology Quarterly*. 43:300-309.

Anderson, G.D., and R.C. Bishop. 1986. The Valuation Problem. *In* Natural Resource Economics, edited by D.W. Bromley, 132-52. Hingham, Mass.: Kluwer-Nijoff.

Bishop, R.C. 1982. Option Value: An Exposition and Extension. *Land Economics*. 58:1-15.

Bishop, R.C. 1986. Resource Valuation under Uncertainty: Theoretical Principles for Empirical Research. *In* Advances in Applied Microeconomics, edited by V.K. Smith, 133-52. Greenwich, Connecticut: JAI Press.

Bishop, R.C., and T.A. Heberlein. 1979. Measuring Values of Extramarket Goods: Are Indirect Measures Biased? *American Journal of Agricultural Economics.* 61:926-30.

Bishop, R.C., K.J. Boyle, M.P. Welsh, R.M. Baumgartner, and P.A. Rathbun. 1987. *Glen Canyon Dam Releases and Downstream Recreation: An Analysis of User Preferences and Economic Values.* Report prepared for Glen Canyon Environmental Studies, U.S. Bureau of Reclamation by HBRS, 4513 Vernon Blvd., Madison, Wis.

Bishop, R.C., T.A. Heberlein, and M.J. Kealy. 1983. Contingent Valuation of Environmental Assets: Comparisons with a Simulated Market. *Natural Resources Journal.* 23:619-33.

Bishop, R.C., T.A. Heberlein, M.P. Welsh, and R.M. Baumgartner. 1984. Does Contingent Valuation Work? Results of the Sandhill Experiment. Invited paper read at the joint meetings of the Association of Environmental and Resource Economists, the American Agricultural Economics Association, and the Northeast Agricultural Economics Council, August 5-8, Cornell University, Ithaca, New York.

Bohm, P. 1972. Estimating the Demand for Public Goods: An Experiment. *European Economic Review.* 3:111-30.

Boyle, K.J. 1985. Essays on the Valuation of Nonmarket Resources: Conceptual Issues and Empirical Case Studies. Ph.D. diss., Department of Agricultural Economics, University of Wisconsin-Madison.

Boyle, K.J., and R.C. Bishop. Forthcoming. Welfare Measurement Using Contingent Valuation: A Comparison of Techniques. *American Journal of Agricultural Economics.*

Boyle, K.J., and R.C. Bishop. 1987. The Total Value of Wildlife: A Case Study Involving Endangered Species. *Water Resources Research.* 23:943-50.

Boyle, K.J., R.C. Bishop, and M.P. Welsh. 1985. Starting Point Bias in Contingent Valuation Bidding Games. *Land Economics.* 61:188-94.

Brookshire, D.S., M.A. Thayer, W.D. Schulze, and R.C. d'Arge. 1982. Valuing Public Goods: A Comparison of Survey and Hedonic Approaches. *American Economic Review.* 72:165-77.

Brubaker, E. 1982. Sixty-Eight Percent Free Revelation and Thirty-Two Percent Free Ride? Demand Disclosures under Varying Conditions on Exclusion. *In* Research in Experimental Economics, edited by V.L. Smith, 151-66.

Coursey, D.L., J.J. Hovis, and W.D. Schulze. 1987. On the Supposed Disparity between Willingness to Accept and Willingness to Pay Measures of Value. *Quarterly Journal of Economics.* 102:679-90.

Cummings, R.G., D.S. Brookshire, and W.D. Schulze. 1986. *Valuing Environmental Goods.* Totowa, N.J.: Rowman & Allanheld, Publishers.

Davis, R.K. 1963. Recreational Planning as An Economics Problem. *Natural Resources Journal.* 3:238-49.

Davis, R.K. 1964. The Value of Big Game Hunting in a Private Forest. *Transactions of the Twenty-Ninth North American Wildlife and Natural Resources Conference.* 29:393-403.

Desvousges, W.H., V.K. Smith, and M.P. McGivney. 1983. A Comparison of Alternative Approaches for Estimating Recreation and Related Benefits of Water Quality Improvements. Report to the U.S. Environmental Protection Agency by Research Triangle Institute.

Dickie, M., A. Fisher, and S. Gerking. 1987. Market Transactions and Hypothetical Demand Data: A Comparative Study. *Journal of the American Statistical Society*. 82:69-75.

Dillman, D.A. 1978. *Mail and Telephone Surveys: The Total Design Method*. New York, N.Y.: John Wiley & Sons.

Edwards, S.F., and G.D. Anderson. 1984. Land-Use Conflicts in the Coastal Zone: An Approach for the Analysis of Opportunity Costs of Protecting Coastal Resources. *Journal of the Northeast Agricultural Economics Council*. 13:73-81.

Fisher, A., and R. Raucher. 1984. Intrinsic Benefits of Improved Water Quality: Conceptual and Empirical Perspectives. *In* Advances in Applied Micro-Economics, vol. 3. edited by V.K. Smith and A.D. Witte. pp 37-66. Greenwich, Conn.:JAI Press.

Hanemann, W.M. 1984. Welfare Evaluations in Contingent Valuation Experiments with Discrete Responses. *American Journal of Agricultural Economics*. 66:332-41.

Horvath, J.C. 1974. *Southeastern Economic Survey of Wildlife Recreation*. 2 vols. Atlanta, Ga.: Environmental Research Group, Georgia State University.

Isaac, R., J. Walker, and S. Thomas. 1984. Divergent Evidence on Free-Riding: An Experimental Examination of Possible Explanations. *Public Choice*. 43:113-49.

Kealy, M.J., J.A. Dovidio, and M.L. Rockel. 1987. Accuracy in Contingent Valuation Is a Matter of Degree. Unpublished paper, Department of Economics, Colgate University, Hamilton, N.Y.

Kealy, M.J., J. Dovidio, and M.L. Rockel. Forthcoming. Willingness to Pay to Prevent Additional Damages to the Adriondcks from Acid Rain. *Regional Science Review*.

Knetsch, J.L., and R.K. Davis. 1966. Comparison of Methods for Recreation Valuation. *In* Water Research, edited by A.V. Kneese and S.C. Smith. Baltimore: Johns Hopkins University Press.

Kim, O., and M. Walker. 1984. The Free Rider Problem: Experimental Evidence. *Public Choice*. 43:3-24.

Marwell, G., and R.E. Ames. 1979. Experiments on the Provision of Public Goods I: Resources, Interest, Group Size and the Free-Rider Problem. *American Journal of Sociology*. 84:1335-360.

Marwell, G., and R.E. Ames. 1980. Experiments on the Provision of Public Goods II: Provision of Points, Stakes, Experience and the Free-Rider Problem. *American Journal of Sociology*. 85:926-37.

Marwell, G., and R.E. Ames. 1981. Economists Free Ride, Does Anyone Else? Experiments on the Provision of Public Goods. IV. *Journal of Public Economics*. 15:295-310.

Mitchell, R.C., and R.T. Carson. 1981. An Experiment in Determining Willingness to Pay for National Water Quality Improvements. Draft Report to U.S. Environmental Protection Agency, Office of Policy Analysis, by Resources for the Future, Washington, D.C.

Mitchell, R.C., and R.T. Carson. 1987. *Using Surveys to Value Public Goods: The Contingent Valuation Method*. Washington, D.C. Resources for the Future.

Rae, D.A. 1981a. *Visibility Impairment at Mesa Verde National Park: An Analysis of Benefits and Costs of Controlling Emissions in the Four Corners Area*. Report prepared for the Electric Power Research Institute by Charles River Associates, Boston.

Rae, D.A. 1981b. *Benefits of Improving Visibility at Great Smokey National Park*. Report prepared for Electric Power Research Institute by Charles River Associates, Boston.

Randall, A., and J.R. Stoll. 1983. Existence Value in a Total Valuation Framework. *In* Managing Air Quality and Scenic Resources at National Parks and Wilderness Areas. edited by R.D. Rowe and L.G. Chestnut. 265-74. Boulder, Colo.: Westview Press.

Samuelson, P.A. 1954. The Pure Theory of Public Expenditure. *Review of Economics and Statistics*. 36(4):387-89.

Scherr, B.A., and E.M. Babb. 1975. Pricing Public Goods: An Experiment with Two Proposed Pricing Systems. *Public Choice*. 23:35-48.

Schneider, F., and W.W. Pommerehne. 1981. Free Riding and Collective Action: An Experiment in Public Microeconomics. *Quarterly Journal of Economics*. 97:689-702.

Schulze, W.D., R.C. d'Arge, and D.S. Brookshire. 1981. Valuing Environmental Commodities: Some Recent Experiments. *Land Economics*. 57:151-72.

Sellar, C., J.R. Stoll, and J.P. Chavas. 1985. Validation of Empirical Measures of Welfare Change: A Comparison of Nonmarket Techniques. *Land Economics*. 61:156-75.

Smith, V.K. 1977. The Principle of Unanimity and Voluntary Consent in Social Choice. *Journal of Political Economy*. 85:1125-139.

Thayer, M.A. 1981. Contingent Valuation Techniques for Assessing Environmental Impacts: Further Evidence. *Journal of Environmental Economics and Management*. 8:27-44.

Tideman, N.T. 1983. An Experiment in the Demand Revealing Process. *Public Choice*. 41:387-401.

Welsh, M.P. 1986. Exploring the Accuracy of the Contingent Valuation Method: Comparisons with Simulated Markets. Ph.D. diss., Department of Agricultural Economics, University of Wisconsin-Madison.

Welsh, M.P., R.C. Bishop, and T.A. Heberlein. 1986. Incentive Compatibility in the Contingent Valuation Method. Paper read at Association of Environmental and Resource Economists/Allied Social Sciences Association Annual Meetings, December 27-30, New Orleans, La.

7 Contingent Valuation and the Prospect of a Satisfactory Benefit-Cost Indicator

John P. Hoehn

Introduction

The reliability of the contingent valuation method has proven difficult to assess. Regression analyses have shown contingent valuation results to be systematically related to individual demographic characteristics and generally consistent with preferences revealed by actual market choices (Tolley *et al.* 1984). Direct comparisons of contingent results with market-demand-based measures are less conclusive. Such comparisons often reveal more about the variability of the demand based method than about the performance of contingent valuation.[1] Additionally, relatively few systematic concepts have been available to guide empirical research and testing.

The objective of this chapter is an improved comparison of contingent and market-based valuations. As a first step, previous empirical analyses are briefly reviewed and highlighted by recent conceptual results. Second, the valuation context is considered. Recent travel demand research is combined with Mäler's (1974) notion of weak complementarity to derive a surprisingly simple, market-based measure of site specific surplus. Third, the contingent valuation experiment is described. Because both the travel demand approach and the contingent valuation experiment yield both variances as well as means, the comparison of surplus measures can be based upon standard statistical tests rather than on simple comparisons of absolute values.

---

[1]Experimental markets provide another important avenue of comparison. For example, Bishop and Heberlein (1980) use an experimental market to obtain their measure of "true" value. However, these experimental markets are likely to confront difficulties of uncertainty and unfamiliarity similar to those that arise in CV experiments.

Previous Research

Previous studies have had some difficulty in designing a direct comparison between contingent valuation (CV) and demand-based techniques. More often than not, a given valuation context lends itself to either a demand-based technique or CV, but not both. Nevertheless, two types of market-based comparisons have been made: (1) those based on the travel cost technique and (2) those using the hedonic approach.

Comparison of travel cost (TC) and contingent value data tends to be based on nonstatistical comparisons of mean valuations. In the first study of its type, Knetsch and Davis (1966) compare a contingent willingness-to-pay measure with a TC valuation and find the two estimates to be within two percent of each other. Subsequent research by Thayer (1981), Sellar, Stoll, and Chavez (1985), and Desvouges, Smith, and McGivney (1983) tends to corroborate the Knetsch and Davis results.

Results of Bishop and Heberlein (1979, 1980) shed additional light on these TC-CV comparisons. Three of their results are particularly relevant. First, Bishop and Heberlein find that TC valuations vary widely depending upon the choice of travel cost index that serves as price. Thus, a single travel cost estimate may be unreliable as a value datum. Second, when compared to a range of reasonable travel cost estimates, the contingent estimate of willingness to pay lies almost exactly at the midpoint of possible upper and lower bounds for the TC estimate. Third, both the contingent and TC estimates of willingness to pay understate the Bishop and Heberlein datum of true value.

Brookshire *et al.* (1982) develop a unique comparison based on hedonic analysis. They demonstrate that the true individual valuation must lie below the true hedonic measure. Thus, if CV elicits an accurate individual valuation and the hedonic measure approximates the true market measure of value, then the contingent estimate must not exceed the hedonic estimate. Empirical results from two studies (Brookshire *et al.* 1982, and Brookshire, Ives, and Schulze 1984) do not reject the validity of either the hedonic or CV estimates.

In an extensive review of these empirical results, Cummings, Brookshire, and Schulze (1986), conclude that at least three reference operating conditions must be met if contingent willingness-to-pay measures are to be predictable: (1) CV respondents must be fully familiar with the commodity being valued; (2) respondents must have adequate prior valuation experience with respect to the consumption levels being valued; and (3) there must be little uncertainty.[2] Though these conclusions are not unreasonable in light of the existing data, they do not explain or predict the behavior of CV results in the many cases of greatest pragmatic value (Cummings, Brookshire, and Schulze, 1986); that is, in cases where the environmental or policy impacts are beyond the familiar range of experience.

An analysis by Hoehn and Randall (1987) reaches an alternative conclusion. They note that the typical application of CV involves (1) uncertainty or unfamiliarity, (2) incomplete decision processes, and (3) incentives. To predict the impact of these three effects on CV outcomes, Hoehn and Randall adapt the standard theoretical model of consumer choice to the specific constraints of the CV choice context. The resulting model of constrained choice demonstrates that errors may certainly occur in the valuations of specific individuals. However, the average sample valuation is systematic: on average, individuals tend to overanticipate the utility damages of environmental deterioration and underanticipate the utility benefits of environmental improvement. The degree of error in anticipation depends upon the degree of unfamiliarity and incompleteness in the decision process.

The decision mechanism outlined by Hoehn and Randall results in an important implication for applied benefit-cost analysis: the average Hicksian compensating measure obtained in contingent valuation, HC^c, does not overstate the ideal Hicksian measure, HC^*. Algebraically, letting willingness to pay be positive and willingness to accept be negative, $HC^c \leq HC^*$. Given $HC^c \leq HC^*$, Hoehn and Randall suggest that the contingent compensating measures are generally "satisfactory" (1987, 240) when interpreted in terms of the potential Pareto improvement (PPI) criterion of benefit-cost analysis. That is, in a benefit-cost context, contingent compensating measures correctly identify a subset of truly PPI policy alternatives as having positive net value and all non-PPI proposals as having negative net value.

With the exception of Bishop and Heberlein (1979), almost all of the previous comparison studies consider rather familiar and routine choice contexts, such as familiar recreation sites or neighborhood characteristics. Based on the Hoehn and Randall analysis, *if* market-based measures approximate HC^*, one would expect results paralleling those actually found, $HC^c \approx HC^*$. In the analysis below, we attempt to extend the empirical results beyond the zone of routine familiarity and there by provide an initial test of the more unique aspects of the constrained choice model.

---

[2]Cummings, Brookshire, and Schultz (1986) also suggest a fourth reference operating condition: that a willingness-to-pay—not a willingness-to-accept—measure should be elicited. This fourth condition is not directly relevant to the empirical aspects of the present study.

Study Design

The case examined is that of an urban viewing site, the Hancock Tower Observatory (HTO) in Chicago. Like similar viewing sites in other metropolitan areas, the HTO attracts a large number of visitors (approximately 350,000 per year). Several factors make HTO a unique opportunity for a comparison study. First, regression analysis shows that air quality, specifically visual air quality or visibility, has a significant impact on visitation (Tolley *et al.*, 1984). Second, not only are admission prices recorded at HTO, but prices are occasionally varied by the management over fairly short periods of time. Third, return visits to HTO are at best infrequent.[3] Thus, on any particular visit, individuals are unlikely to be familiar with the view under different air-quality conditions.

To take advantage of the unique attributes of HTO, a demand analysis and CV experiment were designed to value changes in visual air quality or visibility at HTO.[4] The demand analysis uses the literature on urban travel demand to specify an estimable demand function from HTO visitation. The analysis below shows that the price coefficient of the specified demand function is directly and easily related to the per person Marshallian surplus obtained from a visit to HTO. The CV analysis uses the model developed by Hoehn and Randall (1987) to derive hypotheses regarding the relation between the demand-based and contingent valuation estimates of value.

Demand Analysis

The demand for access to HTO is derived from an individual's demand for HTO viewing services. The most notable aspect of demand for access is that at the individual level, it is discrete: an individual either visits HTO or does not. Borrowing from the urban travel demand literature (Domencich and McFadden 1975), aggregate demand can be represented by

$$VST_t = N_t \pi_t \tag{1}$$

where VST_t is total visits to HTO on day t, N_t is a pool of potential visitors on day t, and π_t is the probability that an individual in N_t visits HTO. Variables relevant to the determination of N_t and π_t can be

---

[3]Statistics for return visits are unavailable. However, in the CV sample, over 50 percent of the visitors were from outside the metropolitan area.

[4]A number of studies examined the value of changes in visibility. See, Rowe, d'Arge, and Brookshire (1980) or Brookshire, Ives, and Schulze (1976).

identified by considering the abbreviated "decision tree" (Domencich and McFadden 1975, 42) given in Figure 7.1. On any particular day one can imagine that individuals sort themselves out over mutually exclusive activities as indicated by the direction of the arrows in Figure 7.1. Decisions represented in Figure 7.1 can be partitioned into those made in the longer-run and those made in the short-run. For example, choices above Branch 3 are likely to be relatively fixed by long-term contracts. Such longer-run decisions involve location decisions, housing service choices, and work-leisure choices. For these long-run decisions, the most important observable variables relevant to the HTO visit choice are likely to be time series variables and weather variables. Therefore, it is supposed that the pool of potential visitors at leisure in downtown metropolitan Chicago is

$$N_{tMLD} = N_{tMLD}(s,w,e) \tag{2}$$

where s is a vector of time series variables (e.g., trend, month, day of week), w is a vector of weather and environmental variables, and e is an error term introduced for the impact of unobservable variables.

At Branch 4 the relation between visitation, $N_{tMLDH} = VST_t$, and admission price becomes important. To analyze the visitation choice, indirect utility functions are defined conditioned upon downtown recreational opportunities with and without a visit to HTO.[5] If an individual visits HTO, the indirect utility function is

$$u_h = V_h(p,w,m-p_h) + \delta_h \tag{3}$$

If the individual does not visit HTO, the conditional indirect utility function is

$$u_0 = V_0(p,w,m) + \delta_0 \tag{4}$$

where δ_0 is, again, a random error term due to unobservables. For brevity, let $V_h = V_h(p,w,m-p_h)$ and $V_o = V_o(p,w,m)$ where m is the excursion budget, p is a vector of prices of ordinary (divisible) market goods available downtown, w is a vector of weather and environmental variables at HTO, p_h is the admission price, and δ_h is a random error term due to unobservable individual characteristics.

---

[5]Small and Rosen (1981) have suggested the conditional maximization process in dealing with discrete choice.

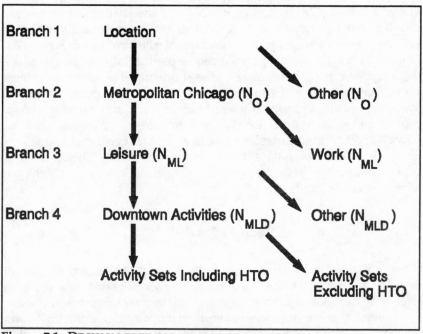

Figure 7.1 DECISION TREE FOR CHOICE OF ACTIVITIES

Under fairly general conditions,[6] the probability that an individual visits HTO is

$$\pi_h = \frac{v_h}{(v_h + v_0)} \tag{5}$$

where $v_h = \exp(V_h)$ and $v_o = \exp(V_o)$.

Aggregate demand for HTO services is the pool of potential visitors times the probability of visitation,

$$
\begin{aligned}
VST_t &= N_{tMLD}\pi_h \\
&= N_{tMLD}\left[\frac{v_h}{v_h + v_0}\right].
\end{aligned}
\tag{6}
$$

Taking the natural logarithm of equation (6) yields

---

[6]For a full discussion and derivation, see the discussion leading to equation (4.39a) in Domencich and McFadden (1974, 33-69).

$$\ln VST_t = \ln N_{tMLD}(s,w,e) + \ln v_h - \ln(v_h + v0). \tag{7}$$

Since no information is available on day-to-day variation in the typical excursion budget size, the logarithm terms which include m—$\ln v_h$ and $\ln(v_h + v_o)$—are replaced by first-order Taylor series approximations. The resulting demand approximation is

$$\ln VST_t = a_1 - b_1 p_h + \ln N_{tMLD}(s,w,e) \tag{8}$$

where a_1 is a constant and p_h enters the equation in level form with coefficient b_1. To estimate equation (8), a general transcendental form is used to represent N_{tMLD}, and the error term, e, is assumed to be lognormal. The demand equation to be estimated is therefore

$$\ln VST_t = a_1 - b_1 p_h + b_2 \ln q_{ht} + b_3 w_t + b_4 s_t + e_t \tag{9}$$

where q_{ht} is visibility at HTO on day t, w_t is a vector of the environmental and weather variables, s_t is a vector of time series variables, and e_t is a normally distributed error term.

The aggregate Marshallian surplus associated with visitation is found by integrating the antilogarithm of equation (9) from the initial HTO entry price to infinity (assuming $b_1 > 0$). Performing this integration, expected aggregate consumer surplus at a given level of visitation, VST_t, is the level of total visitation, VST_t, divided by the coefficient of admission price, b_1. Thus, expected Marshallian surplus obtained per person visit to HT0 is

$$ams = E\left[\frac{VST_t}{b_1}\right]$$
$$= \frac{1}{b_1} \tag{10}$$

Notably, the average Marshallian surplus—ams—is constant as prices or environmental quality changes. That is, as visibility improves from q^o to q^1, the aggregate demand curve shifts from VST^o to VST^1. Those individuals who would have visited HTO at q^o enjoy, at q^1, an additional surplus. However, with the change in visibility, visitation also increases. The additional visitors receive relatively lower levels of surplus. With aggregate demand given by equation (9), the enhanced average surplus of those visitors who would have visited at q^o is just offset by the lower average surplus of the additional visitors attracted by q^1. On average, ams is constant.

The Contingent Valuation Analysis

The objective of the CV analysis was to use the datum given by ams to derive a statistically valid test of the implications of the Hoehn and Randall model of contingent behavior. To provide the contingent value data for the test, a CV questionnaire was designed to elicit three types of willingness to pay valuations: (1) a valuation of HTO services at the time of visitation; (2) a valuation of HTO services given a specified decline in visual air quality or visibility; and (3) a valuation of HTO services given a specified improvement in visibility.

A first set of questions elicited maximum willingness-to-pay for the HTO visit given the environmental conditions prevailing at the time of questioning. Theoretically, this first willingness-to-pay measure, wtp_1^*, is defined by

$$u_0 = V_h(p,w_h,m-p_h-wtp_1^*) + \delta_h \qquad (11)$$

where u_0 is defined by equation (4) and was presumably calculated as part of the individual's visitation decision. Inverting equation (11) about wtp_1^* gives

$$wtp_1^* = m - p_h - e_h(p,w_h,\delta_h,u_0) \qquad (12)$$

where $e_h(\cdot)$ is the minimum expenditure required to maintain the nonvisit level of utility, u_0, when the individual visits HTO. Note that prior to the CV experiment, the individual's visitation decision involves only the utility levels u_0 and u_h. There is no reason to expect the individual to have thought about the values of either wtp_1^* in $V_h(p,w_h,m-p_h-wtp_1^*)$ or $e_h(p,w_h,\delta_h,u_0)$. Thus, to answer the contingent valuation question, the individual must carry out an introspective evaluation or search process.

Hoehn and Randall (1987) suggest that the individual's contingent search process is incomplete due to the time and decision resource constraints of the contingent valuation context. With decisions incomplete, individuals tend to identify something less than maximum prospective utility and something more than minimum expenditure. For instance, in terms of the valuation process given by equation (12), an individual does not instantaneously identify the unique minimum level of expenditure—$e_h(p,w_h,\delta_h,u_0)$—required to maintain the nonvisit level of utility when the individual visits HTO. Instead, the individual iterates toward $e_h(p,w_h,\delta_h,u_o)$ in successive trials. With the decision process cut short by the time and resource constraints of the CV context, the individual identifies a level of expenditure, $\hat{e}(p,w_h,\delta_h,u_o)$ that is greater than the unique minimum, $e_h(p,w_h,\delta_h,u_o)$. Across a sample of respondents, the expected contingent valuation, $E[\hat{wtp_1}]$, is therefore

$$
\begin{aligned}
E[\hat{wtp_1}] &= E[m - p_h - \hat{e}(p,w_h,\delta_h,u_0)] \\
&\le E[m - p_h - e(p,w_h,\delta_h,u_0)] \\
&= E[wtp_1^*].
\end{aligned}
\tag{13}
$$

Given the model of incomplete contingent decision processes, the expected sample valuation of HTO services is less than the ideal valuation. Furthermore, since the amount of income spent on HTO visitation is likely to be a very small fraction of overall income, the results of Randall and Stoll (1980) suggest that

$$
\begin{aligned}
ams &\approx E[wtp_1^*] \\
&\ge E[\hat{wtp_1}].
\end{aligned}
\tag{14}
$$

Equation (14) yields the first hypothesis that stems from the Hoehn and Randall model: the sample mean valuation of current HTO services does not exceed the demand based valuation.

The second set of valuation questions postulated a reduction in visibility and sought to determine whether or not the respondent would visit HTO at the lower level of visibility. If the individual would make the visit despite the lower level of visibility, additional questions obtained a willingness to pay for the HTO services associated with the lower level of visibility. This second measure of willingness to pay, wtp_2, requires the individual to value a qualitatively unfamiliar circumstance—a level of visibility below current experience. Thus, wtp_2 begins to move the valuation context beyond the range of the reference operating conditions described by Cummings, Brookshire, and Schulze (1986). By the Hoehn and Randall analysis, unfamiliarity would accentuate the divergence between the expected contingent valuation, $E[\hat{wtp_2}]$, and the full valuation, $E[wtp_2^*]$. By the arguments leading to equation (14), the second hypothesis is

$$
E[\hat{wtp_2}] \le ams.
\tag{15}
$$

A third set of questions obtained a contingent willingness-to-pay measure for an improvement in visibility. As Figure 7.2 illustrates, an improvement in visibility from an initial q_{ht}^0 to a subsequent q_{ht}^1 shifts the demand function from VST^0 to VST^1 and visitation from VST_t^0 to VST_t^1. The demand shift implies two different effects from an actual improvement in visibility: (1) the aggregate surplus of visitors at the initial and lower level of visibility would increase from area p^0ae to area p^0abd; and (2) the improvement in HTO viewing services would draw in additional visitors with a smaller aggregate valuation given by area abc. For the demand function in equation (9), the two effects cancel out and the average surplus remains unchanged at ams.

In the contingent valuation experiment, however, only current visitors can be queried regarding the value of an improvement in visibility. Given this truncated sample, ams does not provide a valid value datum. Offered an improvement in visibility from an initial q_{ht}^0 to a prospective q_{ht}^1, the expected per person Marshallian surplus for current visitors is, following Figure 2, the area p^0abd divided by VST_t^0 or

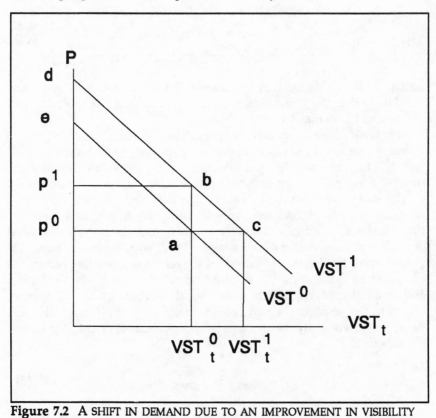

Figure 7.2 A SHIFT IN DEMAND DUE TO AN IMPROVEMENT IN VISIBILITY

$$ams' = E\left(\frac{\left[\int_{p'}^{\infty} VST_t^1 dp + (P^1-P^0)VST_t^0\right]}{VST_t^0}\right) \qquad (16)$$

$$= ams + p^1 + p^0$$

where VST_t^1 is given by equation (9) evaluated at $q_{ht} = q_{ht}^1$, p^o is the initial entry price, and p^1 is the price that results in the initial level of visitation, VST_{tt}^0, at the improved level of visibility, q_{ht}^1. Using equation (9),

$$p^1 - p^0 = \left(\frac{b_2}{b_1}\right)\ln\left(\frac{q_{ht}^1}{q_{ht}^0}\right). \qquad (17)$$

Defined by equations (16) and (17), ams' provides a market-based value measure appropriate for comparison with a contingent valuation obtained from the truncated sample. Analogous to equation (15), unfamiliarity and incomplete decision processes imply that

$$E[w\hat{t}p_3] \leq ams' \qquad (18)$$

where $w\hat{t}p_3$ is a current visitor's contingent valuation of a visibility-induced improvement in HTO services.

Overall, equations (14), (15), and (18) provide three well-defined hypotheses. Each hypothesis asserts that if the Hoehn and Randall model describes contingent valuation decision processes, the average contingent valuation will not exceed the relevant demand-based valuation.

Empirical Results

Both the demand analysis and the contingent valuation experiment were completed during the second and third quarters of 1981. This section presents the demand estimates, the contingent valuation procedures, and the comparison of value results.

The demand analysis was based on daily HTO visitation beginning on March 15 and ending on May 31, 1981. The demand data included daily observations on HTO visitation, admission price, weather variables such as rainfall, cloud or sky cover, and the presence of fog, and a selection of time series variables. The demand function, equation (9), was estimated using ordinary least squares (OLS). OLS was appropriate since the quantity of HTO access supplied was perfectly elastic within the range of realized visitation. Thus, the quantity of access purchased was purely a function of demand.

Table 7.1 presents the demand estimates. Overall, the estimated function explains 87 percent of the variation in visitation. Coefficient estimates are generally statistically precise and consistent with intuition. Importantly, the coefficient of admission price is statistically significant and of the appropriate sign. The statistically significant and positive sign on the logarithm of visibility indicates that a 10 percent improvement in visibility increases visitation by 1.40 percent. Increases in rain, sky cover, fog, and haze reduce visitation. Increases in wind speed and temperature lead to increases in visitation. Relative to April, visitation during March tends to be higher, and visitation during May tends to be lower. Visitation tends to be lowest on Tuesday and highest on Saturday.

The OLS estimator, $\hat{b}_1$, of b_1 is a random variable. To compute the sample mean and variance of ams—the quotient of a random variable, $\hat{b}_1$—the following approximations were used:[7]

$$\bar{x}_{AMS} = \left(\frac{1}{\bar{b}_1}\right) + \left(\frac{1}{\bar{b}_1}\right)^3 var(\bar{b}_1) \tag{19}$$

and

$$s^2_{AMS} = \left[\left(\frac{1}{\bar{b}_1}\right)^2 \frac{s_b^2}{\bar{b}_1}\right] \tag{20}$$

where $\bar{x}_{AMS}$ and s^2_{AMS} are the estimated mean and variance, respectively, of ams, $\bar{b}_1$ is the OLS estimate of b_1, and s_b^2 is the OLS estimate of the variance of $\hat{b}_1$. Since the estimate of ams' also involves a quotient of random variables, approximations similar to equations (19) and (20) were used to compute an estimate of ams' and its variance. Estimates for both ams and ams' are given in Table 7.2.

---

[7]See Mood, Graybill, and Boes (1974, 181) for a derivation.

Table 7.1 AGGREGATE DEMAND ESTIMATES[a] FOR HTO SERVICES, MARCH 15 TO MAY 31, 1981

Independent[b] Variable	Parameter Estimate	Standard Error	Variable Description [mean]
P	-0.533	0.193	Price of admission to HTO in dollars [2.15].
Lnvis	0.140	0.0547	Log of visibility where visibility is measured in miles [2.47]
Rain	-0.927	0.216	Proportion of the day in which rain fell [0.111].
Tsc	-0.00240	0.00154	Total sky cover in percent [69.4].
Fog	-2.296	0.298	Proportion of the day with fog [0.064].
Lnwin	0.0343	0.128	Log of wind speed where wind speed is measured in mph/10 [2.40].
Lntmk	7.137	2.61	Log of temperature where temperature is measured in degrees Kelvin [5.65].
Haze	-0.0906	0.396	Proportion of day with haze [0.043].
Lnt	0.233	0.116	Log of a integer time series variable beginning with 1 on March 15 and ending with 78 on March 31 [3.56].
Mar	0.327	0.196	0-1 variable for March (March=1, 0 otherwise) [0.22].
May	-0.334	0.126	0-1 variable for May (May=1, 0 otherwise) [0.40].
M	-0.172	0.181	0-1 variable for Monday (Monday=1, 0 otherwise) [0.14].
Tu	-0.348	0.160	0-1 variable for Tuesday (Tuesday=1, 0 otherwise) [0.14].
W	-0.127	0.159	0-1 variable for Wednesday (Wednesday=1, 0 otherwise) [0.14].
F	0.376	0.159	0-1 variable for Friday (Friday=1, 0 otherwise) [0.14].
S	0.787	0.159	0-1 variable for Saturday (Saturday=1, 0 otherwise) [0.14].
Su	0.272	0.162	0-1 variable for Sunday (Sunday=1, 0 otherwise) [0.14].
Intercept	-33.48	14.6	

a. $R^2 = .87$, SSE = 7.6, DF = 60, and F = 24.9.

b. Weather observations recorded at O'Hare International Airport were used. Visibility was recorded at HTO.

Table 7.2 ESTIMATES OF THE VALUE OF VIEWING SERVICES AT HTO

Value	Sample Size	Mean ($)	Standard Error Estimate
ams	78	2.12[a]	0.680[a]
ams'	78	2.53[a]	0.749[a]
$\hat{wtp}_1$	319	1.70	0.125
$\hat{wtp}_2$	147	1.03	0.207
$\hat{wtp}_3$	87	2.52	0.284

a. Computed using standard approximation formulas (Mood, Graybill, and Boes, 1974, 180).

The contingent valuation questionnaire was administered in on-site, in-person interviews of HTO visitors. The valuation section of the questionnaire used the iterative bid approach of Randall, Ives, and Eastman (1974) and was divided into three parts. The first part sought to elicit $\hat{wtp}_1$—an individual's maximum willingness to pay for viewing services existing at the time of the interview. $\hat{wtp}_1$ was elicited from all individuals who cooperated in the CV experiment.

Administration of parts two and three depended upon visibility conditions prevailing at the time of the interview. Part two was administered when existing visibility conditions at HTO were better than average. Part two presented the prospect of reduced visibility conditions and then asked whether the individual would have decided to visit HTO under such conditions. The mean proposed reduction suggested an 80 percent decline in visibility. If the individual would have visited despite the reduction in HTO viewing services, $\hat{wtp}_2$ was elicited.

Part three was administered when existing visibility conditions were better than average. This part of the questionnaire presented the prospect of improved visibility and elicited $\hat{wtp}_3$. The mean postulated improvement represented a 400 percent increase over the existing level of visibility.

CV interviews were conducted on nine different days and resulted in 321 initial contacts. Of the initial contacts, 319 individuals answered part one of the questionnaire. Eleven individuals declined to answer further questions after part one; 221 individuals began part two, but 74 of these claimed that they would not have visited HTO given the proposed reduction in visibility. As a result, $\hat{wtp}_2$ was elicited from 147 individuals; $\hat{wtp}_3$ was elicited from 87 individuals.

Table 7.2 displays the results of the CV experiment. The relative sizes of the mean values are consistent with the implications of the Hoehn and

Randall model of contingent valuation. For instance, consistent with the notion of incomplete contingent decision processes, $\hat{wtp}_1$ does not exceed the estimate of ams. Additionally, $\hat{wtp}_2$—subject to both incomplete decision processes and unfamiliarity—is less than estimates of both $\hat{wtp}_1$ and ams. Thus, consistent with the proposed model, unfamiliarity appears to have an important and predictable effect on valuation. Finally, the mean value of $\hat{wtp}_3$ does not exceed ams'.[8]

The statistical hypothesis tests of Table 7.3 confirm the nonstatistical comparison of mean values. In each of the three cases, the contingent valuation of HTO services fails to exceed statistically the demand-based measures of value. These statistical results offer strong support for the implications of the Hoehn and Randall model of contingent behavior. Due to both (1) incomplete decision processes and (2) unfamiliarity, individuals, on average, do not overstate their full willingness to pay for HTO services.

Conclusions

Two methodological problems have made it difficult to assess the reliability of contingent valuation (CV) data. First, situations that allow a direct statistical comparison between CV results and other observable measures of value have proven to be relatively scarce. Second, relatively few systematic concepts have been available to guide empirical research and hypothesis testing.

This chapter has addressed both of these difficulties. First, the chapter described a choice context in which it was possible to obtain statistically precise estimates of value using both the CV method and a demand-based technique. Second, a recently developed theory of contingent valuation behavior was used to specify three well-defined empirical hypotheses regarding the relation between CV and demand-based results.

Test results are consistent with the developed theory: given the constraints of the contingent choice context, individuals tend to underanticipate gains and overanticipate losses. In a Hicksian compensating evaluation framework, these results imply that CV benefit-cost measures will correctly identify (1) a subset of true potential Pareto improvements (PPI) as having positive net value and (2) all non-PPI alternatives as having negative net value. As a result, contingent valuation data are likely to be satisfactory, though not optimal, benefit-cost indicators.

---

[8]Hoehn and Fishelson (1987) analyze a different data series for HTO and give an estimate of ams that averages approximately one order of magnitude larger than the estimates given in this chapter. These larger estimates would only underscore the results of our hypothesis tests.

Table 7.3 HYPOTHESIS TEST STATISTICS

Null Hypothesis, H_o	Pooled Standard Error	t Statistic	Decision[a]
$\hat{wtp}_1 \leq ams$	0.329	-1.28	Do not reject H_o
$\hat{wtp}_2 \leq ams$	0.453	-2.41	Do not reject H_o
$\hat{wtp}_3 \leq ams'$	0.590	-0.02	Do not reject H_o

a. The alternative hypothesis is $\hat{wtp}_i > ams$. H_o is not rejected for any conventional level of significance.

References

Bishop, Richard C., and Thomas A. Heberlein. 1979. Measuring Values of Extramarket Goods: Are Indirect Measures Biased? *American Journal of Agricultural Economics.* 64(5):927-30.

Bishop, Richard C., and Thomas A. Heberlein. 1980. Simulated Markets, Hypothetical Markets, and Travel Cost Analysis. Department of Agricultural Economics staff paper #187, University of Wisconsin-Madison.

Brookshire, D. S., B. Ives, and W. W. Schulze. 1976. The Valuation of Aesthetic Preferences. *Journal of Environmental Economics and Management.* 3:325-46.

Brookshire, David S., Mark A. Thayer, William W. Schulze, and Ralph C. d'Arge. 1982. Valuing Public Goods: A Comparison of Survey and Hedonic Approaches. *American Economic Review.* 72(1):165-77.

Cummings, R. G., R. S. Brookshire, and W. A. Schulze, eds. 1986. *Valuing Environmental Goods: An Assessment of the Contingent Valuation Method.* Totowa, N.J.: Rowan and Allanheld.

Desvouges, William H., V. Kerry Smith, and M. P. McGivney. 1983. A Comparison of Alternative Approaches for Estimating Recreation and Related Benefits of Water Quality Improvements. U.S. Environmental Protection Agency.

Domencich, Thomas A., and Daniel McFadden. 1975. *Urban Travel Demand.* Amsterdam: North-Holland.

Hoehn, John P., and Gideon Fishelson. 1987. Weak Complementarity and Quality Adjusted Prices: A New Approach to Valuing Environmental Services. Paper presented at the joint meetings of the American Agricultural Economics Association and the Association of Environmental and Resource Economists, East Lansing, Mich.

Hoehn, John P., and Alan Randall. 1987. A Satisfactory Benefit Cost Indicator from Contingent Valuation. *Journal of Environmental Economics and Management.* 14(3):226-47.

Knetsch, Jack L., and Robert K. Davis. 1966. Comparisons of Methods for Recreation Evaluation. *In* Water Research, edited by Allen V. Kneese and Stephen C. Smith. Baltimore: Johns Hopkins University Press.

Mäler, Karl Goran. 1974. *Environmental Economics.* Baltimore: Johns Hopkins University Press.

Mood, Alexander M., Franklin A. Graybill, and Duane C. Boes. 1974. *Introduction to the Theory of Statistics*. New York: McGraw-Hill.

Randall, Alan, Berry Ives, and Clyde Eastman. 1974. Bidding Games for the Valuation of Aesthetic Environmental Improvements. *Journal of Environmental Economics and Management*, 1:132-49.

Rowe, Robert D., Ralph C. d'Arge, and David S. Brookshire. 1980. An Experiment on the Economic Value of Visibility. *Journal of Environmental Economics and Management*, 7:1-19.

Sellar, Christine, John R. Stoll, and Jean Paul Chavas. 1985. Validation of Empirical Measures of Welfare Change: A Comparison of Nonmarket Techniques. *Land Economics*. 2:156-75.

Small, Kenneth A., and Harvey S. Rosen. 1981. Applied Welfare Analysis with Discrete Choice Models. *Econometrica*. 49:105-30.

Thayer, M. A. 1981. Contingent Valuation Techniques for Assessing Environmental Impact: Further Evidence. *Journal of Environmental Economics and Management*. 8.

Tolley, George S., *et al*. 1984. Establishing and Valuing the Effects of Improved Visibility in the Eastern United States. University of Chicago report to the U.S. Environmental Protection Agency.

8 Theoretical Aspects of Managing a Multi-Use Congestible Resource: New Zealand Backcountry Angling

Geoff N. Kerr

Introduction

Increased use of New Zealand rivers for recreational angling has caused conflict within the sport. In some regions there are claims of overcrowding destroying the solitude that is an essential part of the sport for many anglers. In order to reduce congestion, some anglers have called for a ban on foreign anglers on some rivers (*Otago Daily* Times 1986a and 1986b).

A further cause of conflict in recreational angling is the varying modes of transport used by backcountry anglers. Many anglers expend considerable effort backpacking into remote areas in pursuit of low angler densities and natural environments. Others, with similar objectives, choose to fly into the same remote areas, usually by helicopter. Backpacker anglers claim that the presence of aircraft in the backcountry destroys the natural values they seek there.

Of particular concern to backpacker anglers is that aircraft are regularly used for access to all remote trout streams in New Zealand. This suggests that alternative allocations of the backcountry fishing resource may be more efficient than the status quo. Under the existing allocation scheme, the whole resource is open to all users, for unrestricted use, at zero use-price, once a fishing license has been purchased. One alternative scheme proposed by some angling groups has been to ban helicopter access to designated areas of the backcountry. The resource manager must decide on the quantity of the resource to be allocated to each type of use. This chapter develops the allocation rules which maximize efficiency for the general case and when constraints are placed on management options. For simplicity, other land uses such as hiking and farming are ignored.

123

Because most backcountry anglers practice "catch and release" fishing, the depletion of fish stocks is not a concern for allocation of the fishery. This makes the allocation decision similar to that for other multiple-use congestible resources. Quality of the resource is dependent upon density of use by, or encounters with, users of each type.

Resource Allocation Choices

In choosing a resource allocation scheme for two competing uses, it is possible to choose from three types of use: backpackers only, helicopters only, and mixed. Special cases of this general allocation occur when the amount of resource optimally allocated to any type of use is zero. The taxonomy of possible resource allocations for backcountry angling, presented in Figure 8.1, assumes that there are no other competing uses for the resource.

Case A in Figure 8.1 is the general case, where the resource manager chooses to allocate the resource among all three uses. The allocation to any particular use may be zero. The special cases constrain the allocation of the resource so at least one of the uses is zero. We can therefore be sure that any optimal solution for the general case is at least as good as for any of the special cases. Likewise, extra special cases can be no better than their related special cases.

The status quo for backcountry angling is represented by case F, where all of the resource is allocated to mixed use. The allocation proposed by some acclimatization societies (the agencies responsible for fisheries administration) is case B. It is immediately apparent that neither of these may represent the most efficient allocation of the resource. However, the status quo can be no better than the optimum under case B, suggesting the possibility of a gain in efficiency by allocating some of the resource to backpacker anglers only.

To test this assertion further requires knowledge of the appropriate demand curves and the optimality conditions for a multiple-use congestible resource.

Theoretical Model

Dorfman's (1984) model of a single-use congestible resource of fixed size will be extended to allow for multiple uses and variable-sized resources. By retaining the amount of each use and amount of the resource in various uses as variables, we may allow them to enter the optimizing process, thereby reducing the number of constraints imposed. This should lead to a more efficient resource allocation. For any use-price (p) and total level of use (X), a user of type i will consume x_i units of the resource, i.e.,

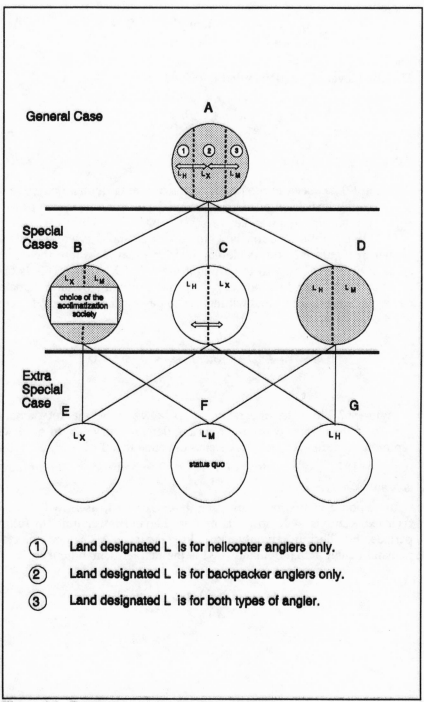

General Case A

Special Cases B C D

Extra Special Case E F G

① Land designated L is for helicopter anglers only.

② Land designated L is for backpacker anglers only.

③ Land designated L is for both types of angler.

Figure 8.1 TAXONOMY OF ALLOCATION CHOICES

$$x_i = f^i(p,X) \quad where \; f^i < 0, \; f_2^i < 0. \tag{1}$$

The Total level of use demanded is then:

$$X^d = \sum_i n_i^i(p,X) \tag{2}$$
$$= F(p,X).$$

Equation (2) has been termed a "constant crowding demand curve" and describes the total level of use demanded for varying use-price p, with constant total expected use, i.e.,

Only one point on the constant crowding demand curve represents as shown in Figure 8.2 is a stable equilibrium—that is, where the actual amount of use is equal to the amount expected ($X^d = X$). This is one point on the market demand curve. Inverse constant crowding demand curves indicate the marginal willingness to pay for the resource ϕ for any X^d, X combination.

$$\phi = \phi(X^d,X) \quad where: \; \phi_1 < 0, \; \phi_2 < 0. \tag{3}$$

Figure 8.2 illustrates the relationship between the market demand curve and the inverse constant crowding demand curves ϕ_1 to ϕ_3. Each represents a different level of expected use such that $0 < X < \tilde{X}$. Suppose use-price is P_B and expected use is $\bar{X} - \varepsilon$. The demand for the resource is $\hat{X}$ and $\hat{X} > \bar{X} > \bar{X} - \varepsilon$.

In response to finding more users than expected, users will change their expectations of X upwards and so demand fewer units in future periods. Equilibrium can only occur along the locus AC, where expected demand equals actual demand. AC is the market demand curve, i.e.,

$$X^d = F(p,X) \; \underline{and} \; X^d = X$$
$$\rightarrow p = G(X).$$

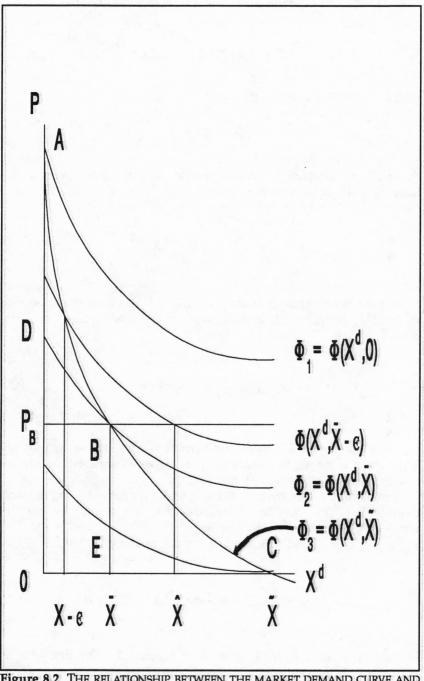

Figure 8.2 THE RELATIONSHIP BETWEEN THE MARKET DEMAND CURVE AND THE INVERSE CONSTANT CROWDING DEMAND CURVES

Consumer surplus associated with any equilibrium level of use is:

$$CS = \int_0^X [\phi(X^d,X) - p]dX^d.$$

Rent accruing to the resource is then:

$$R = X \times p.$$

Assuming, for simplicity, that supply costs are zero for all levels of X, the total value of the resource is:

$$V = CS + R = \int_0^X \phi(X^d,X)dX^d.$$

If use-price is zero and use is maintained at X by some efficient nonprice means, then the full value of the resource is captured by consumers and rent is zero, i.e.,

$$V = CS = \int_0^X \phi(X^d,X)dX^d. \tag{4}$$

For $X = \bar{X}$ in Figure 8.2, consumer surplus is equal to the area ODBE. The market demand curve does not provide an accurate estimate of resource value when congestion effects exist.

For this simple case, the only variable under the control of the resource manager is X. This may be influenced by imposing a use-price p, or by using some nonprice rationing method.

The first-order condition for an internal maximum is then:

$$\frac{\partial V}{\partial X} = \phi(X^*,X^*) + \int_0^{X^*} \phi_2(X^d,X^*)dX^d = 0. \tag{5}$$

Optimality conditions are illustrated in Figure 8.3. The first term in equation (5) is the value of the marginal unit of use and is equal to DEFG in Figure 8.3. This increment in use makes all other users feel more crowded and moves the constant crowding demand curve. The change in value of all existing users is the area between the two constant crowding demand curves—area ABCD in Figure 8.3 and the second term in equation (5).

With open access, and zero use-price, individual users will consider only their own costs and benefits and so will ignore the second term in equation (5). The free, open-access equilibrium is then:

$$\phi(X',X') = 0. \tag{6}$$

The equilibrium occurs at a point like H in Figure 8.3. Since ϕ_2 in equation (5) is assumed to be negative, we have:

$$\phi(X^*,X^*) > 0 = \phi(X',X').$$

For negatively sloping market demand curves, the free, open-access level of use exceeds the optimal level. Potential efficiency gains exist from rationing use of a congestible resource.

Backcountry Angling

The New Zealand backcountry fishery is used by both backpacker anglers (X) and helicopter anglers (H). Use-prices beyond transport costs are zero, and access is not controlled. Total benefits obtained from the fishery are:

$$V = CS_X + CS_H + PS_H$$

where

CS_i = consumer surplus for anglers of type i, and
PS_H = producers surplus for helicopter operators.

The helicopter industry in New Zealand is based upon wild animal recovery. The reduction in animal numbers over recent years has reduced profitability, and many operators are leaving the industry. The surplus of helicopter services indicates that operators will probably supply their services at, or near, marginal cost. For this reason, helicopter operators' profits are subsequently ignored.

130

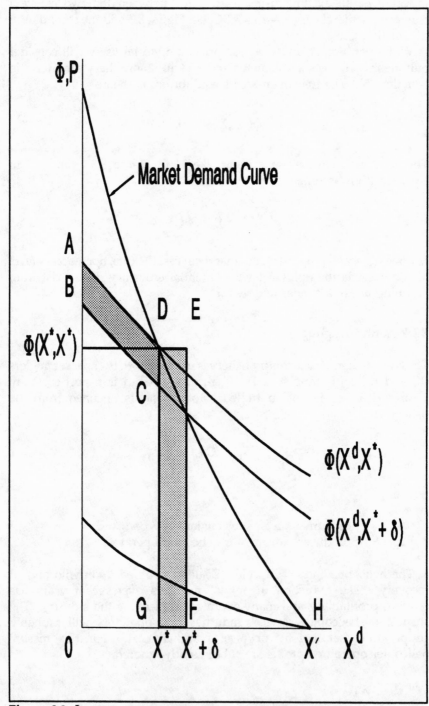

Figure 8.3 ILLUSTRATION OF THE OPTIMALITY CONDITIONS

We assume that willingness to pay is a decreasing function of the numbers of anglers of each type for a fixed-size, mixed-use resource. Let ϕ and Θ be the inverse constant crowding demand functions for backpacker anglers and helicopter anglers respectively:

$$\phi = \phi(X^d, X, H) \quad \phi_i < 0 \ \forall i \tag{7}$$

and

$$\theta = \theta(H^d, X, H) \quad \theta_i < 0 \ \forall i. \tag{8}$$

Total value of the fishery in its present state is:

$$V = \int_0^X \phi(\cdot)dX^d + \int_0^H dH^d. \tag{9}$$

The optimal allocation of this totally mixed resource is given by choosing $X = X^*$ and $H = H^*$ to satisfy the following first-order necessary conditions:

$$\frac{\partial V}{\partial X} = \phi(X^*, X^*, H^*) + \int_0^{X^*} \phi_2(\cdot)dX^d + \int_0^{H^*} \theta_2(\cdot)dH^d = 0 \tag{10}$$

and

$$\frac{\partial V}{\partial H} = \theta(H^*, X^*, H^*) + \int_0^{X^*} \phi_3(\cdot)dX^d + \int_0^{H^*} \theta_3(\cdot)dH^d = 0. \tag{11}$$

With open access and zero user-price, anglers will maximize their individual, rather than social, benefits and so will satisfy the following conditions:

$$\phi(X', X', H'') = 0$$

and

$$\theta(H', X', H'') = 0.$$

For any given level of use by the other group, each group of anglers will make more use of the fishery than is socially optimal. There is a case for rationing use by each group of anglers if this special-case resource allocation is retained.

The General Case

In the general backcountry fishery case there are four relevant functions. Let H and X represent use of the single-use areas and $\hat{H}$ and $\hat{X}$ represent use of the mixed area. The absolute number of users of each type is likely to have little significance on quality of use with variable land allocations. A more appropriate measure of congestion would be some measure of user density, or expected encounters (D). This could be expressed as some function of land area, number of users, and other factors. Individuals will consider the price of the other use area, and the quality at each area, in deciding the value of any particular area.

$$\phi = \phi(X^d, D^X, \hat{D}^H, \hat{D}^X, P_m), \tag{12}$$

$$\hat{\phi} = \hat{\phi}(\hat{X}^d, D^X, \hat{D}^H, \hat{D}^X, P_X), \tag{13}$$

$$\theta = \theta(H^d, D^H, \hat{D}^H, \hat{D}^X, P_M), \tag{14}$$

and

$$\hat{\theta} = \hat{\theta}(\hat{H}^d, D^H, \hat{D}^H, \hat{D}^X, P_H), \tag{15}$$

where

D^X =   some measure of density of backpacker anglers in the back-packer area,

$\hat{D}^X$ =   some measure of density of backpacker anglers in the mixed area,

P_X =   use-price at backpacker-only area, etc.

Total value of the resource is given by:

$$V = \int_0^X \phi(\cdot)dX^d + \int_0^{\hat{X}} \hat{\phi}(\cdot)d\hat{X}^d + \int_0^H \theta(\cdot)dH^d + \int_0^{\hat{H}} \hat{\theta}(\cdot)d\hat{H}^d \tag{16}$$
$$= V_1 + V_2 + V_3 + V_4.$$

The allocation problem is to find the optimal distribution of land to each of the three uses, subject to the constraint on land availability, i.e.,

$$L_X + L_H + L_M = \bar{L} \tag{17}$$

where

L_X = amount of resource allocated to backpacking only,
L_H = amount of resource allocated to helicopters only, and
L_M = amount of resource allocated to mixed use.

Forming the Lagrangian we have:

$$F(X,\hat{X},H,\hat{H},p_X,p_H,p_M,L_X,L_H,L_M,\lambda) = V(\bullet)$$
$$- \lambda(L_X + L_H + L_M - \bar{L}).$$

First-order, necessary conditions for an internal maximum are:

$$\frac{\partial F}{\partial X} = \phi(\bullet) + \int_0^X \frac{\partial \Phi(\bullet)}{\partial X} dX^d + \frac{\partial V_2}{\partial X} + \frac{\partial V_3}{\partial X} + \frac{\partial V_4}{\partial X} = 0, \tag{18}$$

$$\frac{\partial F}{\partial \hat{X}} = \hat{\phi}(\bullet) + \int_0^X \frac{\partial \hat{\Phi}(\bullet)}{\partial \hat{X}} dX^d + \int_0^H \frac{\partial \hat{\theta}(\bullet)}{\partial \hat{X}} d\hat{H}^d + \frac{\partial V_1}{\partial \hat{X}} + \frac{\partial V_3}{\partial \hat{X}} + \frac{\partial V_4}{\partial \hat{X}} \tag{19}$$
$$= 0,$$

$$\frac{\partial F}{\partial H} = \theta(\bullet) + \int_0^H \frac{\partial \theta(\bullet)}{\partial H} dH^d + \frac{\partial V_1}{\partial H} + \frac{\partial V_2}{\partial H} + \frac{\partial V_4}{\partial H} = 0, \tag{20}$$

$$\frac{\partial F}{\partial \hat{H}} = \hat{\theta}(\bullet) + \int_0^X \frac{\partial \hat{\Phi}(\bullet)}{\partial \hat{H}} dX^d + \int_0^H \frac{\partial \hat{\theta}(\bullet)}{\partial \hat{H}} d\hat{H}^d + \frac{\partial V_1}{\partial \hat{H}} + \frac{\partial V_2}{\partial \hat{H}} + \frac{\partial V_3}{\partial \hat{H}} \tag{21}$$
$$= 0,$$

$$\frac{\partial F}{\partial p_i} = \frac{\partial V}{\partial P_i} = 0 \quad \forall i, \; i \in (X,M,H), \tag{22}$$

and

$$\frac{\partial F}{\partial L_i} = \frac{\partial V}{\partial L_i} - \lambda = 0 \quad \forall i, \ i \in (X,M,H), \tag{23}$$

$$\frac{\partial F}{\partial \lambda} = L_X + L_H + L_M - \bar{L} = 0, \tag{24}$$

where λ is the marginal value of land to the backcountry fishery. If use is not restricted, only the first terms in the conditions shown in equations (18-21) will be considered by individuals. These conditions will then reduce to the conditions shown in equations (12-15), which must satisfy the equilibrium conditions. The potential gains from adopting a rationing scheme are found by comparing total benefits evaluated with these two alternative sets of conditions satisfied. Transaction costs are likely to be greater with rationing. These increased costs must be considered in deciding whether adoption of rationing is worthwhile.

Information Requirements

In order to allocate the resource optimally, the resource manager needs to know the inverse constant crowding demand curves for each type of angler, at each user-type area. It is also necessary to know the relationship between encounters, if that is the relevant crowding variable, and user density. This second requirement can be met by employment of tools such as the "Wilderness Travel Simulator" (Smith and Krutilla 1976), which may be estimated from field observations. Of critical importance is the ability to estimate the relationships shown in equations (12-15). These are all similar; recall that equation (12) is:

$$\phi = \phi(X^d, D^X, \hat{D}^H, \hat{D}^X p_m). \tag{12}$$

The most widely accepted methods of identifying these nonmarketed demand relationships are the travel costs method and the contingent valuation, method. The travel cost method may not be useful in the case under consideration. Both types of anglers use all backcountry fisheries, so D^H, D^X, p_X, and p_H do not exist. Without variation in these parameters, it is not possible to estimate relationships such as in equations (12) and (14). However, it is possible to estimate abbreviated forms of equations (13) and (15), where p_X and p_H are infinite, and L_X, L_H, X, and M all equal zero, i.e.,

$$\hat{\phi} = \hat{\phi}(\hat{X}^d, \hat{D}^H, \hat{D}^X) \tag{13a}$$

and

$$\hat{\theta} = \hat{\theta}(\hat{H}^d, \hat{D}^H, \hat{D}^X).\tag{15a}$$

Contingent valuation could be used to estimate individual angler's total willingness to pay (T_i) to use the fishery under varying conditions, or, alternatively, to estimate individual levels of use (x_i). Either of these relationships identifies equation (12), i.e.,

$$T_i = T_i(x_i, D^X, \hat{D}^H, \hat{D}^X, p_M)\tag{25}$$

or

$$x_i = f_i(p_X, p_M, D^X, \hat{D}^H, \hat{D}^X).\tag{26}$$

Three contingent valuation studies of New Zealand sport fisheries have been published (Gluck 1974; Kerr et al. 1984; Cairns, 1985). None of these studies was able to provide accurate estimates of the total value of the respective fisheries in their existing states. All studies reported strong protests against possible use of these values in establishing private property rights over fisheries. These rights do not currently exist in New Zealand, and many local anglers believe that free and open access to fisheries is an intrinsic right (Kerr et al. 1984). Even if this problem did not exist, there are likely to be difficulties in reliably estimating four or five argument demand functions for individuals. This has been successfully attempted for at least two arguments (Cicchetti and Smith 1973). However, as the number of arguments increases, the complexity of weighing the arguments increases. As a result, the response rate is likely to decrease, and the reliability of responses may be questioned. The relatively small numbers of anglers involved in backcountry fishing may mean that it may not even be possible to estimate aggregate demand functions.

It appears as if neither the travel cost method nor the contingent valuation method will be able to provide information to reliably estimate the constant crowding demand curves in equations (12-15). The optimal resource allocation can not be identified in this case.

Alternative Solutions

It may be possible to identify the relationships in equations (13a) and (15a) using the travel-costs method. Alternatively, where it is possible to apply the contingent valuation methods, these relationships may be far more easily, and cheaply, identified than those in equations (12-15).

Knowledge of the relationships in equations (13a) and (15a) provides the resource manager with useful information, as it is possible to determine the efficiency ordering of a subset of special-case resource allocations. This subset comprises the unshaded cases (C,E,F,G) of Figure 8.1. These are all the cases with either completely mixed or completely separated uses. While these cases may not include the optimal resource allocation, they may contain a case which is potentially Pareto superior to the status quo.

Since cases E and G are special cases of C, and the most efficient of this set is found by comparing the most efficient allocation of type C with the status quo. In other words, there may be a gain in efficiency from maintaining a strict spatial separation of user types.

Conclusions

We have concentrated on the efficiency aspects of resource allocation, as measured by total willingness to pay, to gain an understanding of some management alternatives for multiple-use congestible public resources. This is a narrow approach, but it is probably of major concern for most public resource management agencies. The more-market policies of the present government certainly makes these aspects very important in New Zealand.

Many agencies are concerned with equity effects of resource allocation decisions, suggesting several areas for further research. First, there is the case of inter-user-group equity. If no user group is to be made worse off by alternative resource allocations, then the optimal allocations identified here should be made and the losers compensated. Alternatively, new optimal allocations can be identified, with added constraints of minimum-use values to each user group. Second, it is often claimed that price rationing, while efficient, is inequitable because the marginal utility of money varies between socioeconomic groups, to the disadvantage of the poor (Shelby and Danley 1979). There are many different rationing methods available, with differing implications for efficiency and equity. One that is claimed to be inherently fair is the lottery, since all users have an equal chance of gaining access, regardless of socioeconomic status. If a non-efficient rationing mechanism is chosen, then the allocation of the resource among uses will be different than the allocations found here. The expected value of an allocation of X for a fixed-size resource under a lottery will be:

$$E(V) = \frac{1}{X} \int_0^{X^d = F(0,X)} \phi(X^d, X) dX^d,$$

which is less than the value under an efficient choice of X:

$$V = \int_0^X \phi(X^d, X)dX^d.$$

Analysis along these lines indicates the efficiency costs of equitable allocations, allowing decision-makers to make better trade-offs between their competing objectives. The third possible area for further investigation is the distribution of use between New Zealanders and foreigners. Some anglers claim that helicopter anglers are almost exclusively foreigners (*Otago Daily Times* 1962). If this is true, and the fishery is to be managed to provide maximum benefits to residents, the allocation problem becomes trivial unless there are other benefits associated with foreign anglers.

We have departed from the tradition of most congestion studies by not restricting analysis to identifying optimal numbers of users at a fixed-size resource. Resource users may be separated spatially, and the amount of resource devoted to each use, as well as numbers of users, becomes a choice variable. Further areas of specialization of this model could include temporal allocation and the division of user-types into subgroups dependent upon crowd aversion.

Adding refinements to these models increases the costs of obtaining information which, we have seen, may be impossible to find even for the more simple models. Returns to refinements are likely to be decreasing, indicating the need to rely on other means of evaluating alternatives. For New Zealand backcountry angling, the use of economic analysis appears to be limited to comparison of the current totally mixed use of the fishery and the complete separation of helicopter and backpacker anglers.

Reference

Cairnes, N.D. 1985. Assessment of the Kolkoura Amateur Fishery for Rock Lobsters. Master's diss., Centre for Resource Management, University of Canterbury, Christchurch, New Zealand.

Cicchetti, C.J., and V.K. Smith. 1973. Congestion, Quality Deterioration, and Optimal Use. *Social Science Research*. 2:31-40.

Dorfman, R. 1984. On Optimal Congestion. *Journal of Environmental Economics and Management*. 11:91-106.

Gluck, R.G. 1974. An Economic Evaluation of the Rakala Fishery as a Recreational Resource. Master's thesis, Lincoln College.

Kerr, G.N., K.L. Leathers, and B.M.H. Sharp. 1984. Theoretical and Practical Issues in Valuing Instream Flow Benefits for Improved Water Allocation Decisions. Paper presented at the 28th Annual Conference, Australian Agricultural Economics Society, February 7-9, University of Sydney.

Otago Daily Times. 1986a. Anglers React to Call to Ban Foreigners. 9 January.
Otago Daily Times. 1986b. Locals Are Disadvantaged. 13 January.
Shelby, B., and M. Danley. 1979. Allocating River Use. Report to U.S. Department of Agriculture, Forest Service, Oregon State University, Corvallis.
Smith, V.K., and J.V. Krutilla. 1976. *Structure and Properties of a Wilderness Travel Simulator: An Application to the Spanish Peaks Area*. Baltimore: Johns Hopkins University Press.

9 A Note on Population Distributions and the Travel Cost Method

Daniel J. Stynes

Introduction

Recreation opportunities exist within complex spatial markets. Demand for and value of a given recreation site depends upon consumer tastes and preferences, the attributes of the site, the supply of potential substitutes, and the distribution of populations around the site. The travel cost model for valuing recreation sites takes advantage of the fact that populations located at different distances from a park incur different travel costs to visit the park. These differences are used to develop a demand curve for the site (Rosenthal, Loomis, and Peterson 1984).

Travel cost analysis has been primarily carried out by econometricians, who have tended to focus primarily upon the per capita demand function. Considerably less attention has been given to population distributions, which play an important role in the travel cost model. In the traditional zonal or aggregate travel cost model, populations are aggregated into zones defined by distance or (more properly) travel cost (Brown and Nawas 1973; Wetzstein and McNeely 1980). Sutherland (1982) has reported considerable variation in results depending upon how travel cost data are aggregated. Smith and Kopp (1980) have shown that consumer surpluses are sensitive to the market boundary chosen for the analysis. Most reports of travel cost analyses, however, do not devote much attention to how zones are formed or which zones should be included in the analysis. The treatment of population distributions is even more obscure in individual travel cost models, although Brown *et al.* (1983) have recognized that population distributions must be taken into account.

Support from the Wildland Valuation Unit of the Rocky Mountain Forest and Range Experiment Station is gratefully acknowledged.

The obscure role of population distributions in determining recreation use and value has contributed to considerable misunderstanding of the travel cost method among non-economists and some confusion even among economists. For example, a widely held misconception among practitioners is that the travel cost method generates larger values the further a park is located from populations. Even among economists, the lack of attention to population distributions has obscured some important properties of travel cost models. For example, although many have assumed the omission of substitutes in travel cost models gives estimates that are biased upward, Caulkins, Bishop, and Bouwes (1985) have recently shown that the bias can be upward or downward depending upon the distribution of populations relative to the recreation site.

The purpose of this chapter is to seek a better balance in the handling of economic and demographic aspects of travel cost analysis, by focusing more attention on population distributions. This change in focus may help increase our understanding of the travel cost technique, suggest some new directions for improving it, broaden the range of possible applications, and raise some important research questions.

The Travel Cost Model

There are two important components of the demand for a recreation site: (1) the per capita demand function and (2) the distribution of populations around the site. Assuming a homogeneous population with respect to income, tastes, and other determinants of demand, the key feature of populations needed for travel cost analysis is the number of people experiencing each travel cost. Thus, I express population density as a function of travel cost, which may include travel time costs. This yields the following forms for the aggregate demand curve and consumer surplus,

$$Q(f) = \int_0^{p_{max}-f} d(p)q(p+f)dp \tag{1}$$

and

$$CS = \int_0^{p_{max}} d(p)\left[\int_p^{p_{max}} q(s)ds\right]dp = \int_0^{p_{max}} Q(f)df, \tag{2}$$

where

p	=	travel cost,
p_{max}	=	the maximum marginal willingness to pay for the site—intercept of q(p) with the price axis,
f	=	added fee,
Q(f)	=	aggregate demand function (stage II),
q(p)	=	per capita demand curve, and
d(p)	=	population density function, as a function of travel cost.

In this form, the per capita demand function and population density function appear as two equally important determinants of demand and value. For expositional purposes, we select forms for d(p) and q(p) that permit equations (1) and (2) to be easily integrated.

Functional Forms for d(p) and q(p)

For the per capita demand function, we choose simple linear and shifted exponential forms, i.e.,

$$a) \; Linear \qquad q(p) = a - bp \qquad\qquad a,b \geq 0$$
$$b) \; Exponential \quad q(p) = \exp(a-bp) - 1 \quad a,b \geq 0.$$

Each of these functions cross the price axis at a/b, yielding a maximum marginal willingness to pay. This intercept defines the market boundary for the site. Let P denote the population residing within a travel cost of a/b of the site. We then consider three forms of the population density function to distribute this population within the market area.

1. D_n: $d(p) = cp^n$, where n is a nonnegative integer and c is a positive constant. D_0 is a uniform population density function. For $n > 0$, D_n represents population densities which increase with increasing travel cost. This is most typical of the vast majority of rural recreation sites to which travel cost analysis has been applied.

2. D_{DL}: $d(p) = c(p-a/b)$, where $c > 0$ and a/b is the price intercept of the per capita demand functions defined above. This is the case of a population density declining linearly with travel cost to zero at the market boundary. This distribution might apply to an urban park.

3. D_{PG}: $d(p) = P$, if $p=0$ and 0 otherwise. Termed the "park gate" distribution this locates the entire population at the park gate. It is a useful limiting distribution as it generates the largest possible value for a given population size.

D_{DL} and D_n for n = 0, 1, and 2 are shown in Figure 9.1. D_{PG} would be a point distribution with everyone located at zero travel cost. The constant c is defined so that

$$\int_0^{\frac{a}{b}} d(p)\,dp = P.$$

Estimates of Demand and Value

These two per capita demand functions in combination with any of the given population density functions yield integrable forms of equations (1) and (2). After integrating, these equations reduce to fairly simple algebraic expressions which help to reveal the relationships between population distributions and estimates of demand and value.

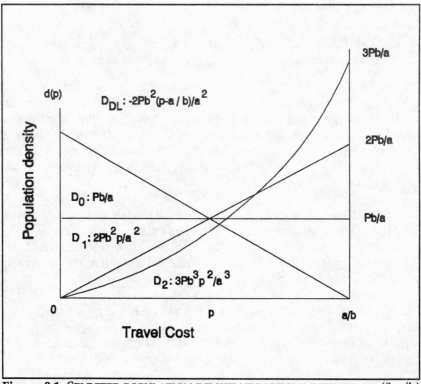

Figure 9.1 SELECTED POPULATION DENSITY FUNCTIONS DEFINED ON (0,a/b) WITH MARKET POPULATION P

The formulas for the linear per capita demand function (Table 9.1) are particularly simple. A number of relationships can be identified from these formulas. Total population size P affects estimates of total use and value, but does not affect average per visit surpluses. The latter do, however, depend upon the distribution of the population around the site. Assuming a linear per capita demand function and a fixed population size P within the market area, a uniform population distribution generates half as many visits as the park gate distribution. Further redistributing populations to increase in density as the square of travel costs cuts use in half again.

Total consumer surplus is more sensitive to population distributions than use, as both the number of visits and the surplus from a given visit increase as populations are located closer to the park. Surplus for a uniform population distribution is one-third of the surplus if everyone is located at the park gate, and surplus from a density which increases as p^2 is one-tenth of the park gate value. Average per visit surpluses are the least sensitive to population distributions. A linearly increasing population density function yields half the per visit surplus of the park gate distribution. Remember that these relationships assume a linear per capita demand function.

The shifted exponential per capita demand function can also be integrated, yielding somewhat more complex algebraic formulas for use and value (Table 9.2). These involve the tail of the MacLaurin series expansion of $\exp(a)$. The formulas for the park gate distribution can be obtained from Table 9.2 by using $n = -1$. Formulas for D_{DL} with the

Table 9.1 RECREATION DEMAND AND VALUATION FORMULAS FOR A LINEAR PER CAPITA DEMAND FUNCTION, $q(p) = a - bp$, AND SELECTED POPULATION DISTRIBUTIONS

Population Density Function*	Visits	Consumer Surplus	Surplus/ Visits
D_{PG}: Park Gate	Pa	$Pa^2/2b$	$a/2b$
D_{DL}: Linearly Decreasing	$2Pa/3$	$Pa^2/4b$	$3a/8b$
D_O: Uniform	$Pa/2$	$Pa^2/6b$	$a/3b$
D_1: Linearly Increasing	$Pa/3$	$Pa^2/12b$	$a/4b$
D_2: Increase as p^2	$Pa/4$	$Pa^2/20b$	$a/5b$
D_n: Increase as p^n	$\dfrac{Pa}{(n+2)}$	$\dfrac{Pa^2}{(n+2)(n+3)b}$	$\dfrac{a}{(n+3)b}$

* Population density functions defined in the text, p = travel cost, P = population size, and n = exponent in population density function.

exponential form, available in Stynes and Donnelly (1987), are not repeated here. Relationships between population distributions and estimates of use and value with the exponential per capita demand function are easier to see with an example.

Park use and value estimates for a specific linear and exponential per capita demand function are given in Table 9.3. Here we assume a population of 1,000 people within the market area of the site, distributed according to different population density functions. The linear example illustrates the more general relationships discussed above. Notice that the exponential per capita demand function yields use estimates that are much more sensitive to population distributions. However, the per visit surpluses are less sensitive to population distributions than observed for the linear form.

Table 9.2 RECREATION VALUATION FORMULAS FOR A SHIFTED EXPONENTIAL PER CAPITA DEMAND FUNCTION AND A POPULATION DENSITY FUNCTION OF THE FORM $D(P) = CP^N$

Per Capita Demand Function
Semi-Log

$$q(p) = e^{a-bp} - 1$$

Demand Function $Q(f)$ $\dfrac{P(n+1)!}{a^{n+1}}\left[e^{a-bf} - S_{n+1}(a-bf)\right]$

Visits $Q(0)$ $\dfrac{P(n+1)!}{a^{n+1}}\left[e^{a} - S_{n+1}(a)\right]$

Consumer Surplus $\mathcal{S}$ $\dfrac{P(n+1)!}{ba^{n+1}}\left[e^{a} - S_{n+2}(a)\right]$

Per Visit Surplus $\dfrac{CS}{Q(0')}$ $\dfrac{\left[e^{a} - S_{n+2}(a)\right]}{b\left[e^{a} - S_{n+1}(a)\right]}$

 • Parameters are defined as follows:

p = *travel cost,*
f = *simulated fee increase,*
n = *a nonnegitive integer, use $n = -1$ for the park gate distribution,*
P = *total population residing within the site's marketing area,*
$c = \dfrac{(n+1)Pb^{n+1}}{a^{n+1}}$, *and*

$S_n(y) = \displaystyle\sum_{i=0}^{n} \dfrac{y_i}{i!}$, *the first $n+1$ terms of the MacLaurin series expansion of e^y.*

Table 9.3 USE AND DEMAND ESTIMATES FOR DIFFERENT POPULATION DISTRIBUTIONS

Population Distribution	Q(0)	CS	CS/Q(0)
Linear Per Capita Demand Function $q(p) = 10\text{-}p$			
Park Gate	10,000	$50,000	$5.00
Decrease Linearly	6,667	$25,000	$3.75
Uniform	5,000	$16,667	$3.33
Increase Linearly	3,333	$ 8,333	$2.50
Increase as Square	2,500	$ 5,000	$2.00
Increase as Cubic	2,000	$ 3,333	$1.67
Beyond Market Boundary	0	$　0	$0.00
Shifted Exponential Per Capita Demand Function $q(p)=\exp(3\text{-}.2p)\text{-}1$			
Park Gate	19,806	$80,428	$4.21
Decrease Linearly	8,149	$30,746	$3.77
Uniform	5,362	$19,309	$3.60
Increase Linearly	2,575	$ 7,873	$3.06
Increase as Square	1,575	$ 4,123	$2.62
Increase as Cubic	1,099	$ 5,497	$2.27
Beyond Market Boundary	0	$　0	$0.00

Population Distributions and Per Visit Surpluses

Average per visit surpluses are increasingly becoming one of the primary products of travel cost studies. Per visit surpluses are empirical estimates of unit day values, still the easiest and most popular means of estimating values at the management level. Per visit surpluses also seem to be the primary focus for comparisons between contingent value (CVM) and travel cost (TCM) studies. The notion of an average per visit surplus or willingness to pay, in itself, tends to obscure the role of population distributions in determining value. Total value of a site is obtained in many cases by multiplying a per visit value times the number of visits. This simple and logical procedure hides the role of population distributions, leading to some faulty notions of recreation value and some misapplication of travel cost results. For example, average per visit surpluses estimated for one site are frequently applied to another site which may have a quite different population distribution surrounding the site. Similar errors may occur if an average per visit surplus estimated for a site at one time is applied at a later time when population distributions may have changed significantly.

Dwyer, Kelly, and Bowes (1977) and Sorg and Loomis (1984) have compared travel cost studies and developed tables of travel cost models and average per visit surpluses from different studies. More attention has been given to the tables of average consumer surpluses than the demand models. Since a wide variety of functional forms and independent variables has been used in different studies, comparing demand functions is difficult. Average consumer surpluses are easier to understand, particularly for non-economists, who interpret them as a rough measure of "price" or "value." Average consumer surpluses replace existing unit day values with numbers that have a stronger empirical basis; however, this once again obliterates the role of population distributions in determining site values. Comparability of per visit surplus estimates across different studies tends to be seen as support for the travel cost method. Sorg and Loomis recognize that differences across sites may be due to variations in quality, substitutes, regional preferences, or locations of sites relative to populations. The latter, while probably the easiest to measure, is often the last to be recognized.

Elsewhere I argue for developing tables of simple per capita demand functions (instead of tables of per visit surpluses) for different classes of sites or activities and letting managers apply these to local population distributions to generate estimates of demand and value (Stynes and Donnelly 1987). This approach would capture the population effects much more explicitly. Also, a per capita demand function should be more generalizable across different sites than a per visit surplus, as it is not dependent upon population distributions.

While per visit surpluses are generally obtained by dividing total surplus by total visits, a better understanding of how population distributions affect per visit surpluses is obtained by observing how the per visit surplus varies with travel cost. I had always assumed that visits from nearby zones generate larger average surpluses than visits from more distant zones, with surpluses dropping to zero at the maximum marginal willingness to pay. The linear and shifted exponential forms of the per capita demand function exhibit this behavior, however, other commonly used forms do not.

For a linear per capita demand function, per visit surplus at travel cost p is $1/2(a/b-p)$, a decreasing linear function of p with slope $-1/2$. The shifted exponential function yields a per visit surplus function that is flat near the site, but that then drops off quickly to zero at a/b, the maximum marginal willingness to pay. For a strict exponential, $q(p)=\exp(a-bp)$, per visit surplus is $1/b$, a constant independent of travel cost. For $q(p)=ap^b$, per visit surplus at travel cost p is $p/(b-1)$, a linearly increasing function of p.

While these relationships are easy to derive and fairly well known, apparently no one has questioned whether these behaviors make sense. These differences in the behavior of per visit surplus relative to travel cost yield quite different implications for recreation planning and management. If the per capita demand function is a power form and the goal is to maximize values per visit, then the travel cost method does indeed yield larger values the further a park is located from populations. Of course, we are generally more interested in total surplus, which will decline as a park is located further from populations.

On further reflection, per visit surpluses that remain constant or increase with increasing travel cost are not that unlikely. They result from per capita demand curves that are very steep near the price axis. If there are a very small number of people with very high willingness to pay and large numbers of people with low willingness to pay, then per visit surpluses can increase with increasing travel cost because travel cost or price increases exclude large numbers of low-valued visitors without substantially reducing the surpluses of high-valued users. Under this scenario, the average surplus per visit can remain constant or increase with increasing travel cost. This pattern can also occur for an individual demand curve if an individual's first visit is highly valued, while subsequent visits decline sharply in value, and many low-valued visits are made if no fee is charged.

This behavior does not seem unreasonable for many kinds of recreation sites, and, indeed, it seems to be supported by most empirical studies that test for functional form. I would note, however, that goodness-of-fit and Box-Cox type tests cannot always discriminate between functional forms that imply different relationships between per visit surplus and travel cost. For example, a shifted exponential function with a suitably small shift cannot be distinguished from a strict exponential function based upon typical travel cost data. However, the two forms will yield quite different estimates of per visit surpluses if populations are primarily located near the market boundary.

Since an estimate of per visit surplus is often a primary product of travel cost models, the behavior of different functional forms with respect to per visit surpluses should be more carefully considered in specification decisions. Since per visit surpluses vary with travel cost (except in the case of an exponential per capita demand function), contingent valuation studies need to pay closer attention to sampling of users from different origins, possibly estimating average willingness to pay for different levels of travel cost. This might shed further light on the relationship between per visit surplus and travel cost that could be helpful in specifying the per capita demand function.

If per capita demand functions for recreation sites tend to have an exponential form, then population distributions are not quite so important since, for this form, per visit values are constant across different travel costs. However, if the per capita demand function is linear, a shifted exponential or some other form, population distributions become more important. When we use exponential forms of the per capita demand function, are we capturing an important property of recreation demand, or are we building into travel cost models hidden assumptions that do not hold? This is just one example of an important question that arises from looking more closely at population distributions.

Conclusions and Recommendations

Population distributions significantly affect the demand for and value of recreation sites. By simplifying the per capita demand function and treating population distributions in more detail, we can better understand these relationships. The effect of population distribution varies depending upon whether our interest is in use, total surplus, or per visit surplus. The relationships also change depending upon the form of the per capita demand function.

A number of sources of confusion about the travel cost model seem to be related in one way or another to population distributions. Most of the effort to date in refining the travel cost model has gone into improving specifications and estimation methods for the per capita demand function. A balanced treatment of population distributions and per capita demand is necessary for a full understanding of recreation use and value. This holds not just for the travel cost method, but any model purporting to explain recreation use and value.

A more complete treatment of population distributions also suggests a broader range of applications of the travel cost method. Although the method can be applied to a variety of problems, it has been used almost solely for valuation purposes. Focusing on population distributions suggests a number of other potential uses. For example, travel cost models can be used to predict changes in use, demand, and value resulting from changing population distributions. The methods can also be applied to location decisions. In these two applications one would fix the per capita demand function and vary population distributions over time or space.

References

Brown, W.G., and F. Nawas. 1973. Impact of Aggregation on the Estimation of Outdoor Recreation Demand Functions. *American Journal of Agricultural Economics*. 55:246-49.

Brown, W.G., C. Sorhus, B. Chou-Yang, and J.A. Richards. 1983. Using Individual Observations to Estimate Recreation Demand Functions: A Caution. *American Journal of Agricultural Economics*. 65:154-57.

Caulkins, P.P., R.C. Bishop, and N.W. Bouwes. 1985. Omitted Cross-Price

Variable Biases in the Linear Travel Cost Model: Correcting Common Misperceptions. *Land Economics*. 61:182-87.

Dwyer, J.F., J.R. Kelly, and M.D. Bowes. 1977. Improved Procedures for Valuation of the Contribution of Recreation to National Economic Development. Water Resources Research Center report no. 128, University of Illinois at Urbana-Champaign.

Rosenthal, D.H., J.B. Loomis, and G.L. Peterson. 1984. The Travel Cost Model: Concepts and Applications. U.S. Department of Agriculture, Forest Service General Technical Report RM-109. Rocky Mountain Forest and Range Experiment Station, Fort Collins, Colo.

Smith, V.K., and R.J. Kopp. 1980. The Spatial Limits of the Travel Cost Recreation Demand Model. *Land Economics*. 56:64-72.

Sorg, C.F., and J.B. Loomis. 1984. Empirical Estimates of Amenity Forest Values: A Comparative Review. U.S. Department of Agriculture, Forest Service General Technical Report RM-107. Rocky Mountain Forest and Range Experiment Station, Fort Collins, Colo.

Stynes, D.J., and D.M. Donnelly. 1985. Simplifying the Travel Cost Method. *Transactions of the American Fisheries Society*. 116:432-40.

Sutherland, R.J. 1982. The Sensitivity of Travel Cost Estimates of Recreation Demand to the Functional Form and Definition of Origin Zones. *Western Journal of Agricultural Economics*. 7:87-98.

Wetzstein, M.E., and J.G. McNeely. 1980. Specification Error and Inference in Recreation Demand Models. *American Journal of Agricultural Economics*. 62:798-800.

Part III Methods and Applications

10 Evaluating National Policy Proposals by Contingent Valuation

Alan Randall

Warren Kriesel

Introduction

A recent development in natural resource economics is the application of benefit-cost analysis (BCA) to national policy proposals concerning pollution control. This work commenced in the universities and not-for-profit research institutions in the 1960s, and has been actively encouraged by U.S. Environmental Protection Agency funding since the early 1970s. Executive Order 12991, issued in 1981, established a benefit-cost filter for regulatory initiatives.

Some of the national pollution control BCAs sponsored by USEPA in the 1980s were confined to the impacts of particular pollutants on the market sectors of the economy. For example, Adams, Hamilton, and McCarl (1984) estimated the national economic effects of ozone damage on a set of agricultural commodities. Schwartz et al. (1985) estimated the benefits of a national policy to reduce gasoline lead content, for both market and nonmarket sectors. The research on which this chapter is based (Randall et al., 1985) estimated the nonmarket benefits to the household sector of a national policy that would reduce air and water pollution loads. We provided alternative benefit estimates derived from a specially adapted contingent choice format and a national multimarket hedonic analysis.

The extension of the contingent valuation method (CVM) into analyses of national policies involved two important departures from the mainly localized contingent market studies to which the method was initially applied: first, the introduction of a contingent policy choice format, in place of the customary contingent market; and second, the development of formats that treat national policy as national policy, rather than as the aggregate of local impacts. This chapter focuses on the innovations introduced in our research to adapt CVM for evaluating policies at the

153

national level. Section 1 introduces the national policy evaluation referendum (NPER) model developed for the Randall et al. study, and discusses its advantages. Section 2 describes the survey questionnaire used in the study. Finally, a short summary of the study's benefit estimates is presented.

The validity of CVM in general is not at issue here. For a detailed discussion of the general validity issue, the reader can consult Cummings, Brookshire and Schulze (1986), and Mitchell and Carson (1986). Our purpose is to report an innovative adaptation of CVM, and in so doing, we are unable to resist some comments addressed to its particular validity.

The National Policy Evaluation Referendum Model

Following widely cited studies by Davis (1963) and Randall, Ives, and Eastman (1974), there has been rapid development in the theory and methods of contingent valuation. It has become standard practice to design and implement a contingent market to elicit Hicksian compensating measures of welfare change which, upon interpersonal aggregation, can be interpreted as benefits (or costs) in the potential Pareto improvement (PPI) framework. Contingent markets may be implemented in laboratory or survey settings, and surveys may be administered by face-to-face interview, by telephone, by mail questionnaire, or by various combinations of these. Nevertheless, any contingent market has certain features that have become standard. The *status quo* is described with respect to institutions and the provision level of the nonmarket good at issue; and—in the context of well-specified rules concerning the conditions under which the alternative level will be provided and individual payments will be collected—the participant states a contingent valuation or a contingent choice in a form that permits the researcher to infer the participant's valuation. In the well-structured contingent market, the researcher will have ensured that the participant has been motivated to (1) undertake a thorough valuation search, and (2) truthfully report his or her valuation (Randall, Hoehn, and Brookshire 1983).

A hallmark of practiced CVM research has been an adherence to the private market ideal as a foundation for the contingent market, even where the goods to be valued were recognized as public. Public opinion polls, often designed to simulate referendum elections, had long been used to gather information about citizen attitudes to environmental policies and other public actions to provide nonmarket goods (*Public Opinion Quarterly* 1972). These polls had the clear virtue that they treated public policy as a public matter. Nevertheless, early CVM researchers made a conscious departure from this tradition for at least two reasons: (1) the alternative package of public goods presented in public opinion polls was frequently poorly specified as to quality, quantity, and cost

("Would you make an economic sacrifice for cleaner air? Yes, No, No opinion"); and (2) there was, at that time, no conceptual basis for interpreting the results of such polls in terms of an acceptable economic theory of welfare change measurement.

Adherence to the private market ideal seems to explain certain features commonly found in CVM applications, e.g., iterative bidding and explicit payment vehicles. Cummings, Brookshire, and Schulze (1986) summarize the findings of their state-of-the-art assessment by stating four reference operating conditions (ROCs), adherence to which will assure reasonably valid benefit estimates via CVM. As they readily admit (104), the ROCs are rooted in the private market analogy model of CVM.

The private market ideal has fostered a focus on goods rather than policies in CVM. While economic theory permits markets in nonhomogeneous goods (consider, for example, hedonic price theory), analysis of homogeneous goods is more common. In CVM, this approach has led to contingent markets that seek to standardize goods and services (i.e., the impacts of policy) across individuals. Standardizing some reference points is required for statistical testing and interpretation of value data in PPI terms. However, the practice of standardizing impacts has some obvious disadvantages when individuals are exposed differently to the impacts of policy, and that, we argue, is typically the case. The problem is that any standard description of baseline and with-policy conditions, in terms of goods and services enjoyed by the individual household, will be at least a little inaccurate from a particular individual's point of view. When evaluating policies of broad geographical scope, the problem is exacerbated.

CVM practitioners must be aware that participants do not approach the exercise *tabula rasa*. They have prior beliefs about the *status quo* and about how policy will affect them. To the extent that these prior beliefs deviate   from   the   researcher's   impact-standardized   scenario,   the participant's posterior beliefs will deviate from the scenario. There are two consequences: first, impact-standardization is futile, and second, a credibility gap arises which may undermine the CVM effort. The obvious solution to this second problem is to instruct the participant to respond as if the standardized scenario fit his or her case, but this would likely serve to notify the participant that the whole exercise is more hypothetical than real. These arguments serve to construct a strong general case against the standardized presentation of policy impacts.

National Policy Evaluation

We posit that the CVM participant is a citizen accustomed to forming opinions about policy alternatives, and to making choices as a voter, responding to surveys, and in some cases acting as a member of organizations and interest groups. Citizens receive information (from government, interest groups, the media, etc.) that describes national and regional effects of policy, in rather general terms. They then combine this information with their own stock of prior information, specialized local knowledge, and personal knowledge about their own susceptibility to damage from pollution and their ability to take evasive action. Finally, they arrive at a personal decision in favor of (or opposed to) the proposed policy, given its likely implementation cost.

To implement the national policy evaluation model, the CVM scenario presents the same policy alternatives to all participants, who then make their own inferences about how policy affects them. While the policy choices are standardized, the policy impacts are unique to each individual. Upon description of the national policy, each participant forms an individualized expectation of policy impact on his or her own welfare. As argued in the preceding paragraph, we believe this process is familiar to citizens in a democracy. We argue, further, that PPI evaluation of a standardized policy is entirely consistent with relevant theory. There is no violation of any important theoretical requirement by departing from the ideal of markets in homogeneous private goods. To the contrary, there is reason to prefer a theoretical structure that recognizes policy as a process in which the level of public goods is chosen publicly.

Value Elicitation by Referendum

Two recent developments have revived the earlier discarded referendum approach to collecting value information: (1) value elicitation by referendum has been shown to be an incentive-compatible demand revelation device, and (2) appropriate statistical procedures have been developed for analyzing data in dichotomous choice form, to generate welfare change estimates in PPI terms.

Hoehn and Randall (1987) define an optimal benefit-cost indicator as one that correctly identifies potential Pareto improvements (PPIs), and a satisfactory benefit-cost indicator as one that will never incorrectly identify non-PPIs as PPIs. If a satisfactory BC indicator is used as a filtering device, non-PPIs cannot be passed by a BC test, and while some PPI opportunities may be filtered out, progress will always be made in the direction of greater societal product. Note that while a satisfactory BC indicator permits the under- (over-) estimation of benefits (costs), the reverse is prohibited.

With a satisfactory benefit cost indicator thus defined, Hoehn and Randall undertake a conceptual analysis of the incentive structure of various CVM formats. The participant completes two processes: (1) value formulation, where the issue is the effect of a decision by the participant to restrict effort devoted to the introspection that is necessary to discover his or her "true" valuation; and (2) value reporting, where the issue is concern for whether there exist incentives for individuals to act strategically, misreporting their "true" valuations in order to benefit themselves by influencing the outcome of policy research.

Hoehn and Randall conceptualize a contingent policy evaluation referendum, in which a participant records a dichotomous vote (yes/no) to a proposed policy change after having been presented information about (1) the quantity and quality of goods and services the policy offers; (2) the public decision rule for implementing the proposed policy or not; and (3) the payment to be exacted from the individual in the event of implementation. Note that the Hoehn and Randall referendum is considerably more structured than the instruments commonly used in public opinion polls.

Within the policy referendum framework, the value formulation stage proceeds as follows. The individual is informed that he or she is a member of a sample of citizens participating in the exercise, and therefore he or she probably expects enhanced influence vis-à-vis that of a participant in a plebiscite. Furthermore, it can be assumed that the individual believes that the results of the valuation exercise will have some impact on policy implementation. Thus, the individual will devote some effort to formulating a response intended to influence policy in a direction favorable to himself or herself. However, the value formulation process is time- and resource- consuming because information has to be acquired and assimilated. Limited effort may cause the valuation process to be incomplete, so that the process will yield values that include some error.

If valuation is performed in the Hicksian compensating framework, the direction of error can be identified. In formulating WTP, the participant first solves an expenditure minimization problem, constrained by the initial utility level. An imperfect solution to this problem, arising from limited effort, must yield an expenditure that is larger than the minimum. Then, the overestimation of minimum expenditure must lead the participant to underestimate his or her compensating surplus, WTP. Therefore, in the Hicksian compensating framework, value formulation errors will lead to understated WTP, which is permitted under the definition of a satisfactory BC indicator.

The value-reporting stage must be analyzed to identify any incentives for strategic behavior. The Hoehn and Randall analysis assumes that the participant gains positive utility from the amenity being valued, but that paying fees or taxes would reduce his or her disposable income. The key issues, then, are how the individual's participation in the exercise is likely to influence the chances that the amenity-increasing policy will be implemented, and how the individual's disposable income will be affected by implementation. For a referendum in which each participant is told (and believes) the amount to be exacted in the event of policy implementation, and that the policy will be implemented by plurality vote, the optimum strategy is truth-telling. The participant's welfare is maximized by voting *yes* if his or her formulated value exceeds his or her stated costs, and *no* if it does not.

The analytical results for the Hoehn and Randall referendum can be summarized as follows. The referendum tends, if anything, to underestimate benefits and overestimate costs at the value-formulation stage; and it is incentive-compatible at the value-reporting stage. Therefore, while the policy referendum may not be an optimal BC indicator, since PPIs may be discarded, the approach fulfills the requirements of a satisfactory BC indicator.

The referendum responses do not directly indicate the full value of each consumer's surplus, but previous research has successfully used the logistic estimation procedure to yield estimates of consumer surplus (Bishop and Heberlein 1979; Sellar, Stoll, and Chevas 1985). Furthermore, the referendum can be iterated to converge on the personal payment that leaves the participant indifferent (i.e., extract the full consumer surplus) without adversely affecting its immunity to strategic behavior (Hoehn and Randall).

The Hoehn and Randall referendum is a satisfactory BC indicator, and its results can be analyzed to generate welfare change estimates consistent with economic theory. These properties eliminate economists' ancient and venerable objections to using referenda to generate BC data. With these concerns allayed, economists can now focus on the long-recognized advantage of referendum formats for evaluating public policies: they use a familiar and thoroughly plausible framework for citizens to communicate their preferences about policy, whereas the private market analogy long standard in CVM always suffers from a degree of implausibility when nonrival and nonexclusive goods are involved.

We have argued for standardization of policy (as opposed to impact) and for the Hoehn and Randall referendum format for CVM data collection. The NPER mode of CVM combines these approaches.

The Policy Evaluation Instrument

This section describes the development and administration of the NPER instrument to estimate the benefits of air and water pollution control policy. A primary consideration in developing the instrument was defining precisely what the resulting benefit estimate should represent. Considering that the estimate would have to be useful for policy purposes, we made four strategic decisions:

Valuation of National or Local Impacts?

Citizens differ in their territorial range, which includes but is not limited to places where they live and work, places to which they may migrate, places they may have visited or may visit in the future, places that are valued by people they care about, and places they care about for whatever reason. For some, this range may extend beyond international boundaries. Nevertheless, people are accustomed to thinking of collective goods and amenities in national terms. For national policy analysis, it is essential to evaluate benefits at the national level. Further, there is no good reason to expect national benefits to equal the sum of local benefits accruing to local residents. Therefore, the primary focus of our study was on national impacts. Participants made their own judgments as to how much weight to place on local impacts, compared with impacts on distant places, when deciding how to respond to the CVM referendum. In future work, it should be feasible to test hypotheses about how the probability of a *yes* vote is affected by place of residence and territorial range.

Total Value, or a Taxonomy of Value Components?

For policy evaluation, total value is the relevant measure. There is a long tradition of attempting to construct total value by developing a taxonomy of value components—e.g., current use values, expected surplus from future use value, option value, quasi-option value, and existence value—estimating each independently by an appropriate method and aggregating across value components. Recent papers by Smith (1987), Boyle and Bishop (1987), and Randall (1987) demonstrate the internal inconsistencies in existing taxonomies of value components. Total value can be measured directly only with CVM, while some components of value can be measured with other methods (e.g., current on-site use values for recreation, using the travel cost method). Nevertheless, the Boyle and Bishop and the Randall papers argue that measuring total value with CVM may be the preferred approach. In this pilot study we followed that approach.

Whole Policy Values, or the Value of Particular Environmental Services?

National pollution control policy provides many environmental services, so we had the choice of valuing individual services and then aggregating over them, or valuing the whole policy. We chose the later course because earlier conceptual work within our main study showed that while holistic valuation of a complex policy is valid, piecewise aggregation (in order to be valid) must be structured so as to be consistent with holistic values. Piecewise aggregation may be attempted in future research.

A Focus on Public Goods

In the case of national pollution control, benefits will accrue to households directly through increased provision of quantity-rationed public goods and indirectly through increased productivity in the agricultural and manufacturing industries. Households will enjoy these derived benefits through price effects from lower production costs faced by affected industries. The welfare impacts of these price effects can be estimated by standard economic analysis of the markets in the affected sectors (see, for example, Adams, Hamilton, and McCarl 1984). We used CVM to estimate the direct benefits to households, focusing on the welfare impacts of increments in quantity-rationed public goods. A complete evaluation of air and water pollution control benefits would include both the direct and derived benefits to households.

Development and Tests of CVM Formats

National air and water pollution control is a complex undertaking. In the United States, it has been conducted under eight major Congressional Acts and their subsequent amendments:

1. Clean Air Act (1970).
2. Clean Water Act (1977).
3. Marine Protection Research and Sanctuaries Act (1972).
4. Safe Drinking Water Act (1974).
5. Federal Insecticide, Fungicide and Rodenticide Act (1975).
6. Toxic Substances Control Act (1977).
7. Resource Conservation and Recovery Act (1976).
8. Superfund (1980).

For each of these legislative programs, we tabulated the important pollutants targeted, their effects on ambient air and water quality, impacts on amenities and services demanded by households, and characteristics of direct and derived demands for abatement.

In developing the instruments for use in the policy evaluation referendum, our strategy was to make the complex pollution control program manageable and comprehensible to citizen-participants, rather than to pretend it is not complex. We posited that citizens value programs in terms of delivered levels of services rather than, for example, concentrations of particular chemicals. Another critical choice was to determine what level of information detail would be sufficient for respondents' valuation process. Various methods of combining visual, numerical, and verbal information were developed. One particularly useful device is a "story picture" that depicts and describes twenty-two separate impacts of air and water pollution on the quality of life, to convey visually the richness of detail that underlies the notion of air and water quality changes.

The preliminary instruments were presented to a series of four focus groups composed of people recruited through a newspaper advertisement. People in these groups could deal with complex materials and, when given the choice, tended to prefer more detail to less. They reacted favorably to the idea of the NPER framework, i.e., standardizing national policy made sense to the participants. While these findings reinforced the prior judgments of the researchers, another finding from the focus groups pinpointed a trouble spot: the relationship between pollution control effort and the levels of prices and taxes. It was apparent that some people (a sufficiently large group to be troubling) tend to think of pollution emission as something that only large corporations do, and that polluting corporations could be required to control emissions at their own expense with no impact on the prices and taxes that ordinary citizens pay. In revising the formats, we stressed the relationship between household demands and pollution (even where corporations are the ostensible polluters) and the economic relationships between pollution, prices, and taxes.

A Sample Format

As previously stated, a major task of this pilot study was to determine how complex a format must be in order to effectively communicate the national pollution control program. Therefore, we developed a master instrument, which used the "story picture" (Figure 10.1) to communicate a base level of complexity, around which four formats could allow subtests on the effects of varying levels of complexity. The general form of the instrument is as follows: a set of environmental knowledge questions, a set of environmental attitude questions, a description of baseline and subsequent national environmental quality resulting from a policy that would change pollution loads by 25 percent, the CVM policy referendum, and a set of demographic questions. Here we present the salient points of the simplest NPER format which provided only two indicators of environmental quality: clean air and clean water.

The NPER module of the survey instrument commenced with the story picture, which is reproduced in full immediately below.

> Figure 10.1 shows some of the many ways in which pollution can affect the U.S. and its people. First, look at some of the sources of pollution in the U.S. Factories dispose of production wastes in the air and water (7). Sewage and other wastes from homes and businesses are routed to a waste water treatment plant (9) but often end up in the nation's inland and coastal waters. Exhaust from cars fouls the air and leaves a residue which can also get into the water (12). When it rains, some pesticides used by farmers (11) and homeowners (14) are washed into waterways. Leaks from toxic waste dumps (17) can contaminate the soil and seep into nearby streams and rivers.
>
> Pollution is produced as people go about activities that benefit them, so stopping all pollution would require large sacrifices. But, pollution is harmful.
>
> As pollutants find their way into the environment they have an effect on the activities people might choose. First, pollution can make people sick (20), so they have to avoid normal activities such as going to work. Some people die (21) earlier than they would have if they had not been exposed to the pollution. Even healthy people find that when pollution gets bad

162

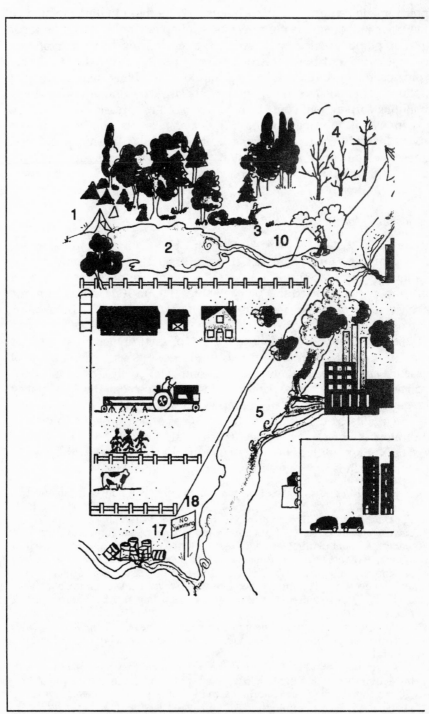

Figure 10.1 THE WAYS THAT POLLUTION AFFECTS PEOPLE

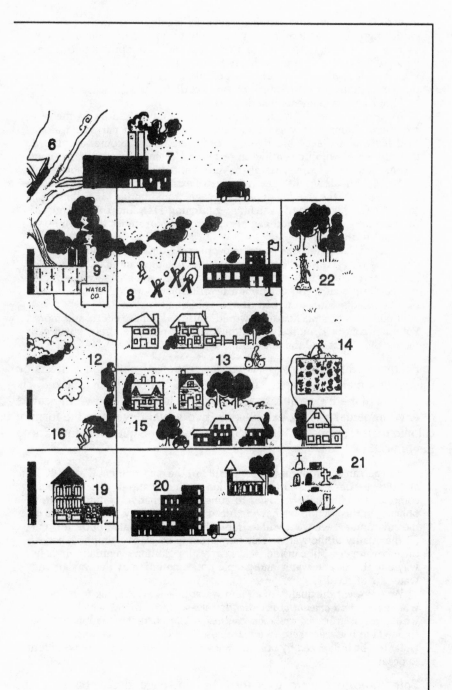

they can't do strenuous activities, such as jogging (16), cycling (13) or gardening (14) for as long as they normally could. Some pollutants such as lead cause birth defects (8). If a city or town has a reputation for being very polluted, tourists are less likely to visit (19).

Materials also can be affected by pollution. Cars rust earlier (12), paint peels from houses (15), plumbing becomes corroded and stained, and public buildings and monuments deteriorate (22).

As with people, the health of plants and animals can be harmed by pollution. Damage to vegetation may be noticeable in parks and along roadsides. Some lakes and rivers (2, 5) have already become so polluted that no fish or wildlife can live in or around them. Fish and game may become contaminated and unsafe to eat. A number of different species of plants (4), animals and fish are in danger of extinction because of pollution. This can reduce the enjoyment people receive from hunting (3), fishing (10), camping (1), hiking, bird watching, gardening (14), and other forms of recreation. Water pollution can also reduce opportunities for swimming (18), and boating (6).

Pollution can reduce the pleasure people get from many activities. Smog or haze in the air can make outdoor activities less pleasant than they would be on a clear, sunny day. And dirty, contaminated water in a local lake can reduce the pleasure you get from a favorite picnic spot. Drinking water may be discolored or taste bad due to pollution.

If pollution was unchecked it would cause all of these effects and more. Pollution control is unlikely to eliminate these effects entirely, but it can reduce the effects and make them more tolerable.

Following this verbal and visual description of pollution's effects on the environment, the next section of the simple format asked six environmental attitude questions. This was followed by two indicators of environmental quality, exhibited as two visual devices in the form of colored dials (Figures 10.2 and 10.3). The following quotation introduced the indicators.

As you can see from the simple picture of the environment (Figure 10.1) and the questions in the previous section, pollution and its effects are very complicated. To make it easier to consider alternative pollution control policies, in this section we have reduced this complexity to two aspects of the environment we want you to think about: (1) the quality of the air, and (2) the quality of the water. This may seem to be an oversimplification of the environment, but consider that nearly all pollution eventually finds its way into the air and water, and people notice pollution by the way air and water are affected.

We represent the quality of air and water by a scale ranging from "best," where a *minimal amount of pollution* is released, to "worst," which is what would result from *no pollution controls*. The current situation will be somewhere between these two extremes. The quality of national air and water can be influenced by policies that would allow more or less pollution to occur.

Both indicators were explained by one-page descriptions of the environmental attributes that they represented. The indicators were devised according to the following criteria.

A water body that is fishable and swimmable has the following characteristics
1) Okay for boating.
2) Game fish like bass can live in it.
3) Human contact is not harmful.
4) Contains some pollution, so you cannot drink it.

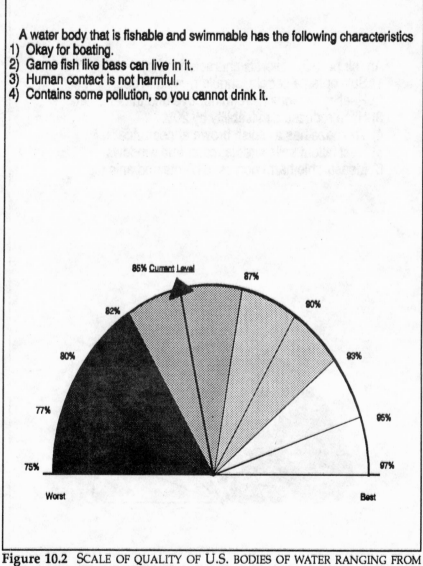

Figure 10.2 SCALE OF QUALITY OF U.S. BODIES OF WATER RANGING FROM CONDITIONS OF NO POLLUTION CONTROLS ("WORST") TO MINIMAL POLLUTION ("BEST")

166

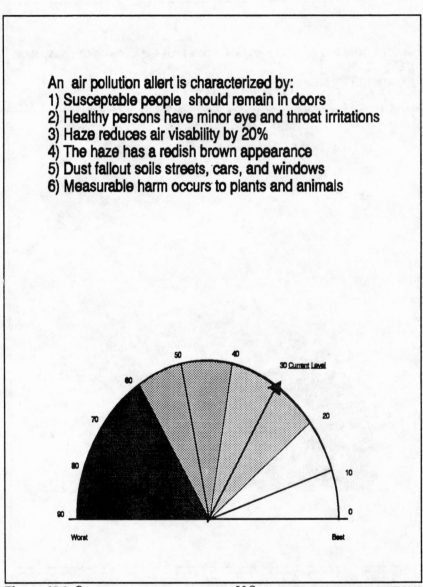

An air pollution allert is characterized by:
1) Susceptable people should remain in doors
2) Healthy persons have minor eye and throat irritations
3) Haze reduces air visability by 20%
4) The haze has a redish brown appearance
5) Dust fallout soils streets, cars, and windows
6) Measurable harm occurs to plants and animals

Figure 10.3 SCALE OF QUALITY OF AIR IN U.S., RANGING FROM CONDITIONS OF NO POLLUTION CONTROLS ("WORST") TO MINIMAL POLLUTION ("BEST")

1) <u>Air quality, in number of air pollution alert days</u>. The measure of smell, soot, and corrosion associated with air pollution was defined in terms of the Pollutant Standards Index. The Council on Environmental Quality (1982, 21) presented data on the annual number of air pollution alert days (i.e., days with PSI>100) for 56 SMSAs. The population of these SMSAs summed to about 100 million, and the average number of air pollution alert days was 30. With the population exposed to alerts held constant, we expressed the impact of policy by varying the number of alert days. The changes in alert days resulting from changes in pollution loads were estimated by the research team, based on the published literature.

2) <u>Quality of water in rivers, lakes, and streams, in percent swimmable and fishable</u>. The current percentage of swimmable and fishable freshwater bodies and the changes attributable to increased and decreased pollution loads were estimated by the research team after consulting the available literature. We note that Mitchell and Carson (1986) have made use of this indicator of recreational water quality.

Next was the NPER question format, which specified the policy cost to the individual (in terms of higher prices and taxes), the policy implementation rule (implicitly, majority vote), and the payment rule (if the policy is approved, you pay the stated price). The policy was offered in Q14 at one of the following prices: $75, $150, $225, $300, $375, $450, $525, $600, $675, $750. This payment institution is a neutral device (i.e., has no "vehicle bias") that accurately models the way that changes in policy extract a price in the real world. The yes/no responses are analyzed via the logit method. The iterative part, Q17 or Q18, extracts a continuous valuation, analyzed via OLS.

Now, let's consider some alternative pollution control policies. It is possible to reduce pollution and improve the environment. However, this costs money and ordinary citizens eventually pay most of the costs. For example, your household may have to buy unleaded gasoline and pay higher taxes for better sewage treatment. Outlawing certain agricultural pesticides would decrease farmers' production, causing an increase in food prices. Forcing electric utilities to reduce pollution would increase their costs, and they would have to charge higher utility rates. The following questions are designed to help us find out how much national environmental quality is worth to you.

PROGRAM A

First, please look at the air and water quality indicators in Figure 10.4 opposite this page. The indicators illustrate the scientifically estimated effects of a pollution control program (Program A) which would reduce the amount of pollution entering the environment by 25 percent. The effects of reducing pollution by 25%, as shown by the indicators are: (1) the number of air pollution alert days would decrease from the current 30 days to 10 days per year; and (2) the percentage of "swimmable and fishable" water would increase from 85 to 90 percent.

Suppose a nation-wide program could be adopted within the next year that would reduce allowable pollution by 25 percent within five years. This would increase the amount of money spent by households, government and industry on pollution control, and you, the end consumer, would have to pay for it. As a result, you (or your household) would have $_____ per year less to spend on other things, beginning next year.

Q14. If the adoption of this national policy were put to a referendum would you vote to accept this program?
Yes _____(go to Q-15)   No _____(go to Q-16)

Q15. Of course, we cannot be certain, in advance, about the costs of this pollution control program. If it turned out that this program would result in you (or your household) having $1,000 less per year to spend on other things, would you vote to accept this program?
Yes _____ (go to Q-17)   No _____(go to Q-18)

Q16. Of course, we cannot be certain, in advance, about the costs of this pollution control program. If it turned out that this program would result in you (or your household) having $50 less per year to spend on other things, would you vote to accept this program?
Yes _____ (go to Q-17)   No _____(go to Q-18)

Q17. Now, think for a moment and write down the very highest amount this pollution reduction program could cost you (your household) and for which you would still vote to accept it. (In other words, if it would cost you any more than this "highest amount," you would have to reject the program.)
The highest amount is $_____ per year.

Q18. Now, think for a moment and write down the very highest amount this pollution reduction program could cost you (your household) and for which you would decide to accept it. (In other words, if it would cost you any more than this "highest amount," you would have to reject the program.)
The highest amount is $_____ per year.

Data Collection

Data for this study were collected in November and December, 1984. To test the relative effectiveness of five formats (offering different kinds and amounts of information about policy impact) and four administration methods (mail, mail-telephone, telephone, and personal interview), data collection was concentrated in the Lexington, Kentucky, SMSA. A national mail survey (excluding Alaska and Hawaii) was also conducted. Response rates varied from a low of 25 percent for telephone administration to 35 percent for national mail administration and 44 percent for personal interview. The close similarity between mail and personal interview is an important finding, given the large differences in cost between these two methods. A comparison of our sample's socioeco-

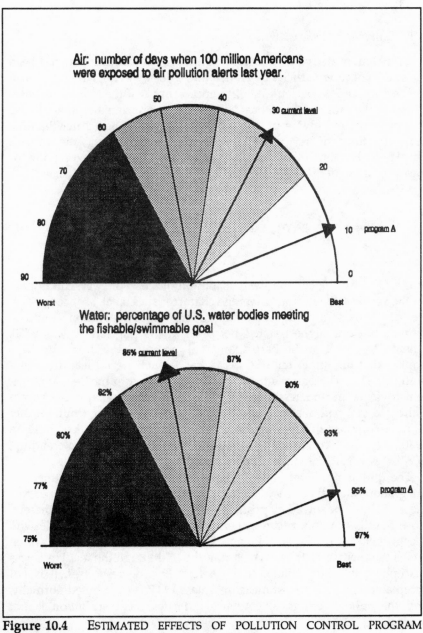

Figure 10.4 ESTIMATED EFFECTS OF POLLUTION CONTROL PROGRAM REDUCING POLLUTION BY 25 PERCENT

nomic characteristics with those of the target population did not reveal any large sampling biases.

WTP Estimation Methods

The problem of deriving valid WTP estimates from voting data has been the subject of recent articles by Hanemann (1984a, 1984b), who focuses on the decision process as a utility difference. That is, if the individual votes to accept the program, then the indirect utility associated with accepting the program and giving up some income, $A, must be greater than the indirect utility of rejecting the program and keeping the money. Employing Hanemann's suggestions yielded the following expression for mean compensated WTP from the sample data:

$$E[WTP|s] = \int_0^{A_{max}} \{1 - [G(A)|s]\}\, da,$$

where G(As) is the cumulative distribution function of WTP, conditional on the vector s, the sample's average characteristics (such as income, age, etc.). By Hanemann's argument, the upper limit of integration should be infinity, but our highest stated tax price in the pilot study was $750, where 60 percent of the participants still accepted the program. This implies that the upper tail of G(A) is "fat," which would lead to a very high E(WTP). Therefore, integration was truncated to the 0—750 range, which yields an underestimate of WTP. The parameters of G(A) were estimated via logit analysis, and integration was calculated numerically using a composite four-point Gauss-Legendre rule (Conte and deBoor, 1980). For the continuous valuations from the iterated referendum, E(WTP) was calculated by simple average.

The problem of fat tails is bothersome, even if truncating the integration interval produces an underestimated WTP. We do not expect the problem to be solved by positing extremely high tax prices, to thereby close the distribution, because there may always be a few people who accept high tax prices. Hanemann suggests another calculation which yields the median of the G(A) distribution. Although the median is less susceptible to being influenced by a few extreme responses, it is not acceptable as a benefit-cost measure unless WTP is distributed normally, and the bulk of empirical evidence indicates the distribution is not normal.

Summary of Benefit Estimates

The basic valuation equation was:

$$VALUATION = f(PRICE, INCOME, AGE, KNOW, ATTIT,$$
$$CELL\ 1,...,CELL\ 7, CELL\ 9,...,CELL\ 13)$$

where

VALUATION =   (a) VALUE (a continuous variable), the log. of the response to Q17 or Q18, and used in OLS analysis. (b) VOTE (=1 if accept the program, O if reject) stating the response to Q14, and used in logit analysis;

PRICE =   log. of offered price of the program ($75 to $750);

INCOME =   log. of household income, 1983;

AGE =   log. of respondent's age;

KNOW =   respondent's score on battery of environmental knowledge questions (0 to 5, with higher scores indicating greater knowledge);

ATTIT =   respondent's core on a battery of environmental attitude questions (6 to 30, with higher scores indicating more "environmentalist" attitudes); and

CELLS 1-13 =   dummy (0,1) variables identifying treatments, i.e., particular combinations of instrument, administration method, and sampling frame (Lexington SMSA, or national).

Complete results of statistical analysis are reported elsewhere (Randall *et al.* 1985). Here we offer a summary of the more interesting findings.

Since this effort was designed to be a pilot study, tests of administration methods and the aforementioned instrument types were an import objective. Administration methods were mailed, for the national survey, and within the Lexington SMSA mail, face-to-face interview, combined mail-telephone, and telephone alone. The results of the Lexington subtest indicated that the mail—telephone and telephone administration methods did not perform as well as the others. Additional tests concerned the appropriate level of information complexity. The telephone format, with abbreviated verbal information and no visual materials, yielded lower valuations than the others, but the difference was not statistically significant. However, this particular format was not tested with a comparable nontelephone administration method. The other four formats, which combined verbal and visual information, performed about equally well. In retrospect, we conjecture that even the simplest of these four formats (i.e., the one presented in this chapter) contained rather substantial information; a less informative verbal-visual presentation may not have performed as well.

The statistical results and value estimates reported below are for the total sample including all treatments, for which there were 872 observations. The valuation equations for the logit and OLS models had the same significant independent variables, at the 0.01 level, and their direction of influence was as we had hypothesized: offered price (- for VOTE, + for VALUE), income (+), and environmental attitude (+). The logit model correctly predicted 74 percent of the votes, while the OLS model had an R-square of 0.22. Annual willingness to pay as estimated from the referendum was $694.42 per household, or $60.4 billion for the nation, in 1984 dollars, for the program that would decrease air and water pollution loads by 25 percent. This estimate is lower than our multimarket hedonic estimate of $983.39 per household, or $85.5 billion.

Concluding Comments

Two recent developments—techniques for estimating welfare change from discrete choice data, and the demonstration that a particular form of referendum is incentive compatible—paved the way for the contingent policy choice form of CVM. This form of CVM has a special advantage when the task is to value the kinds of public goods that are typically provided by public policy. Traditional application of CVM to policy questions introduces a degree of cognitive dissonance by imposing a market analogy on a context that citizens are accustomed to conceptualizing in policy terms. The advantage of the contingent policy choice version of CVM is that it confirms and harnesses the ordinary citizen's intuition that the level of public goods is typically a policy question.

In this chapter, we report a large-scale pilot study using the national policy evaluation referendum (NPER), an adaptation of the contingent policy choice form of CVM. The NPER is distinguished from other contingent policy choice forms in that it standardizes policy rather than its impact on the individual. Rigorous valuation exercises require that something be standardized: impacts or policy. We have argued, above, that there are good reasons to standardize policy rather than its impact on the individual.

Our pilot study (Randall et al. 1985) permitted some initial testing of the NPER in application. The first kind of test is subjective and impressionistic; it implements not a rigorous hypothesis test but something more akin to test-driving an automobile. We used the NPER and came away from the experience with a variety of favorable impressions about its performance characteristics. Secondly, we performed some hypothesis tests. The NPER is a satisfactory benefit-cost indicator (Hoehn and Randall, forthcoming), which implies that, if anything, it understates benefits. Benefits of a 25 percent reduction in pollution loads nationwide estimated with the NPER were of the same order of magnitude as, but lower than, the estimate obtained with a wage-rent multimarket hedonic analysis. A further implication of the NPER's satisfactoriness (Hoehn and Randall) is that, of any pair of benefit estimates, the larger is to be preferred since no satisfactory benefit estimate is an overestimate. Benefits estimated via a telephone-administered NPER, without benefit of the story picture, were significantly lower than the estimates obtained with questionnaires based on the story picture, regardless of which one of four alternative versions were used and whether administration was face-to-face or by mail. The opportunity to look at the picture and read or hear the accompanying text provided sufficient information that reported citizen valuations stabilized at a higher level. We interpret this finding as indicating that a complex national policy can be communicated effectively in a NPER.

These pilot study results are encouraging, while, of course, not definitive. Together with our conceptual arguments in favor of the NPER, they lead us to conclude that a program of systematic implementation and testing of the NPER is justified.

If we have made a convincing case that the NPER is a promising development in contingent valuation methods for policy-provided public goods, this is one more piece of evidence that CVM is a progressing research program.

A recent state-of-the-art assessment (Cummings, Brookshire, and Schulze, 1986) examined virtually the entire corpus of CVM research through the early 1980s and summarized its conclusions in four "reference operating conditions" (ROCs). The implication is that CVM exercises that conform to the ROCs should enjoy a presumption of reasonable accuracy and precision. The ROCs are (104):

1. Subjects must understand, be familiar with, the commodity to be valued.
2. Subjects must have had (or be allowed to obtain) prior valuation and choice experience with respect to consumption levels of the commodity.
3. There must be little uncertainty.
4. WTP, not WTA, measures are elicited.

As a set of proposed sufficient conditions for valid CVM, the ROCs seem quite incomplete. Hoehn and Randall emphasized that CVM is not a collective noun for a homogeneous set of techniques but, rather, a generic term for a set of valuation formats, each of which may have its own incentive characteristics that encourage or discourage biased responses. Other researchers have emphasized framing effects, while others have devised elaborate taxonomies of possible biases. Suffice it to say that it would be a simple task to devise invalid CVM formats that nevertheless conform to the ROCs.

A more interesting question is whether the ROCs are necessary conditions for valid CVM. Since Cummings, Brookshire, and Schulze use the verb "must" in the first three ROCs (and its omission from the fourth appears to be syntactically inconsistent), it seems that necessity was what they had in mind.

The NPER consciously deviates from the ROCs in several important ways. As Cummings Brookshire, and Schulze write (104), "ROCs 1 and 2 derive directly from the market institution," whereas the NPER is built on conscious rejection of the market analogy. NPERs will typically violate ROC 2, since policy change is typically a venture from the known into the unknown. But, we argue, citizens have adapted to the real world of policy and should, by extension, be able to handle the NPER.

We have trouble interpreting ROC 3. If it means that the CVM format itself should not introduce extraneous uncertainty or noise into the valuation process, we concur. Alternatively, however, it may mean that valid CVM must be confined to situations where baseline and with-policy conditions translate into deterministic, rather than stochastic, impacts on the individual household. We would be inclined to reject any ROC interpreted in this way. Citizens, we argue, are able to handle some uncertainty about policy in the real world and the NPER.

Finally, we would counsel against premature acceptance of ROC 4 as necessary for valid CVM. We conjecture that the NPER may be adaptable for valid estimation of WTA. Our understanding of the large divergences between WTP and WTA is as follows. First, with quantity-rationed goods, WTP and WTA may diverge considerably in some cases. The Randall and Stoll (1980) analysis generates formulae for using observations of one measure to generate approximations of the other. It does not provide an argument that they are approximately equal. Thus, some (perhaps considerable) divergence between WTP and WTA is real and not an artifact of measurement error. Second, there is some psychological evidence that people are risk-conservative and loss-conservative. These characteristics would lead to relatively large values for WTA. Economists and psychologists appear to be in some disagreement as to whether this is a kind of measurement error. Third, "market analogy" CVM to estimate WTA invites participants to individually accept (or reject) decrements in public goods in return for individual compensation. Probing of refusals to accept finite compensation reveals a tendency to recoil from "selling out" one's compatriots. The NPER for WTA avoids this third problem—by inviting participants to cast one vote for a policy to reduce, simultaneously, public goods and the prices and taxes everyone pays—and may therefore provide a preferred method of eliciting WTA.

The NPER consciously violates ROCs 1 and 2 and may provide an avenue for overcoming the limiting influence of ROC 4. Nevertheless, we believe it is a promising development in CVM. Surely, there will be other developments that similarly violate the ROCs, yet seem promising. Given that the ROCs are neither sufficient nor necessary conditions for valid CVM, we hope they will not be used to arbitrarily confine and restrict the development of the progressing research program of the contingent valuation method.

References

Adams, Richard M., Scott A. Hamilton, and Bruce A. McCarl. 1984. The Economic Effects of Ozone on Agriculture. EPA-600/3-84-090, U.S.E.P.A., Corvallis, Oregon.

Bishop, Richard C., and Thomas A. Heberlein. 1979. Measuring Values of Extra-Market Goods: Are Indirect Measures Biased? *American Journal of Agricultural Economics.* 61:926-30.

Boyle, Kevin J., and Richard C. Bishop. 1987. The Total Value of Wildlife Resources: Conceptual and Empirical Issues. *In* Toward the Measurement of Total Value, edited by George Peterson and Cindy Sorg USDA Forest Service RMF&RES General Technical Report.

Conte, S.D., and C. deBoor. 1980. *Elementary Numerical Analysis: An Algorithmic Approach.* 3rd ed.New York: McGraw-Hill.

Council of Environmental Quality. 1982. *13th Annual Report of the Council on Environmental Quality.* Washington, D.C. Government Printing Office.

Cummings, R.G., D.S. Brookshire, and W.D. Schulze, eds. 1986. *Valuing Environmental Goods: An Assessment of the Contingent Valuation Method.* Totowa, New Jersey: Rowman and Allenheld.

Davis, Robert K. 1963. Recreational Planning as an Economic Problem. *Natural Resources Journal.* 3:238-49.

Hanemann, Michael W. 1984a. Discrete/Continuous Models of Consumer Demand. *Econometrica.* 52:541-61.

_____. 1984b. Welfare Evaluations in Contingent Valuation Experiments with Discrete Responses. *American Journal of Agricultural Economics.* 66:332-41.

Hoehn, John, and Alan Randall. 1987. A Satisfactory Benefit Cost Indicator from Contingent Valuation. *Journal of Environmental Economics and Management.* 14:226-247.

Mitchell, Robert C., and Richard T. Carson. 1986. *Using Surveys to Value Public Goods: The Contingent Valuation Method.* Washington, D.C. Resources for the Future.

Public Opinion Quarterly. 1972. The Polls: Pollution and Its Costs. 30:120-35.

Randall, Alan. 1987. The Total Value Dilemma. *In* Toward the Measurement of Total Value, edited by George Peterson and Cindy Sorgs. USDA Forest Service RMF&RES General Technical Report.

Randall, Alan, *et al.* 1985. National Aggregate Benefits of Air and Water Pollution Control. USEPA and the University of Kentucky, Cooperative Agreement CR 811-056-01-0, Interim report.

Randall, Alan, John P.Hoehn, and David S. Brookshire. 1983. Contingent Valuation Surveys for Evaluating Environmental Assets. *Natural Resources Journal.* 23:635-48.

Randall, Alan, B. Ives, and C. Eastman. 1974. Bidding Games for Valuation of Aesthetic Environmental Improvements. *Journal of Environmental Economics and Management.* 1:132-449.

Randall, Alan, and John Stoll. 1980. Consumer's Surplus in Commodity Space. *American Economic Review.* 70:449-54.

Schwartz, Joel, *et al.* 1985. Costs and Benefits of Reducing Lead in Gasoline: Final Regulatory Impact Analysis. E.A.D., U.S.E.P.A., Washington. D.C.

Sellar, Christine, John R. Stoll, and Jean-Paul Chavas. 1985. Empirical Measures of Welfare Change: A Comparison of Nonmarket Techniques. *Land Economics*. 61:156-75.

Smith. V. Kerry. 1987. Intrinsic Values in Benefit Cost Analysis. *In* Toward the Measurement of Total Value, edited by George Peterson and Cindy Sorg. USDA Forest Service RMF&RES General Technical Report.

11 Contingent Valuation of Wildlife Resources in the Presence of Substitutes and Complements

Karl C. Samples

James R. Hollyer

Introduction

Valuation of wildlife resources using the contingent valuation method (CVM) is routinely conducted within a partial equilibrium framework. This makes logical sense when the goal is to ascertain the social worth of changes in the supply price or quantity for a single species or a small group of related species. Invocation of *ceteris paribus* conditions effectively keeps the rest of the world at a standstill during the valuation exercise. Value estimates for waterfowl (Bishop and Heberlein 1979; Hammack and Brown 1974), deer (Livengood 1983; Keith and Lyon 1985), grizzly bears and bighorn sheep (Brookshire, Eubanks and Randall 1983), bald eagles and emerald shiners (Boyle and Bishop 1987), and whales and seals (Hageman 1985) have been obtained in this manner.

Adoption of partial equilibrium analysis simplifies the valuation process. It also leads to the generation of numerous wildlife value estimates which are independently obtained and based on *ceteris paribus* assumptions which are often vaguely defined. As the available set of estimated values expands, legitimate questions arise about their usefulness in allocative decisionmaking outside of their original valuation contexts. For example, under what circumstances can estimated values be directly compared with one another, both within and across studies, to help draw conclusions bout relative social worth of wildlife? Also, when is it appropriate to aggregate individually estimated values to arrive at a total value for a collection of different wildlife resources?

This research was supported in part by project PP/R-9, "Economic Benefits and Costs of Marine Mammal Preservation in Hawaii," which is funded by the University of Hawaii Sea Grant Program under Institutional Grant #NA8-5AA-D-SG-082 from NOAA, Office of Sea Grant, U.S. Department of Commerce.

CVM practitioners and scholars offer few definitive answers to these questions. For pragmatic purposes, however, direct cross-study comparisons between CVM estimates of wildlife values are routinely made for validation purposes. Furthermore, it is not uncommon for separate values to be aggregated to demonstrate large collective social worth for a group of wildlife resources.

Despite these practices, a commonly held concern expressed by Rowe and Chestnut (1983) is that considerably more work is needed to understand how CVM estimates are affected by partial equilibrium assumptions, in particular those relating to substitutes and complements.[1] This concern provides the motivation for this chapter. Our purpose here is to explore the sensitivity of wildlife value estimates to partial equilibrium assumptions which underlie the valuation process.

The issue is first analyzed at a conceptual level to illuminate how individual and aggregate wildlife values are conditional upon *ceteris paribus* assumptions that define availability conditions for substitutes and complements. Potential biases associated with valuation sequencing and aggregation are discussed within this context. The conceptual analysis yields a set of hypotheses which are then tested in an empirical study of marine mammal valuation in Hawaii.

The empirical analysis explores the problem of valuing humpback whales and Hawaiian monk seals independently and jointly. Individual and aggregate values are compared. Results of this exercise suggest that summation of individual preservation values consistently overstates aggregate values, and therefore is probably inappropriate. It also appears that individually estimated values are sensitive to the order of valuation; hence direct comparisons between value estimates may not indicate relative social worth, even under ideal conditions where CVM estimates are known to be reliable and robust.

Valuation in the Presence of Substitutes and Complements

The goal of wildlife valuation is to ascertain Hicksian consumer surplus, or a change in Hicksian consumer surplus, accruing to individuals as a result of a change in wildlife supply circumstances. Various surplus measures exist depending on the direction of the change (increment or

---

[1] Concern has also been raised by Randall and Stoll (1983) in regard to aggregating estimated values for vectors of nonmarket goods. In their view, the mere process of summation violates the partial equilibrium assumptions that underlie individual value estimates. This argument has been more formally posed by Hoehn and Randall (1985). They show that upward aggregation biases arise when summing individual project benefits to estimate total benefits of complex multipart public projects.

decrement), the type of change (price, quality, or quantity), and the reference utility level (before or after the change). Regardless of which measure is deemed most proper, consumer surplus is always measured in a partial equilibrium framework. This follows from Hicks, who defined the concept in terms of price variations for single and multiple goods that occur under strict *ceteris paribus* conditions. Utility, wealth endowment, tastes and preferences, and the prices of all other non-affected goods and productive services are fixed. The partial equilibrium nature of the concept is also embodied in work by Mäler (1974) and Randall and Stoll (1980), who extended Hicks's notion of consumer surplus to include quality and quantity variations.

CVM estimates of wildlife values based on Hicksian consumer surplus are therefore inextricably tied to a given set of *ceteris paribus* conditions. The conditions that define the price, quality, and quantity characteristics of substitute and complementary wildlife resources are of special interest here. This is because estimated values for wildlife resources can be affected in a number of different ways by the availability circumstances of related resources. First, values can vary depending on respondents' perceptions of substitutes and complements. Second, estimates can be affected by the number of different resources being valued at one time and the sequencing of the valuation questions. Third, estimated aggregate values for a group of species can differ depending on whether the total is calculated by summing individual values or calculated directly.

These assertions become more transparent by considering some simple valuation cases involving two wildlife resources, A and B, supplied at zero cost. Three policy measures will be considered: (1) total loss of resource A, with resource B remaining intact; (2) total loss of resource B, with resource A remaining intact; and (3) total loss of both A and B, either simultaneously or sequentially. Assuming that the public has no vested rights in A and B, the valuation exercise entails estimating the relevant populations' equivalent surplus for each policy measure. Willingness to pay (WTP) to avoid the supply decrement is the appropriate measure of welfare loss in each instance (Randall and Stoll 1980).

Let the value of A, given the presence of B at current prices and quantities, be called WTP(A|B). Similarly, let the value of B, given the presence of A at current prices and quantities, be called WTP(B|A). WTP(A|B) and WTP(B|A) are the correct values for A and B, respectively, for purposes of evaluating policy measures (1) and (2) above.

Calculated values for A and B will differ from these correct amounts if respondents somehow fail to consider the presence of the other resource when stating willingness-to-pay amounts. This myopia could arise either because of ignorance about the other resource, or uncertainty about personal preference mappings for the resource (Freeman 1986; Samples, Dixon, and Gowen 1986). It could also arise if inadequate attention is devoted to formally defining the complete *ceteris paribus* conditions that prevail in the contingent valuation market. Let the value of A, in the absence of B, be called WTP(A|0). Similarly, let the value of B, in the absence of A, be called WTP(B|0). If A and B are substitutes, it follows that WTP(A|0) > WTP(A|B), and WTP(B|0) > WTP(B|A) because the value of a resource is greater when valued in the absence of its substitutes. If A and B are complements, then the opposite holds and the inequalities are reversed.

These relationships have direct implications for valuing individual resources in a sequential fashion using CVM. Suppose that there is an interest in valuing the loss of two different resources using a single questionnaire survey. If the losses are independent, then the goal is to ascertain WTP(A|B) and WTP(B|A). However, this pair of values is only one of several combinations that could conceivably be obtained. An example of an incorrect alternative pair is WTP(A|B) and WTP(B|0). This combination might occur if respondents are asked for their willingness to pay to avoid the loss of A, and then are asked for their willingness to pay to avoid the additional loss of B, given that A is no longer available. Alternatively, respondents could be asked to value B first and then to value A. The resulting value combination could likely be WTP(B|A) and WTP(A|0).

Deviations from true individual values in both instances stem from the fact that respondents' value assessments for A and B are interdependent, when they actually should be independent. This mistake could occur if *ceteris paribus* conditions are not fully described to respondents. It could also arise if respondents perceive a wealth effect as they are asked to make a sequence of payments to forestall the separate losses of a number of resources.   When confronted with a fixed budget for wildlife preservation donations, respondents may be tempted to "give" generously to save the first resource being valued. Consequently they will have less funds available to donate to subsequent preservation causes. Whatever the cause, the order in which multiple resources are valued can likely affect final outcomes. Aiken (1985) for example, found this true when he tested for the effects of ordering by varying the sequence in which seven separate environmental programs were valued. Estimates of WTP for certain programs differed between 18 and 51 percent depending on order of valuation. WTP for programs was generally higher when the program was placed earlier rather than later in a valuation sequence.

Dealing with substitute and complement effects becomes more complex when valuing multiple rather than individual resources. Consider, for example, the third policy measure discussed above involving the permanent loss of both A and B. Joint losses, whether they occur simultaneously or sequentially, are properly valued by estimating the line integral of the separate demand curves for A and B. The resulting welfare measure, call it WTP(A&B), is independent of the path of integration, provided that cross-price effects in the demands for A and B are symmetric. If so, the order of losses does not influence the final total.

Now compare WTP(A&B) with a second measure of total value derived by summing independently obtained values for A and B. If the individual values account for the presence of related goods, the sum equals WTP(A|B) + WTP(B|A). Notice that regardless of whether A and B are substitutes or complements, this sum, like the line integral, is not affected by which resource is valued first. Nevertheless, if A and B are substitutes, then WTP(A|B) + WTP(B|A) < WTP(A&B). The inequality is reversed if A and B are complements.

A third possible measure of total social worth is obtained by valuing A and B independently, without regard for the presence of the other, and then aggregating the separate estimates. The resulting total would be WTP(A|0) + WTP(B|0). The sum is invariant regardless of which resource is valued first. But if A and B are substitutes, the aggregate will exceed the true total value of WTP(A&B). Conversely, the aggregate will understate WTP(A&B) if the resources are complements.

Finally, the existence of demand interrelationships between resources confuses value measurement when using a residual approach. For example, suppose that the total value of two goods was correctly measured as [WTP(A&B)]. Suppose also that the value of a single good A, in the presence of B, was measured as WTP(A|B). From these two bits of information, can the value of B (WTP(B|A)) be inferred as the difference between the two measures? The answer is no. If B and A are substitutes, then the value of WTP(B|A) is less than the difference. The opposite holds if B and A are complements. Subtraction of values, like aggregation, can lead to errors unless complementary or substitute relationships are fully accounted for.

These relationships between individual and total values are summarized in Table 11.1. The inequalities between the various measures suggest the following hypotheses: (1) individual values may differ depending on questioning order and *ceteris paribus* assumptions that define the valuation context; (2) total values will differ depending on whether the total is arrived at by summing individual values or by calculating a total value directly; and (3) the differences between these measures depends on whether the goods are perceived as substitutes or compliments by respondents.

Valuation of Humpback Whale and Hawaiian Monk Seal Preservation

An opportunity to explore all three hypotheses arose in the context of a benefit-cost study of marine mammal preservation in Hawaii. Two marine mammals, both on the federal endangered species list, were targeted for valuation: the humpback whale (*Megaptera novaeangliea*) and the Hawaiian monk seal (*Monarchus schauinslandi*).

Table 11.1 RELATIONSHIPS BETWEEN INDIVIDUAL AND AGGREGATE WILLINGNESS-TO-PAY (WTP) FOR RESOURCES A AND B UNDER ALTERNATIVE *CETERIS PARIBUS* CONDITIONS

A and B Substitutes	A and B Complements
Individual Values	
WTP(A|0) > WTP(A|B)	WTP(A|0) < WTP(A|B)
WTP(B|0) > WTP(B|A)	WTP(B|0) < WTP(B|A)
WTP(A&B)-WTP(A|B) > WTP(B|A)	WTP(A&B)-WTP(A|B) < WTP(B|A)
WTP(A&B)-WTP(B|A) > WTP(A|B)	WTP(A&B)-WTP(B|A) < WTP(A|B)
Aggregate Values	
WTP(A&B) > WTP(A|B)+WTP(B|A)	WTP(A&B) < WTP(A|B)+WTP(B|A)
WTP(A&B) < WTP(A|0)+WTP(B|0)	WTP(A&B) > WTP(A|0)+WTP(B|0)

The stock of humpback whales visiting Hawaiian waters is a subpopulation of the Pacific humpback whale population. The Hawaiian stock, numbering less than 600 animals, migrates to near shore Hawaiian waters on an annual basis during, the winter and spring months, to mate and calve. The whales, averaging over 50 feet in length, are highly active and visible during their five-month visit. Television and newspaper reports announce their arrival and occasionally provide information about the whales' natural history. A small fleet of whale-watching vessels provides excursions for both residents and tourists. Public interest in protecting the remaining whales has prompted repeated efforts to establish a marine sanctuary in local waters (U.S. Department of Commerce 1983). Media attention devoted to these proposals has given considerable publicity to the humpback whales and their plight for survival.

In contrast, the endemic population of 1,200 Hawaiian monk seals resides on the remote and essentially uninhabited atolls and islands that comprise the Northwestern Hawaiian Islands. Rarely are the seals observed in the inhabited islands of Hawaii. Except for a handful of military personnel and naturalists, few humans have had the opportunity to see a live Hawaiian monk seal in the wild. Public awareness of the seals' natural history and endangered status is therefore comparitively low.

Four different versions of a standard survey instrument were developed to value humpback whales and Hawaiian monk seals individually and jointly. The surveys were identified by (1) the order in which the mammals were valued, and (2) level of species aggregation. In the Seal-Whale (S-W) survey version, both species were valued separately, with seals valued first and whales valued second. In the Whale-Seal (W-S) version, whales and then seals were valued sequentially. The final two versions deviated from this format by first valuing whales and seals jointly and subsequently valuing one or the other species individually. For example, in the Whale&Seal-Seal (W&S-S) version, whales and seals were jointly valued, and then the value of seals alone was measured. The final questionnaire, called the Whale&Seal-Whale (W&S-W) version, was used first to value whales and seals jointly and then to value whales independently. In addition to valuation questions, each survey also incorporated basic demographic questions and a series of inquiries directed at learning respondents' level of knowledge about seals and whales.

The valuation analysis centered on measuring respondents' willingness-to-pay (WTP) to preserve whales, seals, or both at their current population numbers. WTP was measured using CVM with the following fabricated contingent market situation. Depending on the resource being valued, respondents were asked to imagine themselves learning the next morning that a rare disease had killed two seals or two whales. When the interest was in valuing seals and whales *combined* (versions W&S-S and W&S-W), it was explained that two whales and two seals had died of the disease. Respondents were further informed that the disease would rapidly destroy the entire resource being valued unless expensive medical attention was provided. They were told that this medical care, if provided in sufficient quantities, would absolutely guarantee the survival of the remainder of the population(s) from this particular disease. However, no guarantees were made about long-term survival in the face of other maladies. In short, respondents were presented with a dramatic and urgent situation requiring a one-time-only input of resources to ensure preservation over the short run.

After the description of this hypothetical scenario, valuation assessment was conducted in two stages. During the first stage, respondents were asked if they would be willing to contribute to preserving the threatened resource at hand. It was explained that contributions could be made in the form of monetary donations (payable over the next 12 months), or in the form of volunteer time (to be delivered over the next 12 months at home or at a central location preparing medical supplies), or both. The option to allow contributions of time as well as money followed from Bockstael and Strand (1985), and Cory (1985), who convincingly argue that measurement of willingness-to-pay using only money payment mechanisms can lead to significant underestimates of social worth.

All respondents were given the option of not making a contribution at all. Those who selected this alternative amounted to 11 to 31 percent of respondents, depending on the survey version. Individuals in this group were automatically assigned a zero valuation for preserving the resource at hand. Motives of noncontributors were not probed, although less than 1 percent of respondents refused to participate in the valuation exercise altogether.

Respondents who expressed a willingness to make some form of contribution were then asked if they would contribute at least X dollars or Y hours, or both, depending on the contribution method they selected. This presented a relatively simple dichotomous choice situation with the acceptable responses being either "Yes" or "No." Amounts for X and Y were randomly assigned and ranged from $3 to $213 for money payments, and from 1 to 136 hours for contributions of volunteer time. The resulting number of different money-time combinations was one hundred.

The dichotomous choice approach to contingent valuation using fixed payment amounts has been described elsewhere by Sellar, Stoll, and Chavas (1985), and Bishop and Heberlein (1979). The relative merits of the approach vis-á-vis other CVM questioning formats are twofold. First, it more closely replicates the typical consumer purchasing situation in the United States, where goods and services are offered for sale and bought at fixed prices. Secondly, use of randomly assigned fixed prices avoids starting-point and strategic biases sometimes associated with open-ended and sequential bidding approaches.

After completion of the two-stage valuation exercise for the first resource being valued, the process was repeated for the second resource. During the second round of versions W-S and S-W, it was clearly stated that all contributions made to save the second resource would be *in addition* to all earlier contributions made for the first resource. This contrasts with the second round of versions W&S-W and W&S-S, where it was clearly stated that only a single resource was actually threatened and that contributions were needed to save only this resource. Choices were again offered regarding contribution method. Respondents were not permitted to revise their responses to the first set of valuation questions. This restriction is consistent with usual practices governing charitable donations in the United States.

The survey population consisted of Hawaii residents only. Sample size was selected so that each questionnaire version would be administered to approximately 80 individuals, yielding a completed gross total sample of 328. This figure is about .032 percent of the total state population and about .040 percent of the population of Oahu. A stratified quota sampling approach was adopted because of its ease of application and its tolerable bias level relative to other costlier sampling methods (Cochran 1977). The sample was chosen from the adult population (over 18 years) and stratified according to age, income and gender.

All survey work was conducted on Oahu. Pilot interviews took place in December and January, 1986. Final surveys were administered during January, February and October, of that year. All surveys were conducted by a single interviewer to ensure consistency. Each interview averaged approximately 6 minutes in length. To approximate a cross section of the population, interview locations included beach parks, shopping malls, flea markets, and inner-city parks frequented by white-collar workers. Periodic inspection of the survey data allowed for quota monitoring.

For each survey version and particular resource, data on the binary response ("Yes" or "No") and fixed-price amounts were used to fit a logistic probability function. The final logit model was specified as $P(Y_i)= 1/[1 + \exp\text{-}(A + B*P_i)]$, where Y_i equals the probability that the ith respondent will answer "Yes" to a given price P_i, and A and B are parameters to be estimated. Respondent household income was included as an explanatory variable in preliminary model-testing phases. Income was expressed as a series of four dummy variables due to the fact that income data were collected in a categorical format. The income dummies were jointly insignificant at the 0.10 level on a consistent basis and occasionally had incorrect signs. The income variable was dropped in all final estimation models.

The price variable (P_i) was formulated as a linear combination of the money and time amounts proposed to the ith respondent. The variable was expressed in monetary terms by using a constant hourly "wage" rate to value contributions of volunteer time, irrespective of reported income. Wage rates of $1.00 and $3.35 were experimented with. Use of relatively low wage rates was a result of a preliminary analysis to measure implicit wage rates. This was accomplished by specifying the logit model as $P(Y_i)= 1/[1+\exp\text{-}(A + B1*M_i + B2*T_i)]$, where M_i and T_i are the money and time amounts proposed to the ith respondent. The implicit value of time is given by $B2/B1$. This ratio reveals respondents' willingness to trade money for time at the margin. Calculated ratios were generally very close to $0 across the various survey versions. This finding suggests that respondents assign a low opportunity cost to contributing volunteer time to whale and seal preservation.

Eight different logistic equations were independently fit using maximum likelihood estimation. The regression results, based on an assumed value of $1.00 for volunteer time, are given in Table 11.2. Statistical tests indicate that the estimated models have relatively high predictive power as measured by the percentage of correct forecasts. The low goodness of fit is explained by the binary nature of the dependent variable. Observed responses are clustered around 0 and 1, but predicted responses range continuously between these endpoints. The price variable is significantly different from zero at the 0.10 significance level across all equations.

Table 11.2 MAXIMUM LIKELIHOOD ESTIMATES FOR LOGIT MODEL OF WILLINGNESS-TO-PAY FOR WHALE AND SEAL PRESERVATION

Survey Version	Resource	Intercept	Price	N[a]	Goodness of Fit[b]	Percent of Correct Forecasts[c]
S-W	Seal	0.841 (0.473)	-0.013 (0.005)	53	0.30	71
	Whale	1.398 (0.435)	-0.009 (0.004)	65	0.20	66
W-S	Seal	1.917 (0.461)	-0.015 (0.004)	66	0.39	78
	Whale	2.322 (0.549)	-0.016 (0.004)	63	0.43	81
W&S-S	Whale & Seal	3.078 (0.658)	-0.019 (0.005)	72	0.49	83
	Seal	1.418 (0.433)	-0.013 (0.004)	69	0.31	75
W&S-W	Whale & Seal	2.103 (0.503)	-0.017 (0.005)	71	0.43	82
	Whale	1.658 (0.456)	-0.013 (0.004)	72	0.33	72

Notes: Estimated standard errors of coefficients in parentheses.
a. Subsample of respondents who expressed a willingness to make some form of contribution.
b. Analogous to the adjusted coefficient of multiple determination in the ordinary least squares setting.
c. Fraction of observations where predicted response is the same as observed response.

Willingness to pay for preservation was computed in two steps. First, expected willingness to pay was derived by integrating each estimated logit equation from zero to infinity using the formula $E(WTP)=(-A/B)+\ln[1/\{1+\exp-(A)\}]/B$. Evaluating this definite integral is analogous to integrating the area *above* the cumulative distribution function (CDF) for willingness to pay. By definition, the area above a CDF of a random variable equals its expected value. The second step was to weight the resulting integral to reflect the proportion of respondents who were unwilling to commit time or money to that particular preservation effort. For example, if 20 percent of respondents would contribute neither time nor money, the definite integral was multiplied by 0.8 to arrive at a final weighted expected value.

Resulting weighted expected WTP estimates to preserve whales, seals, and whales and seals combined are given in Table 11.3. All are derived from logit models where $1.00 was used to value time contributions.[2] Value estimates are given for each of the four survey versions. Since only two resources were valued in each version, the third resource value is calculated either as a sum or a residual. For example, in the W-S version, whales and seals were valued sequentially. The reported joint value for whales and seals combined is therefore a simple sum of the individual values. By comparison, the value for whales in the W&S-S version is calculated as the difference between the joint whale and seal value and the expected WTP for seals. Four different values are obtained for each resource. Three of these are directly estimated using CVM, and the fourth is indirectly derived from the others.

Discussion of Value Estimates

Calculated expected WTP for preserving seals and whales in survey versions S-W and W-S ranged between $62 and $142, with a simple overall average value of $108. These amounts may seem inordinately high compared with typical values in the range of $5 to $15 reported in the other wildlife valuation studies mentioned above. However, it is important to bear in mind that the values reported in Table 11.3 represent lump-sum WTP amounts rather than annual WTP annuities, as are more commonly reported. These disparities are greatly reduced by either capitalizing the annual values reported elsewhere to arrive at a lump-sum amount, or by amortizing the lump-sum values given in Table 11.3 to estimate annual values; in both cases using a discount rate in the range of 7 percent. For example, the annual equivalent of a $108 lump-sum payment is approximately $7.

Preservation of humpback whales was consistently valued higher than preservation of monk seals across all survey versions. This is consistent with the fact that whales are larger, more accessible, and more popular than monk seals. Consequently, all the components of preservation values—use, bequest, option, and existence—would be expected to be larger for whales (Samples, Dixon, and Gowen 1986).

The statistical significance of differences between calculated whale and seal values was evaluated by testing for structural differences in the underlying estimated logit equations. The null hypothesis in such tests

---

[2]Absolute value estimates were sensitive to the wage rate constant used to value volunteer time contributions. Relative values were less affected. For example, if time contributions are worth $3.35 per hour, the estimated values of seals and whales in the S-W version are $283 and $225, respectively.

Table 11.3 ESTIMATED WILLINGNESS-TO-PAY FOR HUMPBACK WHALE AND
HAWAIIAN MONK SEAL PRESERVATION: EFFECTS OF VALUATION SEQUENCING
AND JOINT MEASUREMENT

Resource Valued	Survey Version			
	S-W	W-S	W&S-W	W&S-S
Whales	$142	$125	$129	$ 38[b]
Seals	103	62	2[b]	108
Whales & Seals	245[a]	187[a]	131	146

Notes: Values are estimates of expected equivalent surplus for
abrupt and complete loss of particular resource.
a. Calculated as a sum.
b. Calculated as a residual.

was that the slope and intercept are the same across equations.[3] In
comparing whale and seal valuation equations, the null hypothesis was
rejected at the 0.10 significance level for version W-S. The hypothesis
was also rejected that the whale valuation equation for version S-W was
structurally identical compared with the seal equation for version W-S.
The hypothesis could not be rejected for all other cross-equation
comparisons for whales and seals.

Effects of sequencing on estimated values was tested using results of
survey versions S-W and W-S. In these versions, the valuation sequencing was reversed. The results show that for seals, expected WTP was
directly related to the order in which the resource was valued. Expected
WTP dropped from $103 to $62, a reduction of 39 percent, when seals
were valued second rather than first in the sequence. Using the
aforementioned statistical test of structural change, the hypothesis that
the seal equations are identical in versions S-W and W-S was rejected at
the 0.10 significance level.

[3]This is a weak test of differences because it accounts for only the response
behavior of individuals expressing a willingness to make some form of
contribution. Dichotomous responses from these individuals were used to fit the
logit models. The test, however, does not account for differences in WTP
estimates that arise due to the variance in weighting factors used to subsequently
adjust expected value estimates to reflect the proportion of respondents who
would contribute neither time nor money.

In the case of whales, the effects of valuation sequencing were less pronounced compared with seals and worked in the opposite direction. Estimated expected WTP rose $125 to $142 (an increase of 14 percent) when whales were valued second in the sequence. However, the structure of the underlying logit equations are not significantly different.

The observed reduction in WTP for seal preservation suggests that respondents may not have fully considered the existence of other resources such as whales when making their initial valuation pronouncements. Part of the problem may have been respondents' lack of familiarity with monk seals. In terms of the earlier discussion of valuing resources A and B, respondents may tend to report something closer to WTP(A|0) or WTP(B|0) when A or B are unfamiliar goods and are valued first in a sequence. In contrast, when A or B are valued second in the sequence, reported values may tend to approximate WTP(A|B) or WTP(B|A). This would especially be true if prior questioning has made respondents aware of substitute alternatives. If A and B are substitutes, then it would be expected that WTP(A|0) > WTP(A|B) and WTP(B|0) > WTP(B|A). This expectation is consistent with the seal valuation results.

It is curious, therefore, that estimated preservation values for whales increased, albeit slightly, when whales were valued second in the sequence. Following the logic just presented to explain the observed variation in seal values, it could be argued that respondents somehow view whale preservation as being complementary to seal preservation. This would explain why whales have greater worth when valued in the presence of seals (version S-W) than when valued in the absence of seals (version W-S). However, this explanation is troublesome because whales and seals cannot be both complements and substitutes with one another at the same time.

An alternative explanation is therefore offered based on debriefing sessions held with the interviewer. Apparently, when respondents valued seals first, they used their behavior in this market situation to guide their responses to whale valuation questions. Since whales are generally more popular than seals, respondents were reluctant to behave more benevolently toward seals compared with humpback whales. Consequently, whale values were inflated in the S-W questionnaire version to maintain a relatively higher value for the humpbacks. This behavioral anchoring effect did not exist in the W-S version, where whales were valued first.

In respect to the issue of value aggregation, the findings of this study show that the sums of individual seal and whale values consistently exceed weighted WTP estimates for preserving both resources combined. There are four different ways that individual preservation values given in Table 11.3 can be summed. The two sums of $245 and $189 are calculated by adding the values obtained sequentially in the S-W and

W-S survey versions, respectively. A third sum is obtained by adding estimated WTP for whales and seals when each is valued first in the sequence. This sum equals $228 ($103 for seals plus $125 for whales). A fourth sum is obtained by adding estimated WTP for the two resources when each is valued second in a sequence. This sum equals $204 ($62 for seals plus $142 for whales).

These four sums can be compared with estimates of WTP to jointly preserve whales and seals. The two estimates of joint value are $131 and $146 for survey version W&S-W and W&S-S, respectively. The $15 difference between the two values is somewhat troublesome because the CVM approaches in both versions were identical. However, no statistically significant differences were detected in the underlying logit equations. More importantly, however, is that both measures are consistently lower than the simple sum of individual values, regardless of how the sum is obtained. On the average, aggregate values using the summing approach are 56 percent higher than joint preservation values obtained directly.

This finding can be partially explained using the relationships given in Table 11.1. If whales and seals are substitute resources, then it would be expected that the sum of individually estimated WTP would exceed the WTP for joint preservation when the individual values do not account for substitute effects. This difference would be expected to reverse when substitute effects were fully accounted for. In the current study, combined estimated values for preserving seals and whales separately always exceed the estimated value for joint preservation. This suggests that respondents consistently did not fully consider the existence of substitute resources when pondering payment amounts for preserving whales and seals on an individual species basis.

Use of the residual approach in versions W&S-W and W&S-S yielded the lowest expected WTP estimates for both whales and seals. Recall that in these versions respondents first valued both resources combined and subsequently were asked to value just one resource. The value of the remaining resource was then interpreted as the difference, or residual, between these two value estimates. The resulting value estimates using this approach were $38 and $2 for whales and seals, respectively. For both species, these values are considerably lower than preservation values calculated on an individual basis. This outcome appears to be a direct result of respondents' tendencies to attribute a large proportion of aggregate preservation value to any single resource, if asked to do so.

Conclusions

The purpose of wildlife valuation is to generate data that are useful in resource-allocation decisionmaking. This investigation suggests that the usefulness of existing wildlife value estimates is very restricted. Most can only be legitimately used to evaluate the particular policy measure that formed the basis for valuation in the first place. Use of the values in policy contexts beyond this may be severely limited. This is because most value estimates have been, and continue to be, derived in partial equilibrium valuation frameworks, each with unique *ceteris paribus* assumptions. For example, the following uses are ruled out: (1) extrapolation of estimated values to a wider population, unless the wider population shares the same *ceteris paribus* circumstances as the sample group; (2) comparisons of values within and across studies to illustrate relative social worth; and (3) aggregation of individually estimated values to illustrate aggregate worth for a set of related resources.

This outlook is based largely on the results of a study of the humpback whale and monk seal, which strongly suggest that estimated preservation values are sensitive to the sequencing of valuation questions. Even in a simple two-good case, differences in value estimates amount to 40 percent. Although the effects of sequencing are complex and were not fully treated here, several hypotheses can be posed for further testing. First, it appears that valuation of resources which are familiar to respondents, like humpback whales for Hawaii residents, is less sensitive to sequencing than the valuation of more obscure resources, such as seals. Second, it appears that sequencing can affect valuation outcomes by altering which resources are valued prior to others. Respondents may tend to anchor their responses to valuation questions based on responses to earlier questions in a sequence.

Empirical findings also show that it is tenuous to aggregate value estimates. Based on the whale and seal value estimates reported here, simple aggregation can overstate combined value by as much as 87 percent in a two-good case. This suggests that respondents tend to overvalue losses of individual resources or to undervalue joint losses. In either case, additional research appears to be warranted on the valuation of wildlife resources in the presence of complements and substitutes.

References

Aiken, R. 1985. Public Benefits of Environmental Protection. Master's thesis, Colorado State University.

Bishop, R. C., and T. A. Heberlein. 1979. Measuring Values of Extramarket Goods: Are Indirect Measures Biased? *American Journal of Agricultural Economics.* 61 (December):926-30.

Bockstael, N., and I. E. Strand. 1985. Distributional Issues and Nonmarket Benefit Measurement. *Western Journal of Agricultural Economics.* 10(December): 162-69.

Boyle, K. J., and R. C. Bishop. 1987. The Economic Valuation of Endangered Species of Wildlife. *Water Resources Research.* 23(5):943-50.

Brookshire, D. S., L. S. Eubanks, and A. Randall. 1983. Estimating Option Prices and Existence Values for Wildlife Resources. *Land Economics.* 59(February): 1-15.

Cochran, W. G. 1977. *Sampling Techniques*. New York: John Wiley and Sons.

Cory, D. C. 1985. Income-Time Endowments, Distributive Equity, and the Valuation of Natural Environments. *Western Journal of Agricultural Economics*. 10 (December):183-86.

Freeman, A. M., III. 1986. On Assessing the State of the Arts of the Contingent Valuation Method of Valuing Environmental Changes. *In* Valuing Environmental Goods: An Assessment of the Contingent Valuation Method. edited by R.G. Cummings *et al*. Totowa, New Jersey, Rowman and Allanhead. 148-61.

Hageman, R. K. 1985. Valuing Marine Mammal Populations: Benefit Valuations in a Multi-Species Ecosystem. Administrative Report LJ-85-22. National Marine Fisheries, Service Southwest Fisheries Center, La Jolla, California.

Hammack, J., and G. Brown. 1974. *Waterfowl and Wetlands: Toward Bioeconomic Analysis*. Baltimore: Johns Hopkins University Press.

Hoehn, J. P., and A. Randall. 1985. A Theory of Benefit-Cost Analysis for Complex Regulatory Programs. Staff paper 85-97, Michigan State University.

Keith, J. E., and K. S. Lyon. 1985. Valuing Wildlife Management: A Utah Deer Herd. *Western Journal of Agricultural Economics*. 10(December):216-22.

Livengood, K. R. 1983. Value of Big Game from Markets for Hunting Leases: The Hedonic Approach. *Land Economics*. 59(August):287-91.

Mäler, K. G. 1974. *Environmental Economics*. Baltimore: Johns Hopkins University Press.

Randall, A., and J. R. Stoll. 1980. Consumers' Surplus in Commodity Space. *American Economic Review*. 70(June):449-54.

_____. 1983. Existence Value in a Total Valuation Framework. *In* Managing Air Quality and Scenic Resources of National Parks and Wilderness Areas. edited by R.D. Rowe and L.G. Chestnut. Boulder, Colorado: Westview Press 265-74.

Rowe, R.D., and L.G. Chestnut, eds. 1983. *Managing Air Quality and Scenic Resources of National Parks and Wilderness Areas*. Boulder, Colorado: Westview Press.

Samples, K. C., J. A. Dixon, and M. M. Gowen. 1986. Information Disclosure Endangered Species Valuation. *Land Economics*. 62(August):306-12.

Sellar, C., J. R. Stoll, and J. P. Chavas. 1985. Validation of Empirical Measures of Welfare Change: A Comparison of Nonmarket Techniques. *Land Economics*. 61(May):156-75.

U.S. Department of Commerce. 1983. Draft Management Plan and Environmental Impact Statement for the Proposed Hawaii Humpback Whale National Marine Sanctuary Program Division, NOAA, Washington, D.C.

12 Contingent Valuation Question Formats: Dichotomous Choice versus Open-Ended Responses

Rebecca L. Johnson

N. Stewart Bregenzer

Bo Shelby

Introduction

As part of a 1985 study of Rogue River users (Johnson, Shelby, and Bregenzer 1986), two alternative contingent valuation (CV) question formats were used to estimate the economic value of noncommercial whitewater recreation. These are referred to as the open-ended and the dichotomous choice (DC) question formats. The study data were gathered through mailed surveys. Benefits were estimated using willingness to pay (WTP) measures. The open-ended format was straightforward; respondents were asked to write in the maximum amount they would pay for a single trip permit for the Rogue River. This open-ended format has been used in other nonmarket good studies (Hammack and Brown 1974; Bishop, Heberlein, and Kealy 1983; Sellar, Chavas, and Stoll 1984). A number of studies have addressed the potential biases involved with the use of this technique (Brookshire, Randall, and Stoll 1980; Thayer, 1981; Cronin, 1982; Bishop *et al.* 1984). Generally, criticism has focused on the presence of hypothetical bias inherent in the survey situation. Since, by definition, this method asks users to respond to a hypothetical situation, there has been concern that what people say they will pay may be quite different than what they would *actually* pay in a situation where money changes hands.

Partially in response to concern over the hypothetical nature of the open-ended format, the DC format was developed to create a more marketlike situation (Bishop and Heberlein 1979). With this format, the respondent is presented with a dollar amount for the price of a hypothetical permit (i.e., a price) to which they respond either "yes," they would pay that amount or "no," they would not. While this question is still hypothetical, the situation has changed from one in which the respondent sets the price to one in which the respondent reacts to a price exogenously set. This format more closely resembles the actual marketplace where individuals commonly face a discrete decision whether or not to buy a commodity at a given price but rarely find themselves setting the price of a commodity.

Dichotomous and multinomial logit analysis has seen widespread application in a number of different areas (Amemiya 1981) and is being used increasingly in nonmarket valuation studies (Loehman and De 1982; Desvouges, Smith, and McGivney 1983; Sellar, Chavas, and Stoll 1984; Boyle and Bishop 1984). However, the methodology is still being refined and there are a number of questions related to model specification and functional form that remain unanswered (Hanemann, 1984; Horowitz, 1985). In this chapter, we compare the empirical results from the two CV question formats, suggest further research areas, and identify needed methodological refinements.

The Study Area

The Rogue River in southwest Oregon is one of the most popular whitewater rivers in the western United States. Demand exceeds the estimated social carrying capacity (Shelby and Colvin 1979), and as a result, a lottery system for distribution of noncommercial permits has been in effect since 1983. Fifty percent of the noncommercial river users receive their permits through the lottery, while the other 50 percent receive their permits from no-shows in the noncommercial and commercial permit system. The fees for both the lottery application and for the permit itself are administratively set at $2.00 and $5.00. These fees do not represent a market clearing price because use is allocated by a lottery system rather than a pricing system. In the absence of a market, nonmarket valuation methods are necessary to establish the Hicksian surplus associated with use of the river. This chapter reports the results of the application of two CV techniques for estimation of the net economic value of noncommercial whitewater recreation on the Rogue River.

Methodology

Open-Ended CVM

The open-ended CV is a method for directly estimating the willingness to pay for the right of access to the Rogue River. This method directly estimates a Hicksian measure of welfare. Since river use is restricted and permits are allocated by a lottery system, people do not currently have the right to run the river without paying for a permit. For the WTP item, when respondents were asked to state the maximum amount they would pay for a permit, the survey instrument was hypothesizing a price-rationing market and asking people to respond to that hypothetical market.

Biases

The open-ended question has the potential to introduce a number of different biases into the benefit estimation. In addition to hypothetical bias caused by its contingent market, the technique may be subject to strategic bias, information bias, and vehicle bias.

Strategic bias occurs when an individual deliberately overstates or understates true WTP in order to make the final results of the experiment reflect the individual's goals. Numerous studies have rejected the hypothesis that strategic bias has a major influence on CV estimates of value (Bohm 1972, 1979; Bishop *et al.* 1984) and some researchers have suggested that it can be rejected as a crucial factor in CV results (Schulze, d'Arge, and Brookshire 1982). On the other hand, Cronin (1982) reports evidence of strategic bias in his results. Cronin suggests that hypothetical bias and strategic bias may be mutually exclusive. If the respondent perceives the CV situation as totally hypothetical, there will be no reason to strategize. Conversely, if the respondent perceives the situation as completely nonhypothetical or "real," there will be a strong impetus toward strategic behavior. The analyst's problem of minimizing strategic bias and hypothetical bias is complicated by this "double-bind" relationship of the two biases. Mitchell and Carson (1981) suggest that this problem can be controlled by creating a high realism level to prevent hypothetical bias and a low consequence level to control strategic bias. Obviously, careful survey design is crucial, and bias-inducing factors were taken into account when the questions for this study were developed. The questions are reproduced in the Appendix.

Information bias results from the respondent's lack of experience in quantifying, in dollars, the value of a nonmarket commodity. Since the respondent's WTP may be uncertain to the respondent, the lack of information on which to base a decision may produce unstable results. Thayer (1981) views the hypothetical market respondent as "information-poor" and consequently very sensitive to information received during the survey process. Thayer explicitly tested for this by giving different respondents different amounts of information, but found no evidence of information bias. Other researchers (Hoehn and Randall 1985: Kolstad and Johnson 1986) suggest that the information search process in CV will never be complete and that hypothetical markets will always underestimate true WTP. Previous studies suggest that information bias is likely to be greatest in situations in which respondents have no experience in valuing the good or service in question. Since respondents in this study have already paid a fee for their river permit, it is hypothesized that information bias will not be a substantial problem but probably will be present to some extent.

Vehicle bias is another possible source of error in CVM. Proper survey design should provide (1) a realistic and familiar setting for respondents to state their WTP for a clearly defined "product" and (2) an appropriate vehicle of payment. Failure to do so can result in either biased responses or unusually large numbers of protest responses. In other words, the respondents must understand the trade-offs involved and be presented with a noncontroversial and equitable method of transaction. In the Rogue River study, since users are already familiar with a permit as a payment vehicle, it was used in the WTP question.

Some researchers (Heberlein-Baumgartner Research Services 1984) suggest viewing protest responses as a form of vehicle bias. Protest responses can either be zero bids or extremely high, unrealistic bids. In both cases, the protest bids must be distinguished from genuine zero bids or high bids that actually reflect a user's value. Techniques for identifying various kinds of protest bids can be found in Desvouges, Smith, and McGiveny (1983). Unfortunately, this study did not include a formal check for zero or protest responses within the survey itself, although most respondents clearly indicated a protest along with a zero bid.

Dichotomous Choice CV

The decision to include the dichotomous choice CV format in the study was a response to the problems of hypothetical bias and information bias and the recognition of the need for further empirical testing of this valuation technique.

There are relatively few market situations in which the purchaser is allowed to state a price instead of taking or leaving the price that is already set. The DC format attempts to avoid this problem and present the respondent with a more realistic situation. The DC format can also help respondents who are "information poor" regarding their actual WTP. Even if they don't know the maximum amount they would pay, they may know if a given amount is acceptable, too high, or too low. With the DC format, this is the only information the respondent (and the analyst) needs. The analyst can estimate the expected value of WTP using the discrete (yes or no) responses of individuals to an offer. Each respondent was presented with a different offer which was randomly generated from a prior distribution. The observations, then, are individual, not grouped.

DC Welfare Measures and Utility Theory

The grounding of dichotomous choice welfare measures in utility theory has been demonstrated in Hanemann (1984). The dichotomous choice logit model is based on a random utility model of consumer decision making.

The logit model that was estimated in this study used a linear form of the utility function and was specified as

$$P_1 = \frac{1}{1 + e^{-(\alpha - BA)}}, \tag{1}$$

where P1 is the probability the individual is willing to pay \$A.

Given this model, welfare measures that are consistent with utility theory can be estimated. For WTP, the dollar amount representing an individual's maximum WTP, E, is to be determined by the value of E that satisfies the equation

$$U(1, Y - E) = U(0, Y), \tag{2}$$

where U (1,Y) represents having access to the river and having income (Y) reduced, and U (O,Y) represents not having access. E is a random variable whose c.d.f. is denoted by $G_E(\bullet)$.

There are a number of different ways to estimate the value of E. Two are used in this study. The first is to calculate the average WTP, the mean of the distribution $G_E(A)$, called E+. When an individual is confronted with an amount, \$A, for the right of access to the river (a permit), the amount will be paid if E, the individual's maximum WTP, is greater than \$A. Therefore, the probability that an individual will pay the amount \$A is

$$P_1 = Pr\{E > A\} = 1 - G_E(A). \tag{3}$$

The mean of this distribution, E+, is

$$E+ = E\{E\} = \int_0^\infty [1 - G_E(A)]dA. \tag{4}$$

A second estimate of E, E*, is the median of the distribution. This is defined as the amount of money needed to keep the individual just at the point of indifference between paying for the permit and doing without. The median is defined as

$$Pr\{U(1, Y - E) \geq U(0, Y)\} = 0.5. \tag{5}$$

Hanemann has shown that both E+ and E* are compatible with ordinal utility theory. However, Hanemann suggests that the median, E*, is less sensitive to outliers, hence more robust and a better measure of central tendency.

Dichotomous Choice Sampling Procedures

If reliable data are to be gathered, proper attention must be paid to the distribution of offers that are presented to respondents. In this study, the open-ended results were used to generate a distribution of DC offers. Specifically, the cumulative distribution of open-ended responses was used to generate a dollar offer for each of a series of random numbers. This method was used so that the range of offers would cover the most likely range of actual values without the surveys listing amounts that were unlikely ever to be accepted. Judging from the fitted logit curve, this procedure appears to have been successful for WTP.

The surveys using the DC format generated a data set of dichotomous dependent variables (yes or no) in response to a continuous independent variable (the dollar amount). From this data, maximum likelihood procedures can be used to estimate a logit model which shows the probability of responding yes or no to any given dollar amount. The resulting equations can be integrated, with numerical methods, over the range of dollar amounts to estimate the expected value of WTP.

Results

Open-ended

Surveys employing the open-ended contingent valuation method were sent to 300 Rogue River users. Of these 300 surveys, 8 were undeliverable and 248 surveys were returned, an overall response rate of 85 percent. The response rate was achieved by a follow-up post card, 2 follow-up letters, a second mailed questionnaire, and a third questionnaire sent by registered mail.

Potential respondents were selected from three groups: (1) permit holders with permits received through the lottery (held in January), (2) permit holders with permits not received through the lottery, and (3) passengers of permit holders. All three groups were asked the WTP question. Using the least significant difference procedure, no two groups were significantly different in their responses at the 0.05 level.

The survey did not incorporate a test for "true" zero responses as opposed to "protest" zero responses. Fortunately, almost all zero responses were accompanied by a written protest to the question. Of the 248 surveys, 229, or 92 percent, showed a positive dollar amount in response to the WTP question. The remaining 19 surveys contained either a zero, a zero and a written protest, or no response.

Our estimates of WTP do *not* include zero responses, since these were most often identified as protests. The mean estimate of WTP was $32.66. The median was $25 with a range of $1 to $200 (see Table 12.1).

Dichotomous Choice

For the second part of the contingent valuation comparison, another stratified sample of 300 Rogue River users was sent surveys with DC questions for WTP. The final step of sending a repeat survey through registered mail was not used due to time constraints. The overall response rate for the second group was 73 percent. Of the 219 surveys that were returned, the response rate for the WTP question was 98 percent.

The dollar amounts, or offers, that were presented to the second set of respondents were generated using 85 of the early responses to the open-ended questions. The WTP offers ranged from $1 to $300. Maximum likelihood techniques were used to estimate the parameters of the logit model, given the "yes" or "no" responses to the bids. The linear functional form provided the best fit and is consistent with utility theory (Hanemann 1984).

The logit equation which was estimated for WTP is reported in Table 12.2. The goodness of fit measure ρ^2 (rho squared), is a so-called "pseudo R^2" (Judge *et al.* 1985). Unlike the R^2 of regression analysis, it does not have an obvious interpretation as percentage of variation explained. Instead, a scaler between 0.2 and 0.4 is considered a "good fit" (Hensher and Johnson 1981). Using the estimated coefficients, the probability of a "yes" response is

$$Pr(Yes) = \frac{1}{1 + e^{-[1.6624 - 0.0344(\$X)]}}. \tag{6}$$

The expected value of WTP (E+) is the area under the logit curve which is specified in Figure 12.1. The integration was truncated at the dollar amount corresponding to the highest offer accepted, called X-max, which was an offer of $175. The value of E+ is $52.93. The median of the probability distribution corresponds to a value of $48.32.

A visual inspection of the estimated logit curve (see Figure 12.1) illustrates two potential problems: (1) the failure of the curve to intersect the origin and (2) the problem of truncation, or what to do with the tails. The predicted probability of a "yes" at $0 for WTP is .82 when 1.0 would be expected. However, the area under the curve would change little by intersecting zero.

Table 12.1 STATISTICS FOR THE OPEN-ENDED CVM

Mean	$32.66	95% Confidence Interval:
Median	$25.00	$28.30 ——— $34.87
Range	$1-200	
Mode	$50.00	
SD	33.6	
SE	2.21	
N	229	

Table 12.2 THE ESTIMATE FROM THE DICHOTOMOUS CHOICE CVM

Dichotomous Choice CVM

$$Log \ \frac{Pr(Yes)}{1 - Pr(Yes)} = 1.6624 - 0.0344(\$X)$$
$$(0.2817) \ (0.0076)(SE)$$

Observation: 200. Percent Positive: 60.

Overall correct prediction percentage: 72.6.

Log-Likelihood at 0: -134. Log-Likelihood at convergence: -107.

$\rho^2 = 0.2015$. $\chi^2 = 54$.

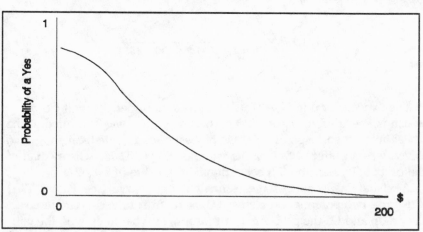

Figure 12.1 LOGIT CURVE

The selection of a point at which to truncate can have a large influence on the estimate (Hanemann 1984). However, the tail of the WTP curve in this case is quite narrow. By truncating WTP at X-max, which corresponds to the .99 probability level, virtually nothing is lost. The truncation question, then, is less critical when the distribution of offers covers the actual range of respondents' WTP, resulting in a smaller tail at the maximum offer.

Conclusion

Estimates of the economic value of noncommercial whitewater recreation on the Rogue River were estimated by two alternative CVM formats. The differences between the welfare measures estimated by the open-ended and the DC formats are relatively large. Although the DC mean and median measures of WTP showed a small relative difference, approximately 8 percent, the difference between the open-ended measures and DC measures was much greater. The mean open-ended WTP of $32.66 is considerably less than either of the DC values, $48.32 for the median and $52.93 for the mean. While this is consistent with the hypothesis that open-ended CVM has a greater problem with information bias, or a less complete information search process, it could also be a result of a number of other factors inherent in survey design and model specification.

The results of this study are encouraging for the use of DC CVM in future studies. The advantage of having the respondent react to a set price is intuitively appealing, especially to those who are skeptical about open-ended CVM formats. We did not find the DC substantially more time-consuming or more expensive to apply. Difficulties do remain, however, with statistical testing of the logit model (Horowitz 1985). Perhaps the biggest drawback to the DC format is in the explanation of the methodology and interpretation of the results for people unfamiliar with the model. Researchers are working on more easily understood explanations of logit models as well as the use of DC logit models as evaluative components in assessments of recreational quality and satisfaction.

References

Amemiya, T. 1981. Qualitative Response Models: A Survey. *Journal of Economic Literature.* 19:1483-536.

Bishop, R., and T. Heberlein. 1979. Measuring Values of Extra-Market Goods: Are Indirect Measures Biased? *American Journal of Agricultural Economics.* 61(5):926-30.

Bishop, R., T. Heberlein, and M. Kealy. 1983. Contingent Valuation of Environmental Assets: Comparisons with a Simulated Market. *Natural Resources Journal.* 23:619-63.

Bishop, R., T. Heberlein, M. Welsh, and R. Baumgartner. 1984. Does Contingent Valuation Work? Results of the Sandhill Experiment. Invited paper, joint meeting of the AERE, AAEA, and the Northeast Agricultural Economics Council, Cornell University, Ithaca, New York.

Bohm, P. 1972. Estimating Demand for Public Goods: An Experiment. *European Economic Review*. 3:111-30.

Bohm, P. 1979. Estimating Willingness to Pay: Why and How?. *Scandinavian Journal of Economics*. 81(2):142-53.

Boyle, K., and R. Bishop. 1984. A Comparison of Contingent Valuation Techniques. Staff paper no. 222. Department of Agricultural Economics, University of Wisconsin-Madison.

Brookshire, D., A. Randall, and J. Stoll. 1980. Valuing Increments and Decrements in Natural Resource Service Flows. *American Journal of Agricultural Economics*. 63:165-77.

Cronin, F. 1982. Valuing Non-Market Goods through Contingent Markets. Prepared for U.S. Environmental Protection Agency, DE-AC06-76RLO 1830. Pacific Northwest Laboratory, Richland, Washington.

Desvouges, W., V. Smith, and M. McGiveny. 1983. A Comparison of Alternative Approaches for Estimating Recreation and Related Benefits of Water Quality Improvement. Prepared for the U.S. Environmental Protection Agency, EPA-23005-83-001.

Hammack, J., and G. Brown. 1974. *Waterfowl and Wetlands: Toward a Bioeconomic Analysis*. Baltimore, Maryland: Johns Hopkins University Press.

Hanemann, W. 1984. Welfare Evaluations in Contingent Valuation Experiments with Discrete Responses. *American Journal of Agricultural Economics*. 66:332-41.

Heberlein-Baumgartner Research Services. 1984. The Grand Canyon Recreation Study. Mimeo graphed paper.

Hensher, D. and L. Johnson. 1981. *Applied Discrete-Choice Modelling*. Halsted, New York.

Hoehn, J., and Alan Randall. 1985. A Satisfactory Benefit Cost Indicator from Contingent Valuation. Staff paper no. 85-4. Department of Agricultural Economics, Michigan State University, East Lansing.

Horowitz, J. 1985. Travel and Location Behavior: State of the Art and Research Opportunities. *Transportation Research*. 19A(5/6):441-53.

Johnson, R., B. Shelby, and N. Bregenzer. 1986. Economic Values and Product Shift on the Rogue River: A Study of Non-commercial Whitewater Recreation. Water Resources Research Institute, Oregon State University, Corvallis.

Judge, G., W. Griffiths, R. Hill, H. Lutkepohl, and T. Lee. 1985. *The Theory and Practice of Econometrics*. New York: John Wiley.

Kolstad, C., and G. Johnson. 1986. Bias in Contingent Valuation. Paper presented at the First National Symposium on Social Science in Resource Management, Corvallis.

Loehman, E., and V. De. 1982. Applications of Stochastic Choice Modeling to Policy Analysis of Public Goods: A Case Study of Air Quality Improvements. *Review of Economics and Statistics*. 64:474-80.

Mitchell, R., and R. Carson. 1981. An Experiment in Determining Willingness to Pay for National Water Quality Improvements. Draft report prepared for U.S. Environmental Protection Agency, Resources for the Future, Inc., Washington, D.C.

Schulze, W., R. d'Arge, and D. Brookshire. 1981. Valuing Environmental Commodities: Some Recent Experiments. *Land Economics*. 57(2):151-69.

Sellar, C., J. Chavas, and J. Stoll. 1984. Specification of the Logit Model: The Case of Valuation of Nonmarket Goods. Working paper TA-18178. Texas Agricultural Experiment Station, Texas A&M University, College Station.

Shelby, B., and R. Colvin. 1979. Rogue River Use levels. Paper no. 63. Water Resources Research Institute, Oregon State University, Corvallis.

Thayer, M. 1981. Contingent Valuation Techniques for Assessing Environmental Impacts: Further Evidence. *Journal of Environmental Economics and Management.* 8:27-44.

Appendix

The Open-Ended and DC Questions

Open-Ended

The following section asks about the dollar value of river running. This is a serious and important research issue. Even though these questions ask you to put yourself in an imaginary situation, please give us the best answer you can for each question. Your answers will not affect the price of river permits.

Think back to the time before you left home for your river trip. Assume you did not already have a permit, but that you could have purchased one for the date of your actual trip. What is the highest whole dollar amount you would have paid for a permit to get on the river? Think of this amount as the price of admission for yourself only, all of which you would have to pay. Even though this is an imaginary price, we would like you to fill in the same amount which you would pay.

The highest dollar amount I would actually have paid for a permit is
$_____.

Once again, think back to the time before you left home for your river trip. Assuming you already had a permit, what is the lowest whole dollar amount you would accept if someone wanted to buy it from you? Assume that the permit you are selling is for yourself only, so you could keep all the money. Even though this is an imaginary price, we would like you to fill in the same amount you would if it were the real cash price which someone would actually pay you. The lowest whole dollar amount I would have accepted to give up my permit is
$_____.

DC

Think back to the time before you left home for your river trip. Assuming you did not already have a permit, would you be willing to pay $ for a permit to get on the river? Think of this amount as the price of admission for yourself only, all of which you would have to pay. Even though this is an imaginary price, we would like you to think of it as if it were the real cash price of a permit which you would pay.

_____Yes, I would actually pay $_____ for a permit.
_____No, I would not pay this amount for a permit.

Once again, think back to the time before you left home for your river trip. Assuming you already had a permit, would you be willing to accept $__i   f someone wanted to buy it from you? Assume that the permit you are selling is for yourself only, so you could keep all the money. Even though this is an imaginary price, we would like you to think of it as if it were the real cash price of a permit which someone would actually pay you.

_____Yes, I would accept $_____in payment to give up my permit.
_____No, I would not accept this amount for my permit.

13 Evaluating the Transferability of Regional Recreation Demand Equations

John Loomis

William Provencher

William G. Brown

Introduction

One longstanding challenge to economists performing Benefit-Cost analysis has been to predict recreation use and net benefits created from policy changes or proposed projects. Creation of new recreation opportunities takes many forms, including the familiar building of new reservoirs and new campgrounds to less familiar restorations of previously unfishable waters via water quality improvements or fish hatcheries. While estimates of use and benefits are critical in these settings, resource economists have devoted relatively little attention to this issue compared to estimation of travel cost method (TCM) demand equations for existing sites. Over 45 studies can be found on demand estimation at existing sites (Sorg and Loomis, 1984), but there are only three published studies of proposed sites.

Several approaches to evaluating the benefits of a proposed site have been put forward. The TCM system of demand equations, the approach of Burt and Brewer 1971 and Cicchetti, Fisher, and Smith 1976, is the most accepted technique among academic economists. Among federal and state economists, two approaches are more commonly used. The first approach, was used by the U.S. Army Corps of Engineers, is called the similar site zonal TCM and involves transferring the per capita demand curve from an existing site to a similar proposed site. A preferred approach among federal and state economists is to build a multisite zonal TCM demand equation relating trips per capita to distance, site characteristics, substitutes, and socioeconomic factors. Dwyer, Kelly, and Bowes (1977, 94-121) devote a substantial number of pages to providing examples of how to perform use estimation at a new site using both the similar site and regional TCMs. Their basic approach involves either (1) applying a regional TCM demand equation to estimate recreation use at a proposed site within the geographic area the regional TCM demand equation was estimated; or (2) if such a demand equation is not available transferring a regional TCM demand equation from another state and applying it to the site of interest. Their basic approach is recommended in the U.S. Water Resources Council Principles and Standards (1979) and more recent Principles and Guidelines (1983) for federal agencies performing benefit-cost analysis. Some state agencies such as Wyoming have adopted this approach for evaluation of state-funded reservoir construction (Andrews 1984). However, no systematic evaluation of the conditions under which such a regional TCM application or transferral will yield reliable predictions of use and benefits has been performed. No empirical comparisons have been made to assess the accuracy of such applications or transfers. That is, how closely do such transferred equations from other sites predict actual use? The purpose of this paper is to provide a theoretical and empirical evaluation of these issues. Such an investigation is of interest not only because such transfers have been recommended by federal agencies to their field offices to conserve survey and analysis budgets, but also because these agencies believe that once estimated, a "demand curve" for a recreation activity should work everywhere.

These issues will be addressed in the context of demand equations for recreation derived by the TCM (Clawson 1959; Cicchetti, Fisher, and Smith 1976; Dwyer, Kelly, and Bowes 1977). In addition, the aggregate or zonal variant of that method will be investigated. Zonal TCM demand curves are likely to be more easily transferred than individual observation TCM for several reasons. First, the effect of size of populations on visitation is explicitly accounted for in the zonal method. Second, trips per capita as the dependent variable account for both probability of a person being a visitor and number of trips by visitors to the recreation site. Third, the zonal model can be applied to the proposed site knowing only the value of variables for potential recreationists rather than all individuals in the population. The individual observation model requires one first to survey the entire population to determine the number of people in the population who would likely be visitors to this proposed site (if it were built). Only then can the individual observation demand equation be applied to the potential visitors to determine the number of trips each visitor would make. The first step is unnecessary with zonal TCM for the reasons discussed above.

Given the greater ease of transferability of zonal TCM relative to individual observation TCM (Brown and Nawas 1973; Gum and Martin 1974) if zonal TCM turns out to be a poor predictor, one would expect even greater errors (in actual field application using secondary data) with individual observations. Thus, we test zonal TCM first; from this, the implications for individual observation TCM should be clear.

The remainder of this chapter discusses the theoretical conditions that would be required for equations to be transferred. The empirical application tests:

1) Whether simple demand equations for Oregon and Washington ocean fishing yield similar fishing visit estimates when the Oregon equation is applied to Washington and the Washington equation applied to Oregon.

2) A comparison of estimated and actual Oregon steelhead fishing visits at nth site (n = 1, ..., 19) when an Oregon steelhead demand equation estimated at n - 1 sites is applied to the nth site.

Theory

Estimated demand equations may take on many forms. Consider a simple demand equation of the following form:

$$\frac{Trips_{ij}}{Pop_i} = B_0 + B_1 TC_{ij} + B_2 INC_i + B_3 Qual_j + B_4 Psubs_k + B_5 Time$$

$$(1)$$

Where:

$Trips_{ij}$	=	trips from recreationists' origin i to site j, where i = 1,..., n where j = 1,..., m;
Pop_i	=	population of origin i;
TC_{ij}	=	round trip travel cost from origin i to site j (our price variable);
INC_i	=	average income of origin i;
$Qual_j$	=	quality of site j (e.g., fish catch, scenic beauty);
$Psubs_k$	=	an index of the price of substitute sites k, k = 1,..., n-1;
$Time_{ij}$	=	travel time from origin i to site j;
B_o	=	intercept term; and
$B_1 - B_4$	=	slope coefficients.

The question posed by application of this model to a proposed site is under what conditions would the intercept and slope coefficients be applicable to the proposed site in the same region. In the case of transferring the model between states, the issue still revolves around the transferability of the coefficients since the analyst can insert the appropriate site-specific values for population, income, travel cost, site quality, etc., to account for these differences between the states.

Consumer demand theory is used to highlight the necessary conditions for successful transference of the slope coefficients and intercept.

Own Price Slope Coefficient

The slope coefficient on travel costs represents how visits per capita changes with a one-dollar change in travel cost. This is essentially the price effect, i.e., $\partial X/\partial P_X$. It is well known that a consumer's response to a change in price can be decomposed into the pure substitution effect (SE) and an income effect (IE), i.e.,

$$\frac{\partial T}{\partial P_t} = \frac{\partial T}{\partial P_t}\Big|_{U \; constant} - T\frac{\partial T}{\partial I} \qquad (2)$$

where:

  T = the number of trips consumed,
  P_t = price of trips (TC_{ij} in Equation 1),
  I = income, and
  U = utility or satisfaction or consumer well-being.

SE reflects the marginal rate of substitution between trips (T) and other goods in producing utility or satisfaction in the recreationists' life. In graphical terms, SE is influenced by the shape of the recreationists indifference curves between recreation and all other goods. For example, recreationists in Utah might have indifference curves pictured in panel A of Figure 13.1 which shows they require a large amount of other goods to give up one skiing trip. Their SE is very small, resulting in a relatively small own price coefficient (and relatively inelastic demand curve) on their demand curve (other things remaining equal). By comparison, recreationists in Illinois may be willing to trade one ski trip for only a small amount of other goods. This results in a larger own price coefficient on their demand curve.

Thus, one condition for demand curves to have the same own price coefficient is for recreationists participating in activity i to have similar tastes and preferences (i.e., identical MRS) in the geographic area where the demand equation was estimated and where it will be applied. This may be a tenable condition if we believe Becker (1976) and Michael and Becker (1973), who claim that differences in behavior often stem from

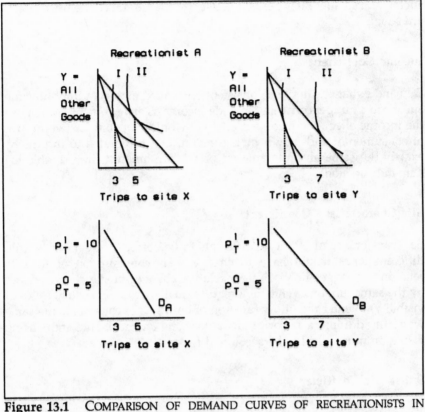

Figure 13.1 COMPARISON OF DEMAND CURVES OF RECREATIONISTS IN DIFFERENT REGIONS

differences in prices, income and opportunity costs of time rather than differences in preferences.

However, having the same substitution effect is insufficient for the slope of the ordinary demand curves to be equal. The income effects must also be equal. In particular, the rate of change in consumption with respect to a change in income ($\partial T/\partial I$) and the proportion of income spent on the good must also be the same.

For example, both the substitution and income effects for recreationists characterized by panel B are larger than recreationists characterized by panel A. Thus, it is not surprising that the slope of the resulting demand curve in panel B is greater (0.8) than panel A (0.4).

If recreationists in two different regions have the same substitution and income effects, they will certainly have the same slope on their ordinary demand curves. However, the slopes on the ordinary demand curves could be the same even if the substitution and income effects are different. This could occur only if, by chance, the differences netted out, such that a smaller SE is perfectly offset by a larger IE, so the price effects are equal.

Income Coefficient

Demand equations derived consistent with maximizing a utility function subject to a budget constraint include income as an argument. Much like the income effect, the income coefficient would be equal for two groups of consumers if and only if their consumption responded to income by exactly the same absolute amount or relative amount (in a double log demand function).

Site Characteristic Coefficients

For transference of quality coefficients to be correct, recreationists from different areas would have to change their consumption of trips in relation to changes in absolute or relative changes in site characteristics by the same amount. This may require quality (e.g., fish catch, miles of visibility) to enter the utility function of both sets of consumers the same way. In addition, a majority of the key site characteristics influencing visitation must (ideally) be accounted for.

Substitute Coefficients

The complexity of factors relating substitutes to benefit estimates is covered in Caulkins, Bishop, and Bouwes 1985. To conserve space, suffice it to say that proximity of other sites must act like substitutes (or complements) to both sets of consumers if the sign on the B_4 coefficient is to be accurate. The equality of the size of the substitute coefficients requires both sets of consumers to respond identically to prices of substitutes.

Constant Term and Omitted Variables

Surely equation 1 does not account for all of the likely explanatory variables. There may be a host of tastes and preference variables (preference for resource characteristics, skill level, etc.) that would influence each individual recreationist's demand. If these variables are omitted from the model, their effects on visitation will show up either in the constant term or, if the omitted variables are strongly correlated with one of the included variables, in the included variables' coefficients. For the demand equation to predict well, not only must the coefficients be transferable, but the relevant variables omitted from the demand equation must be similar. This would likely hold if the basic utility function and preference were the same in the two areas.

Evaluation Criteria

To test whether demand equations can be transferred, it is necessary to determine how well the transferred demand equation would substitute for the site-specific demand equation. In this study we will rely on use of confidence intervals around estimated coefficients to determine how similar the transferred equation is to the site-specific equation. This will allow us to evaluate (1) the degree of certainty (or uncertainty) state and federal agencies can have in use and benefit estimates derived from transferring per capita demand curves, and (2) whether the similarity of utility functions, SE, IE, and other coefficients holds between the two states.

These two factors will be tested (1) by comparing demand equations estimated across different states which have different angler populations and (2) by comparing predicted and actual use at the nth site using a demand equation estimated at n - 1 sites.

The data to perform these simulations came from Oregon steelhead and ocean salmon fishing trips. Data were obtained from surveys performed by Sorhus, Brown, and Gibbs in 1977. Quarterly surveys of Oregon freshwater steelhead and ocean salmon anglers recorded information on trips, expenditures, income, etc.

The Washington ocean fishing data were obtained from the Washington Department of Fisheries and reflect ocean salmon fishing trips during 1983. The data are based on a combination of on-site sampling and a sample of salmon punch card holders.

Cross State Comparison for Ocean Salmon Fishing

Consistency of functional forms, variables included, etc., between the two states coupled with limitations in the two data sets required estimation of a relatively simple model of the following form:

for Oregon Ocean Salmon:

$$\ln\left(\frac{T_{ij}}{Pop_1}\right) = -3.8152 - 1.0261\ln(Dist_{ij}) + 0.4571\ln(Fish_j)$$

$$T \text{ values} \quad (-1.68) \quad (-8.39) \quad\quad\quad (2.19)$$

$$F = 35.3 \quad R^2 = 0.616 \quad N = 47$$

For Washington Ocean Salmon:

$$\ln\!\left(\frac{T_{ij}}{Pop_i}\right) = -6.15 - 0.963\ln\!\left(Dist_{ij}\right) + 0.585\ln\!\left(Fish_j\right)$$

$$T\ values \qquad (-5.43) \quad (-11.73) \qquad\qquad (6.99)$$

$$F = 130.1 \quad R^2 = 0.536 \quad N = 47$$

Where:

T_{ij}	=	trips from origin i to port j,
Pop_i	=	population of origin i,
$Dist_{ij}$	=	distance from origin i to port j, and
$Fish_j$	=	total recreational fish catch at port j.

Comparing these equations in statistical terms, we find *no* statistically significant difference of the distance (price) and fish catch coefficients at the 95 percent level. However, there is a statistically significant difference between the constant terms. This difference is translated into a systematic underestimate of Oregon fishing trips using the Washington equation (inserting the Oregon values of the independent variables and population into the Washington equation) and correspondingly a consistent overestimate of Washington fishing trips using the Oregon equation. This is illustrated in Figures 13.1 (Oregon) and 13.2 (Washington).

These consistent differences attributable to the constant term imply that there are differences between states not accounted for in the model's variables. Possibilities include different propensities to recreate and differences in the year of data collection. The Oregon data were collected in 1977, and the Washington data were collected in 1983. Comparison of use trends in both states shows that 1983 use levels were about 75 percent of 1977 use levels in both states. This may explain some of the difference. Unfortunately, 1977 is the last survey year in Oregon. In addition, part of this difference could arise because of meteorological factors such as "El Niño" affecting availability of fish or because of institutional changes such as fishing regulations. Transference of demand equations between states runs a "double jeporady" of having to deal with differing licensing regulations in two states.

Since R square's are not high in TCM models to begin with (Rosenthal *et al.* 1986) one would not expect extremely accurate estimates between states. The low explanatory power of many TCM models relates to the cross sectional (rather than time series) nature of the data. Cross sectional data is often more heterogenous (i.e., more variability to be explained) and simple models fair poorly. However, since state and

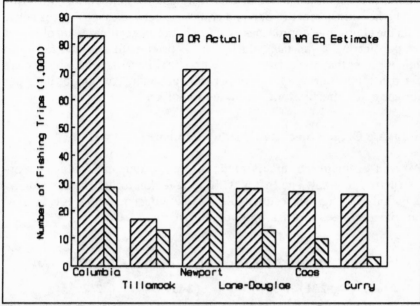

Figure 13.2 THE WASHINGTON EQUATION APPLIED TO OREGON

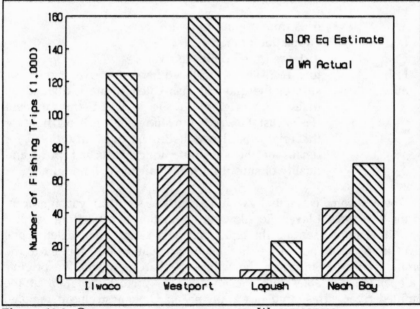

Figure 13.3 OREGON EQUATION APPLIED TO WASHINGTON

federal planners must arrive at a use estimate by some means, the issue
is whether transference of demand equations between states works better
than the alternative approaches. We feel better use estimates are obtained
by transferring a *function* which can be used with site-specific input
values rather than the current agency practice of transferring "angler days
per fish caught" or "angler days per mile of stream" or "angler days per
surface acre" directly from one state to another.

Intrastate Oregon Steelhead Fishing Comparison

We next evaluate the quality of predictions if demand coefficients are
transferred to a new site that is within the region for which the demand
equation was originally estimated. The following equation was estimated
for nineteen steelhead fishing rivers in Oregon.

$$\ln\left(\frac{T_{ij}}{Pop_i}\right) = -3.90 - 0.828\ln(Dist_{ij}) + 0.524\ln(Fish_j) - 0.07745\ln(Subs_{ik})$$

$$T \; values \quad\quad (-2.21) \quad (-5.78) \quad\quad\quad (2.46) \quad\quad\quad (-2.085)$$

$$F = 23.88 \quad R^2 = 0.48 \quad N = 81$$

where:

T_{ij}	=	trips from origin i to river j,
Pop_i	=	population of origin i,
$Dist_{ij}$	=	distance from origin i to river j,
$Fish_j$	=	total recreational steelhead harvest at river j, and
$Subs_{ik}$	=	sum of the quotient Fish catch at site k divided by miles from origin i to site k, where this quotient $(Fish_j/Dist_{ik})$ exceeds the study site's fish per mile for that origin. See Knetsch, Brown, and Hanson 1976, for details of the substitute index reflecting price and quality of substitute sites available to an origin.

Angler income was initially included but was statistically insignificant
at the 0.90 percent level. To allow for simulation of estimating use and
benefits at a proposed site, this equation was re-estimated by deleting one
river from the model. Then, the resulting equation was applied to the
omitted river by inserting the values of that site's and the origin's
independent variables into the equation to predict visitation at the
omitted river. This simulates applying an Oregon steelhead regional
TCM to a new, not currently existing fishing site in the same geographic
region as the model was estimated. This process was repeated for all
rivers. Table 13.1 summarizes the results in terms of use estimates.

Table 13.1 STEELHEAD FISHING OF OREGON RIVERS

River	Actual Trips	Predicted Trips (Demand Equation Including Site)	% Difference	Predicted Trips (Demand Equation Excluding Site)	% Difference
Alsea	29669	7438	-75%	6735	-77%
Chetco	1433	5018	+250%	5656	+295%
Clackamas	47498	47249	-0.5%	47724	+0.5%
Columbia	15091	26620	+76%	27370	+81%
Coquille	10921	5076	-53%	4639	-58%
Coos	2128	1476	-31%	1382	35%
Deschutes	30983	22851	-26%	21805	-30%
Hood	6623	19632	+196%	22695	+243%
John Day	3673	2727	-25%	2348	-39%
Santiam	89496	94628	+6%	94634	+6%
Rogue	42070	44706	+6%	48788	+14%
Salmon	12213	17556	+43%	18058	+48%
Siletz	16641	3227	+40%	25595	+54%
Siuslaw	18727	8289	-56%	7743	-59%
Trask	23135	13632	-41%	11470	-50%
Moqua	70400	38003	-46%	33364	-53%
Willamette	19946	53561	+168%	58068	+191%
Wilson	44260	44517	+0.6%	50212	+13%

As can be seen in Table 13.1, four rivers out of eighteen were estimated within 15 percent of actual use. Of the eighteen rivers, thirteen were estimated within 60 percent of actual use. What is somewhat surprising is that forecasts of visitation made with the reduced model are not much worse than with the full model, and the direction of bias is the same. For the four rivers with estimated use within 15 percent of actual use, Table 13.2 provides consumer surplus benefit comparisons resulting from the two models. Table 13.2 indicates that benefit comparisons are reasonably close on the four rivers where use estimation is also close.

Table 13.2 CONSUMER SURPLUS COMPARISONS FOR THE TWO MODELS

River	C.S. Given Full Model	C.S. Given Reduced Model
Clackamas	$1,563,802	$1,610,191
Santiam	1,759,462	1,754,533
Rogue	1,506,884	1,766,450
Wilson	1,502,845	1,380,123

Assessment of Research Findings

What can we learn and what can we conclude from these findings? Transferability of demand equations between states appears somewhat risky with very simple models since there are likely to be systematic differences between recreationist's preferences and other factors *not* accounted for. The recreationists' response to price stimuli (substitution and income effects) and quality stimuli (fish catch coefficients) were found to be not statistically different between Oregon and Washington ocean salmon anglers. Given these findings on state transferability of equations, one is tempted to argue for inclusion of more taste and preference variables in the demand equation. While this will very likely improve the specification of the equation, this may be of little practical help when transferring demand equations between states for use prediction. The reason is that to apply this more fully specified equation in the new state, the analyst must have information on the values of these independent taste-preference variables in the state to which the demand equation is being applied to. If collection of information on angler incomes, years fishing, percentage of boat ownership, attitude toward trophy fish, etc., requires a survey of anglers, the analyst is caught in a "Catch 22." He or she must transfer an existing demand equation from another state or region to avoid having to perform a survey to build a site-specific demand equation, but transferring a properly specified demand equation for another state requires that a survey be performed to obtain values of the independent variables. By contrast, adding more variables on physical site characteristics should improve model specification, and values of these variables can be more easily obtained without the need for surveys in the region or state to which the model is transferred. If the pattern of errors (differences only in constant term) we found in the Oregon-Washington situation is borne out elsewhere, it may be wise to use the transfer equation approach to arrive only at "initial" site use estimates. These initial site use estimates could be adjusted up or down by using information on regional or state differences in participation rates or intensity of visitation per participant. Such information at a state level is available from secondary sources such as the U.S. Fish and Wildlife Service National Survey of Fishing, Hunting and Wildlife Associated Recreation.

In terms of prediction for sites that are *within the region on which the equation was estimated*, we have greater hope. These estimates were much closer to the actual figures and the prospects for future improvements are greater. Not only can more site characteristics be added, but the addition of taste and preference variables is quite feasible here, the reason being that if the new proposed site draws from the same market area as the existing sites, then values of the taste and preference variables for anglers in that region will already be known.

However, the use estimates derived from an application of a demand curve estimated in a specific region to a site in that region are generally accurate to plus or minus 50 percent. In an absolute sense, this is not very accurate for benefit-cost analysis. However, this may be much closer than state and federal agency analysts can arrive at using their current approaches for calculating use and net benefits which rely on a standardized range of values. Lastly, researchers should keep in mind the potential for transferability of demand models when formulating new modelling approaches. A more general model structure that facilitates transference may be of more practical value than very detailed models specific to one particular area.

References

Andrews, K. 1984. Recreation Benefits and Costs of the Proposed Deer Creek Reservoir. Cheyenne: Wyoming Recreation Commission.

Becker, G. 1976. *The Economic Approach to Human Behavior.* Chicago: The University of Chicago Press.

Burt, O., and D. Brewer. 1971. Estimation of Net Social Benefits From Outdoor Recreation. *Econometrica.* 39:813-27.

Caulkins, P., R. Bishop, and N. Bouwes. 1985. Omitted Cross-Price Variable Biases in the Linear Travel Cost Model: Correcting Common Misperceptions. *Land Economics.* 61:182-7.

Cicchetti, C., A. Fisher, and V. K. Smith. An Econometric Evaluation of A Generalized Consumer Surplus Measure: The Mineral King Controversy. *Econometrica.* 44:1259-75.

Clawson, M. 1959. Methods of Measuring the Demand for and Value of Outdoor Recreation. Reprint 10. Washington, D.C.: Resources for the Future.

Dywer, J., J. Kelly, and M. Bowes. Improved Procedures for Valuation of the Contribution of Recreation to National Economic Development. Research Report #128. Urbana, Ill: Water Resources Center, University of Illinois at Urbana-Champaign.

Knetsch, J., R. Brown, and W. Hansen. 1976. Estimating Expected Use and Value of Recreation Sites. *In* Planning for Tourism Development: Quantitative Approaches. edited by C. Gearing, W. Swart, and T. Var. New York: Praeger.

Michael, R. and G. Becker. 1973. On The New Theory of Consumer Behavior. *The Swedish Journal of Economics.* 75:378-95.

Rosenthal, D., D. Donnelly, M. Schiffhauer, and G. E. Brink. 1986. User's Guide to RMTCM: Software for Travel Cost Analysis. GTR RM-132. Ft. Collins, Col.: Rocky Mountain Forest and Range Experiment Station, U.S. Forest Service.

Sorg, C. F., and J. B. Loomis. 1984. Empirical Estimates of Amenity Forest Values: A Comparative Review. U.S. Department of Agriculture, Forest Service General Technical Report RM-107. Ft. Collins, Col.: Rocky Mountain Forest and Range Experimental Station.

Sorhus, C., W. Brown, and K. Gibbs. 1981. Estimated Expenditures by Salmon and Steelhead Sport Anglers for Specified Fisheries in the Pacific Northwest. Special Report 631. Corvallis, Ore.: Agricultural Experiment Station, Oregon State University.

Author Affiliations

Gregory Alward is a Research Forester at the Rocky Mountain Forest and Range Experiment Station, U.S. Department of Agriculture Forest Service, Fort Collins, Colorado.

Richard C. Bishop is a Professor in the Department of Agricultural Economics at the University of Wisconsin, Madison, Wisconsin.

Perry J. Brown is the Associate Dean of Instruction for the College of Forestry and Professor in the Department of Forest Resources at Oregon State University, Corvallis, Oregon.

William G. Brown is a Professor in the Department of Agriculture and Natural Resource Economics at Oregon State University, Corvallis, Oregon.

N. Stewart Bregenzer is lawyer in Bend Oregon.

Beverly L. Driver is Project Leader for the Valuation of Resource Benefits at the Rocky Mountain Forest and Range Experiment Station, U.S. Department of Agriculture Forest Service, Fort Collins, Colorado.

Robin Gregory is affiliated with Decision Research, Eugene, Oregon.

Charles C. Harris is an Associate Professor in the Department of Wildlife Recreation Management at the University of Idaho, Moscow, Idaho.

Thomas A. Heberlein is a Professor in the Department of Rural Sociology at the University of Wisconsin, Madison, Wisconsin.

John P. Hoehn is an Assistant Professor in the Department of Agricultural Economics at Michigan State University, East Lansing, Michigan.

James R. Hollyer is in the Department of Agricultural and Resource Economics at the University of Hawaii at Manoa, Honolulu, Hawaii.

Gary V. Johnson is an Associate Professor in Residence in the Center for Food Policy Management, Department of Agricultural and Resource Economics at the University of Connecticut, Storrs, Connecticut.

Rebecca L. Johnson is an Assistant Professor in the Department of Forest Resources at Oregon State University, Corvallis, Oregon.

Alan Jubenville is an Associate Professor in the School of Management at the University of Alaska-Fairbanks, Fairbanks, Alaska.

Geoff N. Kerr is a Resource Economist in the Centre for Resource Management at the University of Canterbury and Lincoln College, Christchurch, New Zealand.

Warren Kriesel is at the Rural Development Center, Tifton, Georgia.

John Loomis is an Assistant Professor in the Division of Environmental Studies, Department of Agricultural Economics, University of California, Davis, California.

Mary McGown is a Graduate Assistant in the Department of Wildlife Recreation Management at the University of Idaho, Moscow, Idaho.

Donald MacGregor is affiliated with Decision Research, Eugene, Oregon.

Scott C. Matulich is an Associate Professor in the Department of Agricultural Economics, Washington State University, Pullman, Washington.

Frederick Norbury is Land Management Planning Specialist on the Land Management Planning Staff, U.S. Department of Agriculture Forest Service, Washington, D.C.

George L. Peterson is Project Leader for the Valuation of Resource Benefits at the Rocky Mountain Forest and Range Experiment Station, U.S. Department of Agriculture Forest Service, Fort Collins, Colorado.

William Provencher is in the Department of Agricultural Economics at the University of California, Davis, California.

Alan Randall is a Professor in the Department of Agricultural Economics and Rural Sociology at Ohio State University, Columbus, Ohio.

Karl C. Samples is an Associate Professor in the Department of Agricultural and Resource Economics at the University of Hawaii at Manoa, Honolulu, Hawaii.

Bo Shelby is an Associate Professor in the Department of Forest Resources at Oregon State University, Corvallis, Oregon.

Daniel J. Stynes is an Associate Professor in the Department of Parks and Recreation Resources at Michigan State University, East Lansing, Michigan.

Dennis Schweitzer is Assistant Director of the Land Management Planning Staff, U.S. Department of Agriculture Forest Service, Washington, D.C.

William G. Workman is an Associate Professor in the School of Management at the University of Alaska-Fairbanks, Fairbanks, Alaska.